GLUTEN-FREE
Celebrations

Memorable Meals without Wheat

Other books from Savory Palate, Inc.

Gluten-Free 101:
Easy, Basic Dishes without Wheat
By Carol Fenster, Ph.D.

Wheat-Free Recipes & Menus:
Delicious Dining without Wheat or Gluten
By Carol Fenster, Ph.D.

Special Diet Solutions:
Healthy Cooking without Wheat, Gluten, Dairy, Eggs, Yeast, or Sugar
By Carol Fenster, Ph.D.

Food Allergy Field Guide:
A Lifestyle Manual for Families
By Theresa Willingham

GLUTEN-FREE
Celebrations
Memorable Meals without Wheat

Carol Fenster, Ph.D.

Savory Palate, Inc.
8174 South Holly, # 404
Centennial, CO 80122-4004
www.savorypalate.com

Library of Congress Catalog Card Number: 98-96752
ISBN 1-889374-06-7
Printed in the United States of America

First Edition, 1999; Second Edition, 2003

SUMMARY
1. Wheat-free, gluten-free, celiac, diabetes, autism, cookbook
2. Wheat intolerance, gluten intolerance, food sensitivity, food allergy

Edited by Mary Bonner
Cover design by MacGraphics Services, Aurora, CO
Illustrations by Jeanne VonWyl

For orders and information, contact:
Savory Palate, Inc., 8174 So. Holly, # 404, Centennial, CO, 80122-4004
(800) 741-5418   (303) 741-5408   www.savorypalate.com

~ CONTENTS ~

Recipes

Appendices 223

To husband Larry, son Brett, and daughter-in-law Helke

~ ACKNOWLEDGEMENTS ~

Celebrations are special times— regardless of what is being celebrated. This cookbook was a joy to write because I know it will be used to make special occasions— or everyday meals— more memorable. I am deeply indebted to the following people who gave so generously of their time so you could celebrate with your favorite food.

To those who helped with testing recipes and providing excellent feedback, I truly appreciate your input--and please extend my thanks to your family and friends who lent their taste buds to the tasting process: Jane Dennison-Bauer, Julie Cary, Mary Courtney; Sandy Dempsey; Terri Ditmer; Laura Dolson; Donna Franz; Caroline Herdle; Jane Holcomb; Ruth Horelica; Janene Lenard; Alicia Pitzer; Janet Rinehart; Denise Roth; Lynn Samuel, L.P.N.; Judy Sarver; Chris Silker; Jenny View; Peggy Wagener; Anne Washburn; Cecile Weed; and Sue Weilgopolan.

To those who helped with reviewing the manuscript and providing extremely valuable feedback, I sincerely appreciate your help: Rosanne G. Ainscough, R.D., C.D.E., Diabetes Dietitian Educator; Mary Bonner, Contributing Writer, *Living Without* Magazine; Gail Bright, R.D., Colorado Allergy & Asthma Centers; Sheila E. Crowe, M.D., Department of Internal Medicine, University of Virginia, Charlottesville, VA; Kathy Gibbons, Ph.D., Healthy Actions nutritional counseling; Leon Greos, M.D., Colorado Allergy & Asthma Centers, P.C.; Dianna S. Hayton, R.N., Patient Educator, Colorado Allergy and Asthma Centers, P.C.; Cynthia Kupper, C.R.D., Executive Director, Gluten Intolerance Group of North America; Anne Munoz-Furlong, Founder, The Food Allergy & Anaphylaxis Network, Fairfax, VA; Janet Y. Rinehart, Chairman, Houston Celiac Sprue Support Group and Past President, CSA/USA, Inc.; Nancy Carol Sanker, OTR, former Education and Support Group Project Director, Asthma and Allergy Foundation of America; Ellen Speare, B.S., Clinical Nutritionist, Wild Oats Markets; Gail Spiegel, M.S., R.D., CDE ; Joanne M. Vitanza, M.D., Colorado Allergy and Asthma Centers, P.C.; Peggy A. Wagener, publisher of *Living Without* magazine; Ann Whelan, publisher of *Gluten-Free Living* newsletter; and Maura Zazenski.

What People Are Saying About
Gluten-Free Celebrations

Lots of tips, simple instructions. You take the fear out of making these foods.
-Cynthia Kupper, CRD – Executive Director
Gluten Intolerance Group of North America

Well-written, informative, appealing, unique.
-Sheila E. Crowe, M.D., Associate Professor
Department of Internal Medicine,
University of Virginia, Charlottesville, VA

I like the idea of targeting dietary needs for special occasions.
-Joanne M. Vitanza, M.D.
Colorado Allergy & Asthma Centers, P.C.

A great source of information. Much needed by our patients.
-Dianna S. Hayton, R.N., Patient Educator
Colorado Allergy & Asthma Centers, P.C.

It will shorten the amount of time I have to spend educating clients about recipes and substitutes. You made another wonderfully great and useful book that can fix any "special" dietary needs.

-Ellen Speare, B.S., Clinical Nutritionist
Wild Oats Markets

I think it's great. Thanks for including nutritional values.
-Janet Rinehart, Chairman
Houston Celiac Sprue Support Group
and Past President, CSA/USA, Inc.

A normal cookbook for special people.

-Ann Whelan, publisher
Gluten-Free Living newsletter

~ SPECIAL DIET PHILOSOPHY ~

Birthdays, anniversaries, parties— celebrations of any kind. This is the good stuff, the stuff life is made of. These are the occasions we use to the mark significant stages in our lives, to bond with our family, to connect with friends, and to re-affirm our connections to treasured rituals, traditions, and customs. Inevitably, food takes center stage.

And, yet for those of us with food sensitivities, these joyous occasions can be downright dangerous. The food we once ate— and that everyone expects us to continue eating— is now off-limits. But the good news is that you can continue to eat these foods— if they're prepared with appropriate substitutes for the problem ingredients.

Food Plays a Symbolic Role in Our Lives

Perhaps I am more aware than others of the symbolic role that food plays in our lives. In addition to being a culinary professional, my sociological background keeps me aware of how we use food to communicate with others. It is the celebrations, the holidays, the special occasions in our lives where food becomes the celebratory medium. Rituals associated with food become the memories of a lifetime. Fortunately, my training as a home economist gives me the technical ability to transform recipes into dishes that are safe, delicious to eat, and appropriate for *any* occasion— from everyday dining to special events.

If you've purchased my earlier books, you know my story. I suffered from chronic sinusitis most of my life until I learned to avoid my own particular food villains— especially wheat and certain wheat-related grains. For someone raised on a farm in Nebraska and who married into a wheat-farming family, this was unsettling to say the least!

Today, I am an expert in helping people with special diet needs manage a healthy diet. Once they identify their own particular food villains (with the help of a health professional), I help them eat the foods they love—without the ingredients they don't want.

There is almost always an appropriate substitute for a particular problem ingredient—the secret lies in knowing what the substitute is and how to use it. I've created this cookbook so you can cook for those special occasions without wheat or gluten— and, also— without dairy or eggs. You can also avoid corn or soy if you're careful to read ingredient labels.

Gluten Free Diet is Special— Not Limited or Restrictive

You'll notice I don't refer to my diet as restricted, limited, or alternative. Instead, I refer to it as a "special" diet because it is tailored to suit my body and its needs. I'm very aware of the psychological aspects of adjusting to this diet. However, it is very important to refer to our diets with positive, rather than negative words. Our bodies hear what our brains are thinking, so I try to keep my thoughts and actions positive at all times. To me, "special" is a positive term.

Whenever I'm tempted by forbidden food, I say to myself— *Nothing tastes as good as feeling good feels.* I then imagine how I will feel if I eat the forbidden food— that's enough to make me realize it isn't worth it.

Getting in Touch with Your Inner Chef

Some people love to cook. However, many others tell me they don't like to cook, don't have time to prepare meals, or feel inadequate in the kitchen. Despite the growing availability of mixes and ready-made foods, you will need to prepare some dishes yourself.

Yes, this usually requires preparing most dishes from scratch. But, as I remind my students in cooking classes—there are two major benefits when you cook from scratch: (1) you gain control over what you eat, and (2) you control the standards under which that food is prepared. And remember the psychological aspects—it's very rewarding to create a tasty dish that you, your family, and your guests enjoy.

I hope you, your family, and your guests truly enjoy these dishes everyday or at your celebrations. Bon Appetit! Celebrate everything with food!

Carol Fenster

~ INTRODUCTION ~

How to Use This Book

This book is a resource for people on special diets. It is meant to help you eat the dishes you want— after your health professional tells you which ingredients to avoid. Specifically, this book is for people who *know* they must avoid wheat, gluten, dairy, and eggs.

This book should not be used to "self-diagnose" yourself or others, to determine whether you have a particular condition that warrants a special diet, or to determine the particular ingredients you should avoid. Let a health professional guide you in this process.

Can This Book Help You?

If you belong to any of the following groups of people, then the recipes in this book are appropriate for your diet:

> 1. People who <u>must</u> avoid gluten in their diets. This includes persons with celiac disease (also known as celiac sprue, gluten intolerance, gluten sensitive enteropathy, and dermatitis herpetiformis). In addition, 5% of people with insulin-dependent (Type 1) diabetes have celiac disease, so the recipes include nutrient values for managing diabetes.

> 2. People who must avoid wheat and all wheat-related grains because of wheat allergies or intolerances or other special dietary considerations. For those with additional sensitivities, substitutes may be used for dairy and eggs.

> 3. Vegetarians and vegans who avoid dairy and eggs.

Why People Must Avoid Certain Ingredients

Celiac Disease

Celiac disease (also called celiac sprue and related forms of gluten intolerance or gluten-sensitive enteropathy) is a genetically transmitted condition in which gluten (a protein in certain grains) destroys the small intestine's ability to absorb nutrients from food. Another form of the disease is dermatitis herpetiformis (DH) with symptoms of skin rashes and blisterlike spots. The Center for Celiac Research says about 1 in every 180 persons in the United States has celiac disease.

Persons with celiac disease must avoid all forms of gluten, which is present in wheat and wheat-related grains such as barley, rye, spelt, oats and the lesser known grains of kamut and triticale. All recipes in this book avoid these grains by using gluten-free flours and by specifying gluten-free substitutes for other ingredients as well.

The recipes are designed so you can make them without gluten— plus instructions for omitting additional problem ingredients such as dairy and eggs,— if necessary. If you want to experiment with using alternative sweeteners, see Baking with Alternative Sweeteners in the Appendix for guidance.

Celiac disease is a lifelong condition which requires strict adherence to a gluten-free diet. This condition must be managed with the help of a gastroenterologist, who performs a series of tests before a final diagnosis can be made.

A particularly useful resource is the Cooperative Gluten-Free Commercial Products Listing from the Celiac Sprue Association. This publication lists products and ingredients that are gluten-free. Many other national associations provide beneficial information as well such as the Tri-County Celiac Support Group. (See Appendix.)

Celiac Disease and Diabetes
Approximately 1 in every 20 (or 5%) of people with insulin-dependent (Type 1) diabetes also have celiac disease. And some celiacs have Type 2 diabetes. Both groups must avoid all forms of gluten— while monitoring the rest of their diets, as well.

How can celiacs with diabetes use this book? Each gluten-free recipe contains nutrient values for monitoring daily nutrient intake.

The combination of celiac disease and diabetes demands a very careful diet. Persons using these recipes are urged to work closely with a health professional to assure a balanced diet. See Appendix for associations that provide information on diabetes.

Food Allergies and Intolerances
Although there is not one official national statistic, food allergies are thought to affect anywhere from 1 to 5% of the general population. The Food Allergy and Anaphylaxis Network says 1 to 2% of adults have true food allergies. Others estimate that nearly 25% of Americans suffer

from food intolerances and sensitivities. Whether you are allergic (your reaction is usually sudden and more pronounced) or intolerant (your reaction may be delayed and more subtle), these recipes show you how to cook without the problem ingredients.

Diagnosis of a food allergy or intolerance should be made by a board-certified allergist or other health professional who specializes in this area. There are a variety of tests and procedures used to confirm a diagnosis; not all experts agree on a single approach. There are also many associations dedicated to helping people with these conditions. See the Appendix for a list of these associations.

Labels
Reading labels is very important when shopping for special diets. Learn to recognize the various names used for certain ingredients Also, *continue* to read labels on all ingredients— even the ones you've used for a long time. Manufacturers may change the contents of an ingredient, perhaps adding a substance. They may change the manner in which it was prepared, such as dusting the item with wheat flour to prevent sticking. Or the manufacturing process may introduce cross contamination with other problem ingredients. Call the manufacturer if you have concerns. Phrase your questions as clearly and concisely as possible and be sure to thank them for responding to your questions.

Nutritional Content
Managing a healthy diet is important to all of us, so nutrient values are offered as an aid to managing your nutritional intake. These values are based on the United States Department of Agriculture (USDA) guidelines and are only approximate. Exact nutrient values may vary according to serving sizes or brands used. MasterCook is the software program used to calculate nutritional data.

Serving Size
Serving sizes recommended by the American Diabetes Association are used in the calculation of nutrient values. Because we Americans are accustomed to eating very large portions, these serving sizes may seem quite small and it may take several servings to satisfy you.

Flour
Instead of wheat and gluten flours, the recipes in this book use a variety of flours—e.g., rice, corn, bean, potato starch, sorghum, and tapioca. Why these flours? These flours are safest for the largest number of

people, the flours are least likely to compete with the flavors of the dish, and combinations of these flours produce the most pleasing results.

In place of rice flour, many recipes use sorghum flour, which is in the corn family. Others use garbanzo/fava bean flour which is made from a combination of garbanzo (chickpea) and fava (broad) beans. This flour is ideal for people who want to increase their protein intake, provided they're not allergic to or intolerant of legumes. The flour does not alter the dish's flavor, but does impart a slightly sweeter taste than rice flour. (One caution: avoid this flour if you have a condition called glucose-6-phosphate dehydrogenase (G6PD) deficiency in which fava beans cause digestive problems.)

In place of potato starch, cornstarch can be substituted in a 1:1 ratio—provided you can eat corn. And 1 cup of tapioca flour can be replaced with ⅞ cup sweet rice flour. See Wheat-Flour Equivalents chart in the Appendix to customize your own recipes. Gf means gluten free.

Eggs
Most of the baked goods in this book can be made without eggs. Of course, using eggs produces a "lighter" baked item. See the Appendix for Baking with Egg Substitutes.

Dairy
People avoid dairy products for three reasons: 1) allergies, 2) lactose intolerance or 3) vegan diets. If lactose intolerance is your concern, you may use lactose-reduced milk in place of regular milk in these recipes. If you are allergic to dairy products or just want to avoid all dairy products for personal reasons, there are suggestions for using milk substitutes made from rice, soy, or nut milk. Df means dairy free.

According to the Food Allergy & Anaphylaxis Network (FAAN) newsletter (Vol. 5, #4, April-May, 1996), goat milk, goat yogurt, or goat cheeses are not recommended for those with milk allergies since the proteins are believed to be similar. Some people with lactose intolerance say they can tolerate goat products, but FAAN does not recommend this. Ask your physician. Be sure to read the label on these milk substitutes to make sure no other offending ingredients are present. For example, some "dairy-free" items contain casein, a milk protein that must be avoided by milk-allergic persons. And, celiacs should avoid oat milk.

There are also dairy-free yogurts and sour cream, but make sure they don't contain additional problem ingredients. See the Appendix for additional information on Baking with Dairy Substitutes and Hidden Sources of Dairy in prepared foods.

Baking without Conventional Ingredients

All conventional baked goods usually contain wheat, eggs, milk, and a leavening agent, and each ingredient plays a unique role in producing tasty, pleasingly textured results. What happens when we omit these ingredients? Let's take each separately.

Baking without wheat flour produces a somewhat heavier and denser product because the missing gluten can't establish a cell structure in which the leavening agent does its job. However, using xanthan gum helps alleviate this situation to the extent that many people can't distinguish between the same cake made with and without wheat flour.

Eliminating eggs has as dramatic an impact on baking as omitting wheat flour. In fact, eliminating wheat flour and eggs are the two biggest challenges to allergy-free baking. Eggs not only bind ingredients together and provide moisture, they are also leavening agents. This is the function we miss the most in baking. Several other ingredients can bind and moisturize a recipe, but eliminating eggs produces baked goods that are decidedly heavier and denser. For example, a cake that is light and airy when made *with* eggs becomes more like pound cake when made *without* eggs— but is still delicious!

Using milk substitutes is quite easy and usually has a minimal impact on the final product. In fact, most non-dairy milks can be used interchangeably with cow's milk in baking. Each type of milk has subtle taste differences and may produce slight color variations in the finished product (for example, soy milk may darken the product during baking). Decide which type of milk you prefer and stick with it. Be sure it doesn't contain problem ingredients such as casein (a milk protein) or barley malt extract (which contains gluten).

So, what does all this mean? Cooking without conventional ingredients is not harder— it's just slightly different. While there are a few more ingredients in each recipe, these ingredients are essential and require only a few more seconds of measuring. Also, certain ingredients cost somewhat more than conventional versions— a small price to pay for being able to resume eating your favorite dishes and maintain a healthy diet.

Principles of Cooking without Wheat or Gluten
Although cooking without conventional baking ingredients requires unique cooking techniques, omitting wheat and gluten present special challenges. Here are some guidelines for successful baking which have been incorporated into each recipe:

- Use rice, corn, bean, potato starch, sorghum, or tapioca flours for wheat flour
- Use a mixture of flours (2-3) rather than a single flour
- Use xanthan gum, soy lecithin, and gelatin as well as different preparation techniques to restore texture and appearance
- Use herbs, spices, and flavorings to restore flavor
- Use bread machines and heavy-duty stand mixers since gluten-free dough is softer, moister, and stickier than traditional dough

In addition to these guidelines, it is important to measure dry ingredients correctly. Use dry measuring cups or spoons and level the top off with a straight-edged knife. Don't pack the flour into the cup or spoon. Use liquid measuring cups for liquids. And, use standardized measuring cups and spoons from a reputable manufacturer for consistent results. Read through the recipe entirely before proceeding to make sure you know which substitutes, if any, you'll use.

Flour Blends: Mixes versus Individual Ingredients
Even though you can buy an increasing number of ready-made food items or mixes, the fact remains that 1) you can't buy everything, 2) some of us can't afford to buy lots of ready-made foods, *or* 3) we really prefer to make our own food.

Many of you have already learned that wheat flour can't be replaced with one single flour in baking. Instead, it takes a blend of flours carefully selected for their unique properties. Measuring all those flours makes baking a bit more time consuming. Isn't there an easier way?

I've pondered the issue of pre-mixed flour blends (several flours blended to measure as one flour) for some time now. Yet, for every customer who wishes I would use flour blends (rather than individually listed ingredients), there are those who are glad I don't because their food sensitivities don't allow the inflexibility of ready-made blends.

Furthermore, I know that certain dishes are better when made with varying amounts of the typical gluten-free flours— e.g., rice, bean, corn, potato starch, sorghum, and tapioca flour. For example, chewier foods like cookies or bars require more tapioca flour than delicate items such as cakes. Therefore, it makes sense to tailor the flour blend to suit the dish rather than use the same blend for everything.

Nonetheless, I am an extremely practical person and— like you— need to minimize my time in the kitchen. For some time now, I have experimented with different blends, using a wide variety of flours. And I've become quite fond of the convenience of using a flour blend rather than always measuring 2 or 3 flours per recipe.

At the same time, I haven't forgotten that some of you can't or don't want to eat legumes (which rules out the bean flours), some of you don't like rice flour, or some of you are allergic to nut flours.

I've developed a gluten-free flour blend that works well with every baked item in this book. This way, you can mix up a large batch and store it on your pantry shelf or in your refrigerator and it will be ready the next time you bake. If the recipe in this book calls for 1 cup of rice flour, ½ cup of potato starch, and ¼ cup of tapioca flour— use 1 ¾ cup of the following flour blend (1 ½ + ½ + ¼ = 1 ¾ cups).

Carol's Gluten-Free Sorghum Flour Blend*

1 ½ cups sorghum flour	1 cup tapioca flour
1 ½ cups potato starch or cornstarch	½ cup corn flour or almond flour or bean flour

*Makes 4.5 cups

These ingredients are readily available at your health food store or possibly your grocery store, but if they're new to you— read on. To order, check Mail-Order Sources in the Appendix.

Sorghum: Sorghum flour has been around for ages, but has just recently received attention as a nutritious alternative to wheat. Find it at health food stores, order it from gluten-free vendors (see Appendix), or directly from a grower at www.twinvalleymills.com.

Corn flour: Corn flour is not the same as cornstarch. It is the whole corn kernel ground into flour rather than just the starch. You can buy it at health food stores, some grocery stores, and certain mail-order companies and on-line vendors. You can also buy yellow or white cornmeal (available at any grocery store) and grind the meal into a flour-type consistency with a small coffee or spice grinder. Both the yellow and white cornmeal work well, but baked goods made with the white corn flour will be somewhat lighter in color and may not brown as deeply as yellow corn flour.

Almond flour. Almond flour is available at some health food stores and from certain mail order companies. Make your own by grinding blanched almonds to a fine, powdery consistency with a coffee or spice grinder. You may also purchase ready-made almond meal. The meal will add important fiber to your diet, but the almond skins will lend a brown tint to baked goods.

Almond flour and almond meal should be refrigerated so you must also refrigerate the flour blend. Bring to room temperature before using.

Potato starch: Potato starch (not potato flour) and tapioca flour (some-times called tapioca starch) are old standbys for us. Find them at your health food store. Cornstarch can replace potato starch, if necessary.

Bean Flour. If corn or almond flour doesn't suit your tastes— or if you want a change— try using bean flour. This could be white bean flour from Bob's Red Mill or a blend of garbanzo/fava bean flour from the same company, or from Authentic Foods or Ener-G Foods. Bean flours, like corn flour and almond flour, add protein and fiber to the diet and nicely complement sorghum flour.

Which Flour Should You Use?
Almond flour has a higher fat content than corn flour and tends to make baked goods that have a lovely golden color. It is also somewhat higher in fiber. The flavor is not appreciably different whether you use almond or corn flour, but almond flour introduces a bit of texture. You should *definitely* store the almond flour blend in the refrigerator.

Bean flour lends its own distinct "bean" flavor, but also offers a good fiber and protein content. Egg-free baked goods are especially good made with bean flour.

You might experiment with the variations of this flour blend to see which ones you like best. Or, just use the recipes as they're written which means you'll measure more individual flours each time you bake. The choice is yours; either way, the recipes will turn out great!

~ GLOSSARY OF INGREDIENTS ~

R ead this section carefully so you know what the ingredient is, what it looks like, and where to find it (if not available in grocery stores). No endorsement of products is intended, but certain brands are mentioned to help you find the ingredient in the U.S.

Read labels carefully to make sure you know what you're eating. Continue to read labels since manufacturers can change the ingredients and the processes under which the ingredient is handled. And remember... *if in doubt about any ingredient, don't eat it!*

Agave Nectar: Honey-like liquid from agave plant; 90% fructose. Found in baking aisle of natural food store.

Ascorbic Acid: Also called Vitamin C crystals or powder. Choose unbuffered version for maximum leavening boost in baked goods. Found in supplements at natural food stores. (See **Vitamin C.**)

Applesauce: Also available as baby food, but choose those (e.g., Gerber First) without extra fillers such as rice or tapioca. Organic versions are usually darker and will cause baked goods to be somewhat darker.

Arrowroot: Flour made from a West Indies root. Excellent thickener for fruit sauces or other sauces that do not require high heat. Binds baked goods. Found in natural food stores.

Baking Powder: Ener-G®, Featherweight make gluten-free versions.

Brown Rice Syrup: Made from brown rice. Lundberg's is gluten-free. Found in natural food store.

Brown Sugar: Generally made from cane sugar, this is white refined sugar to which a little molasses has been added.

Butter: If cow's milk butter is unsuitable, use margarine or use canola oil spread (Spectrum™), vegetable shortening, or same amount (may need to reduce by 1 tablespoon) of your favorite cooking oil. (See also **Canola Oil Spread, Oleo,** and **Oil** below.)

Butter Flavored Salt or Sprinkles: Durkee makes a gluten-free version and Butter Buds are gluten-free, but both may contain dairy.

Canola Oil: One of the most heart-healthy oils, it has a very low smoking point so it won't cause baked goods to brown too quickly. You may substitute other oils, such as safflower, corn, or vegetable oil.

Canola Oil Spread: Sold under the brand name Spectrum™ from Spectrum Naturals, this 100% canola oil spread looks and tastes like butter with the consistency of mayonnaise. Non-hydrogenated, it bakes quite well but does not melt or blend into sauces cooked on the stovetop. Its fat is mostly mono-unsaturated, so it is a healthy substitute for vegetable shortening, margarine, or butter—which you may use instead. Found in refrigerated section near the butter in natural food stores and some supermarkets.

Cheese: See **Parmesan Cheese** below and also see Baking with Dairy Substitutes in Appendix for more information on related dairy products.

Chipotle Chiles: Dried jalapeno peppers. Found on Mexican shelf in supermarket or natural food store.

Chocolate and Chocolate Chips: "Dairy-free" chocolate chips and bars are available in natural food stores, but may actually be processed on dairy equipment. Carob chips may be used instead of chocolate chips, but they may be sweetened with barley malt.

Cocoa Powder: Use unsweetened cocoa powder. Carob powder may be used, but with significant loss of flavor and color.

Coffee Powder: Taster's Choice® makes a gluten-free instant coffee powder. Espresso powder (Medaglia D'Oro) may be used instead.

Cooking Spray: Put your favorite oil in a non-aerosol pump-spray bottle, available at kitchen stores. Vegetable shortening or oil may be used to grease baking pans instead of cooking spray.

Cornstarch: Made from corn, this white powder is the same ingredient used to thicken sauces and puddings. Can be used as a flour in wheat-free cooking, but it is not the same as corn flour (which is yellow and has a heavier texture).

Dry Milk Powder: White milk powder adds sugar and protein to baked goods. Better Than Milk, Solait, and DariFree are non-dairy substitutes. Found in natural food stores. Carnation® instant milk doesn't measure the same as dry milk powder, so use twice as much.

Eggs: Use large eggs, which equal about ¼ cup each.

Egg Replacer: White powder made of various starches and leavening. Use in addition to eggs in certain recipes or in place of eggs in others. Helps stabilize baked goods. Ener-G® brand in natural food stores.

Flaxseed or Flaxseed Meal: Seeds or meal (partially ground seeds) used as egg substitute. Found in natural food stores.

Garlic Powder or Garlic Salt: Or use fresh garlic instead.

Gelatin Powder: Available in regular version (common brand name is Knox® or Grayslake®) or kosher, which is made from vegetable sources. Adds moisture and helps bind ingredients together. Kosher versions are at some natural food stores and may be marked "pareve".

Guar Gum: Plant-derived gum used to provide structure to baked goods so leavening can do its job. Contains fiber so could irritate in large amounts. Can be used in place of xanthan gum, but use half again as much guar gum. Found in baking aisle of natural food stores.

Italian (Herb) Seasoning: A blend of spices and herbs.

Lecithin Granules or Liquid: Made from soy, lecithin emulsifies, stabilizes and texturizes baked goods (especially bread). Granular and liquid versions found in the supplement section of natural food stores (sometimes in the refrigerated sections.) Usually light or beige-yellow in color, the limited amount required (about ¼ tsp.) does not change the flavor or appearance of the dish, but does enhance the texture and makes the dish seem to have more fat. Buy only pure soy lecithin.

Lemon Peel (Rind): Outermost portion of lemon. Adds flavor to baked goods. Use a microplane or zester or grater to remove peel from lemon. Use organic produce to avoid pesticides.

Maple Syrup: Made from maple tree sap and available at supermarkets and natural food stores. Most flavorful version for baking is Grade B, which is often sold in bulk in natural food stores. Choose organic maple syrup to avoid formaldehyde.

Margarine: Don't use diet margarines in baking. Non-hydrogenated brands are made by Spectrum and Earth Balance.

Milk: People with dairy allergies or lactose-intolerance should use alternatives such as rice, soy, or nut milk (called beverages). Choose casein-free substitutes if you're allergic to dairy or lactose-free products if you're lactose-intolerant. The Food Allergy & Anaphylaxis Network newsletter (Vol. 5, #4, April-May, 1996) forbids goat milk for the truly dairy-allergic and lactose-intolerant. Check with your physician.

Celiacs should avoid milk substitutes with barley malt or oats. Read labels to choose one appropriate for your condition. Choose low-sugar milks for savory dishes. See Baking with Dairy Substitutes in Appendix.

Molasses: Use regular (unsulphured) molasses, not blackstrap molasses.

Mustard: For dry mustard powder, grind mustard seeds to a fine powder with coffee grinder. Coleman's contains gluten. Dijonnaise (which is gluten-free) can be substituted for Dijon mustard.

Oil: Heart-healthiest oils are canola and olive; safflower canola, and corn oil work well in baking due to low smoke points.

Onion Powder, Onion Salt, and Dried Minced Onion: Look for gluten-free versions or use freshly grated onion, instead.

Parmesan Cheese: Often from cow's milk, but may be made from goat or sheep's milk (check with your physician— milk-allergic and lactose-intolerant persons should avoid). Found in the refrigerated sections of natural food stores. Soyco® makes a brown rice version that contains casein (a milk protein) and another made of soy, labeled 100% dairy free and casein-free, and it contains texturized soy vegetable protein (TVP). Store on pantry shelf until opened, then refrigerate.

Potato Starch: Also called potato starch flour. Fine, white powder made from the starch of potatoes. Adds light, airy texture to baked goods. Found in flour section of natural food stores. Don't confuse with the heavy, dense potato flour made from potatoes and their skins.

Puréed Fruit: Several fruits work nicely to help bind ingredients, add sweetness and moisture, and replace fat. Puréed pears impart little flavor or color. Puréed apples (applesauce or apple butter) impart a slight apple flavor, especially if the apple butter is spiced. The darker color and flavor of puréed prunes or dates make them useful only in darker, more strongly flavored dishes such as spice cakes or chocolate items.

Rice Bran: This is the outside layer of the rice kernel which is removed to make brown rice. Contains bran and part of the rice germ. Found in natural food stores by Ener-G®, near the flours or in the baking aisle. Adds fiber to baked goods. Refrigerate after opening.

Rice Flakes: Also called rolled rice or rolled rice flakes. Looks like oatmeal. Found in natural food stores or www.vitamincottage.com

Rice Flour: Most common flour used in gluten-free baking. White rice flour is the rice kernel stripped of most of its nutrients. Brown rice flour contains more layers of the rice kernel—and more nutrients. Store brown rice flour in the refrigerator or freezer to extend shelf life and avoid rancidity. Found in baking aisle or bulk sections of natural food stores and some supermarkets. See Wheat-Free Flours in Appendix.

Rice Milk: (Also called rice beverage.) Made from rice, this milk is an effective substitute for cow's milk. Available at natural food stores or supermarkets. Refrigerate after opening. Choose enriched or fortified versions. Celiacs must avoid those with barley-based brown rice syrup or malted cereal extract (which may contain barley). See Baking with Dairy Substitutes in Appendix.

Rice Polish: Portion of brown rice kernel removed in the process of making white rice. Contains part of the rice germ and bran—high in fiber. Refrigerate after opening. Found in Ener-G® box in the baking aisles of natural food stores.

Rolled Rice: See **Rice Flakes**.

Safflower Oil: Made from safflower plant, oil works well in baking or sautéing because of relatively high smoke point (won't burn as quickly).

Salt: Use your favorite salt, but check the fillers that make them free-flowing. I prefer sea salt because it has no fillers—but it is more expensive. You may reduce salt in recipes to suit your individual taste and dietary needs, but overall flavor is affected.

Sorghum Flour: Made from sorghum (milo) plant. Available at health food stores or by mail order (See Mail-Order Sources in Appendix).

Sour Cream Alternative: Made from soy; performs like real sour cream. Found in dairy section of natural food stores. Some brands contain casein or other problematic ingredients, so read labels carefully.

Soy Flour: Derived from soy beans, this yellowish-tan flour is found in regular and lower-fat form— usually in the flour section of natural food stores. Refrigerate to avoid rancidity due to fat content. Works best in baked goods with fruit such as carrot cakes. Persons who are allergic to legumes should avoid this flour. See Wheat-Free Flours in Appendix.

Soy Milk: (Also called soy beverage.) Available at natural food stores or supermarkets. Refrigerate after opening. Read labels to avoid problem ingredients. See Baking with Dairy Substitutes in Appendix for guidelines on using soy milk to replace cow's milk.

Soy Sauce: Look for wheat-free tamari versions. May use Bragg's Amino Acids (non-fermented soy sauce without wheat and yeast.)

Sugar: Bleached or unbleached cane sugar may be used. Beet sugar may also be used. See Baking with Alternative Sweeteners in the Appendix.

Sun-Dried Tomatoes: Dehydrated tomatoes which are packaged dry or packed in oil. Choose dry packaged version if you prefer the lower fat version.

Sweet Rice Flour: Derived from short grain rice, this white powder produces baked goods that are more moist and firm than if "long-grain" rice flour is used. Sometimes called "sticky" or "glutinous" rice, it *does not* contain wheat gluten. Sold in boxes by Ener-G® in baking aisle or near flours in natural food stores. See Wheat-Free Flours in Appendix.

Tapioca Flour: Made from the cassava plant, this is a fine, white flour that adds chewiness and elasticity to baked goods. Sold in natural food stores in package or bulk form. See Wheat-Free Flours in Appendix.

Tofu: Be sure to use the soft silken version (made by Mori-Nu®) in baked goods (unless otherwise specified). Store the aseptic (shelf-stable) packages on pantry shelf until opened. Refrigerate in closed container and use within two days. Found in natural food stores in refrigerated section or in displays near the baking aisle.

Vanilla Extract: Acceptable for gluten-free diets.

Vanilla Powder: Derived from vanilla beans, this white powder may also have sugar added. Powdered vanilla bean is dark brown in color. May be used interchangeably with liquid vanilla extract, but may need to add a teaspoon of water to restore moisture to the batter or dough.

Vegetable Oil: The best oils for baking are canola, safflower, and sunflower oil due to their higher smoking points, which means they won't burn as quickly (see p. 248). Canola oil is one of the more heart-healthy oils, but you may use your favorite oil. Avoid using olive oil in baking unless specified in the recipe. Most oils are found in baking aisle of supermarkets and natural food stores.

Vinegar: Except for malt vinegar, acceptable for gluten-free diets.

Vitamin C Crystals or Powder: Derived from the fermentation of corn, this powder adds acid to yeast dough and strengthens the protein structure. Also acts as acid leavening component in quick breads which are baked in the oven, not in a bread machine. Sold in supplement section of natural food stores. Make sure label says wheat and gluten-free. Choose unbuffered Vitamin C or it will not add acid to the bread.

Yeast: Red Star® and SAF® are gluten free. In this book, dry yeast is the term used to indicate regular yeast.

Yogurt: Choose yogurts with good acidophilus content. Lactose-reduced yogurt is a possible solution for the lactose-intolerant. Goat's milk yogurt is not a good solution for either the milk-allergic or lactose intolerant person according to the Food Allergy & Anaphylaxis Network (FAAN). Soy yogurt does not work well in baking. See Baking with Dairy Substitutes in Appendix.

Xanthan gum: Derived from bacteria in corn sugar, this gum lends structure and texture to baked goods and thickens sauces. Probably the most indispensable ingredient when baking without wheat or gluten. Found in baking aisle or near flours in natural food stores. Seems expensive, but lasts a long time since only a tiny amount is used in recipes.

Can be used interchangeably with guar gum, but use half again as much guar gum as xanthan gum.

Water: Some cooks prefer to use filtered water instead of tap water because it produces a sweeter, fuller flavor in baked goods. Feel free to use the water of your choice.

~ CELEBRATION MENUS ~

T hese menus are designed to help you plan and execute the perfect special occasion. Each menu is designed to provide a balance of flavor, color, texture, and overall appearance so that the food you serve looks and tastes wonderful.

Page numbers are listed beside the dish to you locate the recipe in this book. No page number means the dish has no recipe.

Afternoon Tea

Miniature Focaccia Sandwiches • 193
with
Focaccia Fillings • 194

~

Scones with Citrus Butter • 79

~

Ginger Pound Cake • 109

~

Assorted Teas

Brewing Tea: Start with kettle of fresh water. Bring water to boil. While water is heating, warm teapot by filling it with hot water. Let stand for about 1 minute. Then pour water out and dry pot.

In teapot, place 1 heaping tsp. of loose tea leaves per cup (plus one for the pot). Let leaves steep for 3 to 5 minutes. Stir once, allow leaves to resettle. Then pour tea through strainer into cups.

What kind of tea should you serve? Some people prefer Earl Grey (sweet, citrusy with bergamot), Darjeeling (fine, delicate), and Ceylon (pale, malty). But you could use Orange Pekoe and Pekoe (the old standby) or your favorite herbal tea––or perhaps green tea. Whatever you like! And, if you choose to serve iced tea, then follow your palate's desire.

Anniversary Dinner for Two

Salmon in Parchment • 40

~

Brown Rice Pilaf • 174

~

Steamed Asparagus

~

Mixed Greens with Basic Vinaigrette • 164

~

Heart Cake • 110

Anniversary Buffet Dinner

Chicken Breasts with Mango Chutney • 22
Pork Tenderloins with Ginger Sauce • 36
Lamb Chops with Rosemary Marinade • 46

~

Cooked White Long-Grain Rice

~

Mixed Greens with Basic Vinaigrette • 164

~

Italian Breadsticks • 63

~

Steamed Broccoli, Baby Carrots, & Asparagus

~

Wedding Cake • 113-119

Birthday Cakes

Butterfly Cake • 121

Candle Cake • 123

Down on the Farm Cake • 127

Halloween Spider Web Cake • 128

Indy 500 Race Track Cake • 131

How Old Are You? Cake • 129

Choice of Frostings • 136-140

Bridal Shower Luncheon

Walnut Shrimp Salad • 46
Pasta Salad • 52

Italian Breadsticks • 63

Steamed Asparagus Spears

Chocolate Dipped, Filled Strawberries • 144

Bridal Shower Brunch

Breakfast Fruit Pizza • 83

Breakfast Sausage • 90

Brown Rice Pilaf • 174

Fruit Bowl

Lemon Poppy Seed Raspberry Cake • 85

Chinese Take-Out

Chinese Hot-Sour Soup • 56

Pork Fried Rice • 34

Sweet-and-Sour Pork • 38

Pad Thai • 51

CHINESE

Cinco de Mayo

Green Chile Stew • 57

Cornbread with Green Chiles • 67

Tomatillo Rice • 178

Vegetables with Avocado Bean Salsa • 197

Mexican Chocolate Cake • 100

Congratulatory Dinner

Paella • 42

Mixed Greens with Basic Vinaigrette • 164

Italian Breadsticks • 63
French Bread • 62

Chocolate Mocha Fudge Trifle • 145

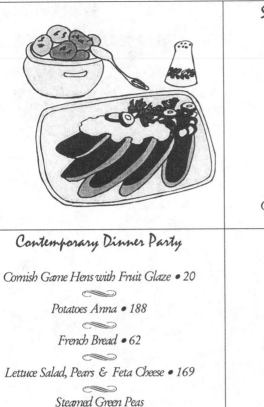

Small, Intimate Dinner Party

Oven-Baked Crab Cakes • 196

Potatoes Anna • 188

Caesar Salad without Eggs • 166

French Bread • 62

Steamed Broccoli

Chocolate Macaroon Tunnel Cake • 107

Contemporary Dinner Party

Cornish Game Hens with Fruit Glaze • 20

Potatoes Anna • 188

French Bread • 62

Lettuce Salad, Pears & Feta Cheese • 169

Steamed Green Peas

Double Chocolate Cherry Torte • 108

Elegant Dinner Party

Pork Medallions with Cherry Sauce • 35

Brown Rice Pilaf • 174

Spinach Salad with Strawberries • 170

Steamed Vegetables

Frozen Tiramisu • 147

Holiday Menu for Thanksgiving/Christmas

Turkey & Gravy • 21

Stuffing • 176

French Bread • 62

Pumpkin Pie • 142

Your favorite holiday dishes

Fall Dinner

Pork Chops with Apple-Dijon Sauce • 33

Roasted Potatoes • 187

French Bread • 62

Mixed Greens with Basic Vinaigrette • 164

Sautéed Brussels Sprouts • 184

Applesauce Spice Cake • 97

Father's Day

Grilled Pork, Orange-Rosemary Sauce • 32

Garlic Mashed Potatoes • 186

Waldorf Salad • 170

Corn-on-the-Cob
or
Steamed Green Peas

Rocky Road Brownies • 156

Dad

HAPPY DAD'S DAY

Fireworks on the Fourth

Barbecued Chicken • 20

Roasted (Grilled) Vegetables • 182

Garlic French Bread • 62

Chocolate Ice Cream Sandwiches • 153
Rocky Road Brownies • 156

Aprés Golf Party

Barbecued Ribs
with 19th Hole Barbecue Sauce • 31

Cabbage Coleslaw • 174

Potato Salad • 169

Fruit-Sweetened Gelatin Salad • 171

Garlic French Bread • 62

Double Chocolate Cherry Torte • 108

Fireside Candlelight Dinner

Coq Au Vin • 27

Pasta (Homemade Egg Pasta) • 176

Roasted Fennel • 181

Italian Breadsticks • 63

Mixed Greens with Basic Vinaigrette • 164

Chocolate Cherry Cake • 106

Graduation Day

Tuna Burgers (or Hamburgers)
With Grilled Pineapple Slices • 45

Roasted Potatoes • 187

Fruit-Sweetened Gelatin Salad • 171

Italian Breadsticks • 63

Celebration Cookies • 152
Chocolate Cappuccino Ice Cream • 158

Halloween

Cakes
Basic Cake • 98-99

Basic Chocolate Cake • 100-101

Halloween Spider Web Cake • 128

Cookies, Bars, Muffins, Etc.
Bug Cookies • 150

Colorado Chocolate Chip Cookies • 154

Cookie Monsters • 150

Flower Pot Treats • 146

Granola Bars • 93

Pumpkin Muffins • 75

Snake Cookies • 150

Basic (Cut-Out) Cookies • 157

8

Mardi Gras

Bayou Red Beans & Rice • 37

Cornbread with Green Chiles • 67

Platter of Fresh, Bite-Size Vegetables
with
Chutney Appetizer Spread • 198

Pecan Nut Torte with Chocolate Ganache • 112

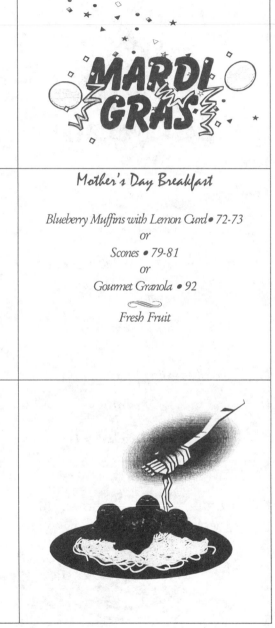

Happy Mother's Mom

Mother's Day Breakfast

Blueberry Muffins with Lemon Curd• 72-73
or
Scones • 79-81
or
Gourmet Granola • 92

Fresh Fruit

O Sole Mio Supper

Spaghetti Sauce & Meatballs • 50

Mixed Greens
with Tomato-Basil Vinaigrette • 165

Roasted Fennel (on salad)• 181

Italian Breadsticks • 63

Frozen Tiramisu • 147

Ice Cream Social

Chocolate Sorbet • 158

Raspberry Sherbet • 160

Strawberry Sherbet • 160

Vanilla Ice Cream or Frozen Yogurt • 161

Cookies of Choice • 151-157

Caramel Sauce • 134
Chocolate Syrup • 136

Ice Cream

Pasta Party

Fresh Tomato Basil Sauce with Pasta • 50

Spicy Fettuccini with Basil • 54

Spicy Shrimp & Pasta • 44

Mixed Greens
with Tomato-Basil Vinaigrette • 165

Focaccia • 61

Chocolate Mocha Fudge Trifle • 145

Pizza with Panache

Pizza with Pizza Sauce • 53
Toppings: Sausage • 47
Pineapple & Ham or Vegetarian

Mixed Greens with Basic Vinaigrette • 164

Chocolate Cherry Cookies • 152

Portable Feasts
(Picnic, Tailgate Party)

Barbecued Chicken • 20

∽

Couscous Salad • 174
Potato Salad • 169
Jicama & Mandarin Orange Salad • 168
Fruit Salad with Balsamic Vinegar • 167

∽

Focaccia • 61

∽

Celebration Cookies • 152

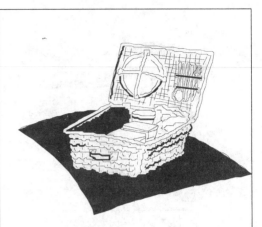

Rites of Spring Dinner

Lamb Chops with Rosemary Marinade • 46

∽

New Potatoes & Peas with Lemon & Dill • 187

∽

French Bread • 62

∽

Strawberries & Kiwi in Orange Juice

∽

Lemon Sorbet • 159
Basic (Cut-Out) Cookies • 157

Spring Luncheon

Asparagus Soup • 55

∽

Spinach Salad with Strawberries • 170

∽

Scones with Ham • 78

∽

Strawberry Sherbet • 160
"Oatmeal" Cookies • 155

Hot Summer Days

Pasta Salad • 52

French Bread • 62
or
Italian Breadsticks • 63

Raspberry Sherbet • 160
Chocolate Cherry Cookies • 152

Hot Summer Nights

Grilled Chicken
with Mango/Black Bean Salsa • 23

Jicama & Mandarin Orange Salad • 168

Italian Breadsticks • 63

Roasted Potatoes • 187

Steamed Green Beans or
Corn on the Cob

Peach Melba Ice Cream Pie • 149

Sunday Dinner

Baked Ham • 30

Duchesse Potatoes • 185

French Bread • 62

Minted Peas

Fruit-Sweetened Gelatin Salad • 171

Chocolate Macaroon Tunnel Cake • 107

Super Bowl Party

Colorado Chili • 57

Corn Bread with Green Chiles • 67

Platter of Ready-to-Eat Fresh Vegetables
(baby carrots, celery, broccoli, radishes)

Corn Chips & Mexican Tomato Salsa Dip • 200
or
Avocado Bean Salsa • 197

Celebration Cookies • 152

TOUCHDOWN!

St. Patrick's Day

Corned Beef & Cabbage • 48

Colcannon • 184

Irish Soda Bread with Dried Cherries • 69

Steamed Broccoli or Green Peas

Irish Apple Cake • 111

Valentine's Day Dinner

Red Snapper in Parchment • 40

Mixed Greens with Basic Vinaigrette • 164

Steamed Broccoli

French Bread • 62

Heart Cake & Chocolate Strawberries • 110

HAPPY VALENTINE'S DAY

Wedding Reception Dinner

Raspberry-Basil Chicken • 25

Brown Rice Pilaf • 174

Steamed Vegetables of Choice

Spinach Salad with Strawberries • 170

French Bread • 62

Wedding Cake • 113-119

Wedding Breakfast

Blueberry Muffins with Lemon Curd • 72-73

Cappuccino Chocolate Chip Muffins • 74

Bran Muffins • 75

Gourmet Granola • 92

Bowl of Fresh Fruit

Wedding Cakes

Chocolate Raspberry Groom's Cake • 113

Coconut Wedding Cake • 114

Lemon Wedding Cake • 115

Spice Wedding Cake • 116-117

Yellow Tiered Wedding Cake • 119

White Wedding Cake With Fruit Filling • 118

Frostings • 136-140

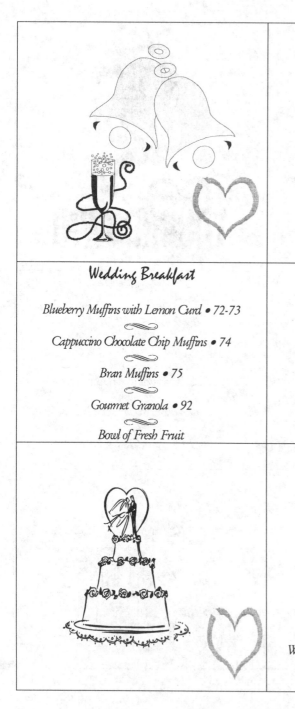

Wedding Reception Buffet

Miniature Focaccia Sandwiches • 193

Grilled Shrimp with Wraps • 195

Herbed Rice Salad • 177

Couscous Salad • 175

Grilled (Roasted) Vegetables • 182

Platter of Ready-to-eat Vegetables
(carrots, celery, radishes, broccoli, bell pepper)
Tuscan Bean Dip • 198

Platter of Ready-to-eat Fruits
(pineapple, melon, strawberries, kiwi, berries)

Wedding Cake • 113-119

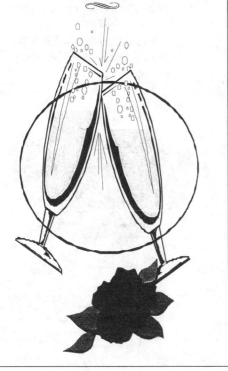

Buffet Tips

1. Allow at least 8 hors d'oeuvres per person if you're not serving a meal afterwards.

2. Choose a few make-ahead dishes to reduce preparation on the day of the event.

3. Balance the menu with hot dishes next to room-temperature salsas; crunchy vegetables next to creamy dips; decadent dishes next to low-calorie options. Use bright colors in food and some serving platters, neutrals in others.

The idea is to provide variety in many ways so your guests enjoy the food from a visual, tactile, and aromatic perspective. Also, by providing variety your guests can choose foods that work for them. And, various textures, shapes, and sizes make the table visually appealing.

4. Envision the traffic flow up to and around a buffet table. Place plates, utensils, etc. at the most convenient, obvious location so guests aren't leaning over or around dishes or backtracking to pick up things they missed.

5. If you won't always be near the table to answer questions, put miniature place cards beside each food listing the contents.

6. Use attractive garnishes, but make sure they're edible . . . or clearly marked as inedible.

7. If you're serving outdoors, consider covers for the food to thwart bugs and pests.

8. Centerpieces add visual drama and help carry out the theme of the special occasion.

9. Introduce your guests to a new flavor or dish each time you entertain. Many people like to experiment with their taste buds. With a buffet, those who don't like to experiment aren't forced to eat something they know they won't like.

Breakfast

Gourmet Granola • 92

Breakfast Trifle • 90

Fresh Fruit

Cappuccino Chocolate Chip Muffins • 74

Brunch

Banana Pecan Waffles
with Maple Raisin Syrup • 86

Breakfast Sausage • 90
with
Brown Rice Pilaf • 174

Fruit Bowl

Lunch

Pizza Crust • 55
with
Pizza Sauce • 55

Mixed Greens with Basic Vinaigrette • 164

Platter of Fresh Ready-to-eat Vegetables
with
Sunny Tomato-Basil Dip • 201

Colorado Chocolate Chip Cookies • 154
Chocolate Cappuccino Ice Cream • 158

Dinner

Veal (or Pork) Scaloppini • 52

Pineapple Coconut Rice • 180

French Bread • 62

Mixed Greens with Basic Vinaigrette • 164

Sautéed Brussels Sprouts • 184

Double Chocolate Cherry Torte • 108

~ Secret Anniversaries of the Heart ~

For some of us, the most precious times are not the holidays on the calendar, but rather those we observe silently, in private. Let's call them "secret anniversaries of the heart." These special times are evoked by our senses and— of these— scent is one of the most powerful emissaries.

For example, the smell of roses makes me think of my maternal grandmother who used a rose-scented hand lotion. When I think of her I recall the cookies she always had waiting for her grand-children. To this day, I associate those cookies with her.

Think back over your life and your secret anniversaries. For many of us, certain memories trigger thoughts of food and celebratory times. Perhaps it is winning the coveted part in a school play... or the music that played on your first date or ... when you found out you were pregnant with your first child. Maybe it's a sad memory such as the loss of a parent... or an unexpected job transfer that separated you from loved ones.

If these memories— whether they're happy or sad, evoke thoughts of food— then let those foods be markers for those anniversaries. Though she's been dead for nearly 20 years, I still have fond, warm thoughts as I prepare some of my Mother's favorite recipes. And, sometimes I prepare those dishes simply because I have that longing to reconnect with her using food as the medium. You don't have to explain why you're serving a particular dish. If it makes you happy or arouses melancholy thoughts that allow you to indulge your feelings, that's your secret.

I like to use food to celebrate life and the rituals we embrace. So my motto is "Celebrate anything and everything--with food". Use the next page to record secret anniversaries of your heart. Encourage your family to think of foods (or aromas) that evoke pleasant memories and prepare those foods for them as a tribute. They'll be grateful.

~ Notes ~

~ MAIN DISHES ~

W hether you're entertaining in grand style, hosting a small, informal dinner party, or just fixing a special meal for your family . . . you'll find plenty of flavorful dishes in this chapter to take center stage for those special occasions.

Beef & Lamb
Chorizo 47
Corned Beef & Cabbage 48
Lamb Chops/Rosemary Marinade 46
Orange Beef Stir-Fry 49
Sausage 47
Spaghetti Sauce & Meatballs 50
Veal (Pork) Scaloppini 52

Pork & Ham
Baked Ham 30
Bayou Red Beans & Rice 37
Barbecued Ribs/19th Hole Sauce 31
Grilled Pork/Orange-Rosemary Sauce 32
Pork Chops/Anise-Prune Sauce 30
Pork Chops/Apple-Dijon Sauce 33
Pork Fried Rice 34
Pork Medallions with Cherry Sauce 35
Pork Tenderloin with Ginger Sauce 36
Sweet-and-Sour Pork 38
Thai Pork Noodle Bowl 35

Pasta, Pizza, & Miscellaneous
Fresh Tomato Basil Sauce/Pasta 50
Pad Thai 51
Pasta Salad 52
Pizza Crust & Pizza Sauce 53
Spaghetti Sauce & Meatballs 50
Spice Rub for Meat 54
Spicy Fettuccini with Basil 54
Spicy Shrimp & Pasta 44

Fish & Shellfish
Coconut Shrimp/Orange Marmalade 39
Red Snapper in Parchment 40
Paella 42
Poached Salmon 43
Salmon in Parchment 40
Shrimp Creole 41
Spicy Shrimp & Pasta 44
Tuna Burgers/Grilled Pineapple 45
Walnut Shrimp Salad 46

Soups & Stews
Asparagus Soup 55
Chinese Hot-Sour Soup 56
Colorado Chili 57
Green Chile Stew 57

Chicken & Poultry
Barbecued Chicken 20
Chicken Breasts/Mango Chutney 22
Grilled Chicken/Mango-Bean Salsa 23
Chicken Cacciatore 26
Coq Au Vin 27
Cornish Game Hens/Fruit Glaze 20
Southwest Chicken/Grilled Peaches 24
Raspberry-Basil Chicken 25
Stir-Fry Lemon Chicken 28
Stir-Fry Orange Chicken 29
Turkey & Gravy 21

For additional main dishes without wheat, gluten, or dairy see *Gluten-Free 101: Easy, Basic Dishes without Wheat*, 2003, or *Wheat-Free Recipes & Menus: Delicious Dining without Wheat or Gluten*, 2002.

~ Barbecued Chicken ~

This sauce is so simple and easy, yet your guests will love it. You can make it the day before, chill, and it is ready to use when you are.

1 small can (5.5 oz) tomato juice
¼ cup fresh lemon juice
1 Tbsp. butter or oleo
1 tsp. grated lemon peel
1 tsp. Worcestershire sauce
  (Lea & Perrins)

½ tsp. onion powder
¼ tsp. black pepper
¼ tsp. cayenne pepper
1 garlic clove, minced
1 lb. chicken pieces

Combine all sauce ingredients in small, heavy saucepan. Simmer over low-medium heat 10-15 minutes. Brush on chicken as it grills. Serves 4.

Calories	Fat	Protein	Carb	Chol	Sodium	Fiber
190	9g	24g	4g	80mg	225mg	<1g

~ Cornish Game Hens with Fruit Glaze ~

These are especially pretty to serve at company meals. The fruit glaze provides a wonderful complement to the crispy skin and assures a beautifully browned bird.

2 Cornish game hens, halved
½ tsp. salt
¼ tsp. black pepper
½ cup fruit-only raspberry jam
¼ tsp. dried thyme leaves

¼ tsp. dried tarragon leaves
1 tsp. olive oil
¼ cup red wine vinegar
1 small garlic clove, minced

1. Wash game hens and pat dry. Season with salt and pepper. Arrange game hens skin side up in oiled roasting pan. If possible, place hens on roasting rack in pan so they do not sit in fat while roasting.

2. Combine remaining ingredients in small bowl to make glaze and microwave until jam is melted. Stir mixture thoroughly.

3. Bake hens, covered, in 400° oven 45 minutes to 1 hour, brushing frequently with glaze. Serves 4.

Calories	Fat	Protein	Carb	Chol	Sodium	Fiber
400	25g	29g	12g	170mg	400mg	1g

~ Turkey ~

*This particular method works best with a fresh turkey (which has no questionable additives).
The brining imparts moisture and flavor and works best with turkeys under 16 lb.*

1 cup coarse (kosher) salt
⅓ cup honey
2 large bay leaves
1 Tbsp. dried thyme leaves
6 whole cloves

½ tsp. ground allspice
6 black peppercorns, crushed
2 gallons water
1 fresh turkey, 14-16 lb.

1. In very large stockpot or canning pot, combine salt, honey, bay leaves, thyme, cloves, allspice, peppercorns and 2 cups water. Bring to boil, stirring until salt dissolves. Remove from heat, add remaining water. Cool.

2. Rinse fresh turkey; check for pin feathers. Remove giblets; wash cavities thoroughly. Place turkey, breast side down, in brine, covering completely. If not, add more water. Cover and refrigerate overnight.

3. Rinse turkey; discard brine. Roast in your preferred method.

~ Gravy ~

Adjust the herbs and spices to suit your taste. Each thickener produces different textures.

1 ¾ cups low-sodium gf chicken broth
½ cup strained drippings of turkey
Thickener of your choice:
  Cornstarch: 2 Tbsp.
  Rice flour: 4 Tbsp.
  Tapioca flour: 6 Tbsp.

¼ tsp. salt
¼ tsp. black pepper
¼ tsp. ground sage
¼ tsp. dried thyme leaves
¼ tsp. poultry seasoning

1. Combine strained drippings and broth to heavy saucepan, reserving ½ cup of the broth.

2. Place pan over medium-high heat; add seasonings. Stir thickener into ½ cup reserved broth, making thin paste. Gently whisk thickening mixture into pan, continuing to whisk until mixture thickens and boils. Adjust consistency by adding more thickener or chicken broth. Remove from heat. Strain, if desired. Taste and adjust seasonings, if necessary. Makes 2 ¼ cups. Serves 8 (about ¼ cup gravy each).

Calories	Fat	Protein	Carb	Chol	Sodium	Fiber
140	14g	1g	2g	14mg	186mg	<1g

~ Chicken Breasts with Mango Chutney ~

Mango chutney has been called the "king of chutneys". You'll see it in many gourmet recipes and, of course, there are commercial versions on the shelf. But, you can make your own and have complete control over what goes into it. Prepare the chutney ahead of time and bring to room temperature before serving.

Chicken Breasts
4 chicken breast halves
1 tsp. salt
¼ tsp. black pepper
1 Tbsp. cooking oil

Mango Chutney
⅓ cup cider vinegar
¾ cup sugar
½ cup seedless raisins or dried currants
1 small onion, finely chopped
2 tsp. mustard seed
1 jalapeño or serrano chile pepper, diced
1 large garlic clove, minced
1 Tbsp. grated fresh ginger
1 tsp. ground ginger
¼ tsp. salt
½ tsp. ground nutmeg
½ tsp. ground allspice
½ tsp. ground mace
⅛ tsp. cayenne pepper
⅛ tsp. ground cloves
1 large mango, peeled and diced

Chutney
Combine all chutney ingredients, except mangoes, in large kettle. Cook over low heat, uncovered, 45 minutes or until liquid is clear and syrupy. Add mango and continue cooking until fruit is tender, about 20-25 minutes. Stir occasionally to prevent scorching. Remove from heat and cool while chicken is browning.

Chicken
As chutney simmers, wash chicken breasts and pat dry with paper towels. Season with salt and pepper. Brown chicken in olive oil in heavy skillet over medium heat until nicely browned on both sides. Serve with warm chutney. Serves 4.

Calories	Fat	Protein	Carb	Chol	Sodium	Fiber
370	6g	15g	67g	36mg	768mg	3g

~ Grilled Chicken, Mango/Black Bean Salsa ~

Salsas are very popular in fine restaurants, but you can produce the same results at home. Salsas are very colorful, healthy, and introduce fiber and a variety of interesting flavors into our meals. This one is also great on grilled fish.

Salsa
1 medium ripe mango (peeled, diced)
½ cup minced red onion
¼ cup chopped red bell pepper
¼ cup cooked black beans
¼ cup chopped fresh cilantro, packed
1 Tbsp. fresh lime or lemon juice
1 Tbsp. sugar
1 Tbsp. red wine vinegar
1 chipotle pepper*
1 Tbsp. olive oil
¼ tsp. ground cumin
¼ tsp. salt
¼ tsp. black pepper

Chicken
4 chicken breast halves
1 tsp. salt
¼ tsp. black pepper
1 Tbsp. olive oil

Salsa
1. Combine ingredients in medium-size bowl. Cover and chill. Leave at room temperature for 15 minutes before serving.

Chicken
2. Pat chicken dry with paper towels. Season with salt and pepper. Brown in olive oil in heavy skillet over medium heat until nicely browned on both sides. Or, grill on barbecue grill. Serve immediately with salsa. Serves 4.

Calories	Fat	Protein	Carb	Chol	Sodium	Fiber
195	9g	15g	15g	36mg	760mg	3g

*Bring 2 Tbsp. water to boil. Remove from heat. Soak 1 dry chipotle pepper in water 20 minutes. Finely chop pepper and add it with water to salsa. If you have never used chipotle peppers before (they're actually smoked, dried jalapeños), use ½ chipotle pepper and 1 Tbsp. rather than 2 Tbsp. of chipotle-flavored water. Taste salsa and add ½ chipotle and 1 Tbsp. of water, if desired, for hotter dish. Or, if you prefer, use a finely chopped fresh jalapeño pepper in place of chipotle pepper. Wear rubber gloves to protect hands while cutting chiles.

~ Southwest Chicken & Grilled Peaches ~

You've seen fancy restaurant dishes with multiple sauces, decoratively placed on the plate in exotic patterns. The secret? Fill empty, plastic squeeze bottles such as those that contain mustard or ketchup. Refrigerate unused sauce for up to 1 week.

<u>Chicken & Peaches</u>
4 chicken breast halves
Fresh cilantro, parsley and cherry
    tomatoes for garnish
2 firm, ripe peaches (unpeeled)
<u>Chipotle Sauce</u>
1 dried chipotle pepper
¼ cup boiling water
½ cup milk (cow, rice, soy)
1 tsp. grated fresh ginger
¼ tsp. salt
1 tsp. fresh lemon or lime juice
1 tsp. nut butter (almond or cashew)

<u>Southwest Marinade</u>
¾ cup fresh lime juice
½ cup minced fresh cilantro
2 Tbsp. olive oil
2 small garlic cloves, minced
2 tsp. chili powder
2 tsp. dried oregano
½ tsp. cayenne pepper
½ tsp. cumin powder
½ tsp. salt
½ tsp. cornstarch
2 tsp. water
<u>Balsamic Syrup</u>
1 cup balsamic vinegar
1 tsp. sugar
1 tsp. ground coriander

Chicken
Assemble marinade ingredients (except cornstarch and water) in shallow glass or ceramic dish. Arrange chicken breasts, turn to coat thoroughly, cover, and chill for 2-4 hours. Grill over coals or brown in a ridged skillet until done.

Southwest Marinade Sauce
While chicken is cooking, heat marinade juices in small, heavy pan.

Chipotle Sauce
Bring ¼ cup water to boil. Place dried chipotle pepper in water and soak 5-10 minutes. Finely chop chipotle pepper (wearing rubber gloves to protect hands), and reserve liquid. In food processor, combine chopped chipotle, soaking liquid, milk, ginger, salt, lemon (or lime) juice, and nut butter. Purée until very smooth. Heat mixture in small, heavy saucepan over medium heat until thick.

Balsamic Syrup
Bring balsamic vinegar, sugar, and coriander to boil in small, heavy pan. Reduce heat to low; simmer until liquid is reduced to about ⅔ cup.

Grilled Peaches
1. Cut peaches in half; remove pits. Place cut side down on grill. Brush with Balsamic Syrup; grill on both sides until grill marks are visible.

2. Just before serving, stir cornstarch into 2 tsp. water to form paste. Stir paste into marinade over medium heat until slightly thickened. Place 2 Tbsp. hot Southwest Marinade in pool on plate. Place cooked chicken breast in pool.

3. Spoon Chipotle Sauce over each chicken breast. Drizzle Balsamic Syrup over chicken breasts in decorative. Add peach half. Garnish plate with cilantro sprigs and cherry tomatoes. Serve immediately. Serves 4.

Calories	Fat	Protein	Carb	Chol	Sodium	Fiber
240	10g	16g	24g	37mg	513mg	2g

~ Raspberry-Basil Chicken ~

Raspberry and basil seem to complement one another in this truly delicious dish.

6 chicken breast halves
⅓ cup fruit-only raspberry jam
¼ cup pineapple juice
3 Tbsp. gf tamari soy sauce
1 Tbsp. rice or balsamic vinegar
1 tsp. dried basil leaves
¼ tsp. salt

¼ tsp. black pepper
¼ tsp. dry mustard*
1 small garlic clove, minced
¼ tsp. chili powder
¼ tsp. curry powder
Fresh basil leaf for garnish
Grind mustard seeds with small coffee grinder

1. Place chicken breasts in greased, shallow baking dish.

2. Whisk together remaining ingredients and pour half over chicken, reserving other half. Marinate chicken 30-45 minutes in refrigerator.

3. Preheat oven to 350°. Bake chicken 30-45 minutes or until done, basting occasionally,. Heat remaining sauce and serve over chicken. Garnish with a sprig of fresh basil, if desired. Serves 6.

Calories	Fat	Protein	Carb	Chol	Sodium	Fiber
108	2g	14g	89g	37mg	635mg	1g

~ Chicken Cacciatore ~

The aroma of this dish will fill your kitchen, inviting you and your guests to a marvelous dining experience. Serve with hot cooked rice or pasta and a crunchy tossed salad. It is especially wonderful on a cold winter day.

4 chicken breast halves
1 Tbsp. olive oil
3 cups fresh mushrooms, halved
1 small green bell pepper, chopped
1 large onion, sliced
1 garlic clove, minced
½ cup dry red wine
1 can (20 oz.) tomatoes, chopped
2 Tbsp. tomato paste

2 Tbsp. fresh lemon juice
2 tsp. dried basil leaves
1 tsp. sugar
1 tsp. dried thyme leaves
¼ tsp. crushed red peppers
½ tsp. salt
¼ tsp. black pepper
2 Tbsp. tapioca flour
2 Tbsp. water

1. In large, heavy skillet or Dutch oven, brown chicken on all sides in olive oil. Add mushrooms, green bell peppers, onion, and garlic to skillet. Cook until vegetables are tender. Add wine, bring to boiling and simmer, uncovered, until liquid is nearly evaporated. Add undrained canned tomatoes, tomato paste, lemon juice, basil, sugar, thyme, crushed red peppers, salt, and pepper.

2. Return chicken to pan and simmer, uncovered, for 15 minutes-- either on the range or in 350° oven. If sauce is not thick enough, stir 2 Tbsp. tapioca flour with 2 Tbsp. water and add to sauce, stirring until thickened. Serves 6.

Calories	Fat	Protein	Carb	Chol	Sodium	Fiber
148	4g	12g	15g	24mg	233mg	3g

~ Coq Au Vin ~

A popular French dish, this is actually just chicken cooked in wine. It is an elegant blend of flavors and the dish cooks slowly on its own, leaving you free to do other things. It's absolutely delicious and perfect for a fall or winter day.

1 bacon slice, uncooked
1 tsp. olive oil
4 chicken breast halves
1 pkg (9 oz) frozen pearl onions
3 garlic cloves, peeled
½ lb. fresh mushrooms
1 cup low-sodium gf chicken broth
½ cup dry red wine
1 tsp. dried thyme
1 tsp. sugar

1 tsp. dried rosemary, crushed
1 tsp. paprika
½ tsp. celery salt
½ tsp. black pepper
1 lb. small new potatoes
1 lb. baby carrots
¼ tsp. salt
1 Tbsp. cornstarch
2 Tbsp. water
½ cup chopped fresh parsley

1. In heavy, ovenproof Dutch oven, brown bacon slice until crisp. Remove bacon; add 1 tsp. olive oil to pan and cook chicken pieces until browned on all sides. Remove chicken from pan; set aside.

2. In same Dutch oven, brown onions and garlic about 5 minutes. Add mushrooms and sauté 5 minutes more. Slowly pour in chicken broth and wine. Add thyme, sugar, rosemary, paprika, celery salt, and black pepper. Return chicken to pan and add potatoes and bacon slice.

3. Bake, covered, 30 minutes at 400°. Reduce heat to 350°, add carrots and continue cooking another 30 minutes. Remove chicken and vegetables from Dutch oven with slotted spoon. Keep warm on serving platter or bowl. If sauce does not need thickening, it may be served at this point by pouring over chicken and vegetables.

4. If sauce needs thickening, combine cornstarch and water to form paste. With Dutch oven over low-medium heat, stir in cornstarch mixture; boil until sauce thickens. Use more cornstarch for thicker sauce.

5. Pour sauce over chicken and vegetables. Garnish with parsley. Serves 4.

Calories	Fat	Protein	Carb	Chol	Sodium	Fiber
318	8g	20g	37g	42mg	688mg	4g

~ Stir-Fry Lemon Chicken ~

One of the secrets to attractive stir-fry dishes is to vary the shapes and colors of the various vegetables. For example, I like to cut the carrots into ¼-inch ridged diagonals, the red or green bell peppers into long, ¼-inch thin slices, and the green onions into 1-inch diagonals.

1 lb. chicken (1-inch pieces)
¼ cup gf tamari soy sauce
¼ cup fresh lemon juice
1 Tbsp. grated lemon peel
¼ cup water
1 tsp. honey
2 tsp. crushed red peppers
2 garlic cloves, minced
½ tsp. ground ginger

1 Tbsp. olive oil
3 green onions (1-inch diagonals)
2 medium carrots, sliced diagonally
½ cup red bell pepper (¼-inch strips)
2 tsp. cornstarch
2 cups hot cooked white rice
Additional green onion & lemon
    peel strips for garnish

1. Place chicken in shallow, glass dish. Set aside. Combine soy sauce, lemon juice, lemon peel, water, honey, crushed red peppers, garlic, and ginger. Pour half of marinade over chicken and reserve remaining half. Marinate chicken, refrigerated, 30 minutes.

2. Meanwhile, prepare vegetables. Set aside. Drain chicken and discard marinade.

3. In heavy skillet over medium heat, sauté chicken in olive oil until lightly browned. Transfer meat to plate, cover with foil.

4. In same skillet, sauté onions, carrots, and red bell pepper until crisp-tender. Whisk cornstarch into reserved marinade. Stir into vegetables and stir-fry until thickened. Return chicken to skillet; bring to serving temperature.

5. Serve immediately over cooked rice. Garnish with additional chopped green onions and lemon strips, if desired. Serves 4.

Calories	Fat	Protein	Carb	Chol	Sodium	Fiber
415	7g	30g	57g	63mg	999mg	3g

Rice contributes 45mg of the 57g of carbohydrate per serving.

~ Stir-Fry Orange Chicken ~

This is a beautiful dish and one that you can prepare in front of your guests. For some reason, guests love to watch the cook— at least at my house! So, make the food preparation part of the entertainment. You may use shrimp in place of chicken, if you wish.

Sauce
½ cup low-sodium gf chicken broth
½ cup orange juice
3 Tbsp. gf tamari soy sauce
2 tsp. rice vinegar
1 tsp. sesame oil
1 Tbsp. canola oil
1 tsp. molasses
1 tsp. sugar
3 Tbsp. cornstarch

Chicken & Vegetables
1 tsp. canola oil
4 chicken breast halves
  (sliced diagonally)
3 Tbsp. grated orange peel
1 garlic clove, minced
¼ tsp. crushed red peppers
1 cup sliced red and/or
  yellow bell pepper
1 cup snow peas (fresh or frozen)
¼ cup diagonally sliced carrots
¼ cup chopped fresh cilantro,
  packed
4 cups hot cooked white rice

Sauce
Whisk together sauce ingredients and set aside.

Chicken & Vegetables
In large skillet or wok, heat oil over medium-high heat. Add chicken slices and cook until nicely browned. Add orange peel, garlic, crushed red pepper, bell peppers, snow peas, and carrots. Sauté 2-3 minutes. Stir in sauce mixture and simmer 4-5 minutes until mixture thickens and reduces slightly. Add cilantro. Serve over cooked rice. Serves 4.

Calories	Fat	Protein	Carb	Chol	Sodium	Fiber
205	6g	17g	64g	37mg	810mg	3g

Rice contributes 44g of the total 64g of carbohydrates per serving.

~ Baked Ham ~

Baked ham is the perfect dish for a Sunday dinner. Leftovers are great, too.

5 lb. ham, fully cooked
2 cups low-sodium gf chicken stock
½ cup dry sherry
1 bay leaf
¼ cup frozen orange juice concentrate

½ tsp. dried thyme leaves
⅛ tsp. ground cloves
1 cup raisins
1 Tbsp. tapioca flour
2 Tbsp. water

1. Bake ham one hour at 325°, or until heated through. Meanwhile, in heavy medium saucepan combine chicken stock, dry sherry, bay leaf, orange juice concentrate, thyme, and cloves. Bring to boil; remove from heat to cool. Add raisins.

2. When ready to serve, return sauce to medium heat. Cook about 10 minutes, or until sauce is slightly reduced. Stir tapioca flour with 2 Tbsp. water; then stir into sauce. Continue stirring constantly until mixture thickens slightly. Makes about 2 cups of sauce. Serve sauce over sliced ham. Serves 12.

Calories	Fat	Protein	Carb	Chol	Sodium	Fiber
460	18g	56g	14g	178mg	230mg	1g

~ Pork Chops with Anise-Prune Sauce ~

Prunes contribute wonderful flavor, interesting texture, and considerable nutrients.

4 medium pork chops (1 ¼ lb.)
1 Tbsp. olive oil
1 large garlic clove, minced
1 tsp. grated fresh ginger
2 Tbsp. gf tamari soy sauce

2 Tbsp. red wine vinegar
¼ cup water
1 Tbsp. brown sugar
1 tsp. anise extract
¼ cup prunes, finely chopped

1. In large, heavy skillet brown pork chops in olive oil over medium heat. Remove meat from skillet.

2. Add garlic, ginger through prunes. Bring to simmer. Return pork chops to skillet and simmer, covered, 15 minutes. Remove cover. Let sauce simmer to desired consistency. Serves 4.

Calories	Fat	Protein	Carb	Chol	Sodium	Fiber
350	13g	45g	11g	130mg	585mg	1g

~ Barbecued Ribs with 19th Hole Sauce ~

This is one of our favorite summertime dishes. By pre-cooking the ribs, they turn out deliciously tender and succulent.

8 lb. pork ribs
1 cup ketchup
½ cup molasses
2 Tbsp. dried minced onion
2 Tbsp. brown sugar
1 Tbsp. mustard seeds
1 tsp. crushed red peppers
1 tsp. dried oregano leaves
½ tsp. black pepper
2 tsp. paprika

1 tsp. chili powder
½ tsp. salt
1 bay leaf
1 garlic clove, minced
1 tsp. grated orange peel
½ cup orange juice
2 Tbsp. olive oil
¼ cup red wine vinegar
2 Tbsp. Worcestershire sauce
  (Lea & Perrins)

1. Wrap ribs in aluminum foil and bake in 250° 3-4 hours. (This step can be done the day before. Refrigerate, covered.)

2. To make sauce, combine remaining ingredients in small saucepan. Bring to boil, reduce heat to low, and simmer sauce 10-15 minutes. Brush sauce on ribs as they cook on grill. Serves 12.

Calories	Fat	Protein	Carb	Chol	Sodium	Fiber
690	45g	42g	20g	170mg	270mg	1g

~ Grilled Pork with Orange-Rosemary Sauce ~

This dish can also be transformed into a last-minute quick dinner—if you skip marinating the pork in the sauce. For a smoother sauce, be sure to grate rather than chop the onion.

4 pork chops (1 ¼ lb.)
2 Tbsp. molasses
½ cup orange juice
1 tsp. grated orange peel
2 tsp. Dijonnaise mustard
1 tsp. olive oil
1 tsp. balsamic vinegar
¼ tsp. salt

¼ tsp. black pepper
1 tsp. crushed dried rosemary
1 small garlic clove, minced
2 Tbsp. grated fresh onion
1 tsp. cornstarch
1 Tbsp. water
Fresh rosemary sprigs for garnish

1. Place pork chops in shallow dish or heavy-duty plastic freezer bag. Combine all sauce ingredients (molasses through onion) and pour over pork. Marinate for 6-8 hours. Remove pork and grill until done.

2. Meanwhile, while pork is cooking, bring marinade to boil in small saucepan over medium heat, reduce to low, and simmer 5 minutes. Baste chops with the cooked sauce as they grill, if you wish.

3. Just before serving, mix cornstarch with tablespoon of water. Whisk into sauce, continuing to stir until mixture thickens. Remove from heat. Serve over pork and garnish with fresh rosemary sprigs, if desired. Serves 4.

Calories	Fat	Protein	Carb	Chol	Sodium	Fiber
252	8g	31g	13g	90mg	268mg	1g

~ Pork Chops with Apple-Dijon Sauce ~

The combination of apples and Dijonnaise mustard makes a tantalizing sauce. Serve with grilled apple rings or applesauce, if desired. You may also use this sauce on chicken breasts, as well.

4 pork chops (1 ¼ lb.)	1 Tbsp. olive oil
½ tsp. dried thyme leaves	½ cup apple juice
½ tsp. dried marjoram leaves	¼ cup finely chopped green onions
½ tsp. black pepper	2 Tbsp. Dijonnaise mustard
½ tsp. salt	1 tsp. cornstarch
⅛ tsp. ground allspice	1 Tbsp. water
⅛ tsp. cayenne pepper	Fresh apple wedges for garnish

1. Combine thyme, marjoram, black pepper, salt, allspice, and cayenne pepper. Rub spice mixture onto both sides of meat. (You can do this step the night before or morning of the day you plan to serve this dish. Refrigerate meat until ready to cook.)

2. In large, heavy skillet over medium heat, brown meat on both sides in olive oil. Cook about 15 minutes, or until meat is no longer pink.

3. Transfer to plate and cover with foil. In same skillet, bring apple juice, green onions, and Dijonnaise to boil. Mixture will look grainy at first, but becomes smoother after cooking. Cook over low-medium heat, scraping up browned bits, for 5 minutes.

4. Combine cornstarch with 1 Tbsp. water to form paste. Whisk into sauce, stirring constantly, until thickened slightly.

5. Return meat to pan and bring to serving temperature. Serve with garnishes of fresh apple wedges. Serves 4.

Calories	Fat	Protein	Carb	Chol	Sodium	Fiber
250	11g	31g	6g	90mg	538mg	1g

~ Pork Fried Rice ~

This is a great way to use up leftover rice. It's quick and easy and the perfect answer when someone says, "Let's order Chinese take-out tonight."

1 Tbsp. canola oil
½ lb. pork (¼-inch thick cubes)
1 small onion, finely chopped
2 small garlic cloves, minced
1 large carrot (¼-inch diagonals)
½ cup chopped mushrooms
1 large egg, beaten (optional)
4 cups cooked white rice

2 Tbsp. gf tamari soy sauce
3 green onions (¼-inch diagonals)
½ cup snow peas
¼ lb. bean sprouts
1 tsp. sesame oil
½ tsp. salt
¼ tsp. black pepper

1. In wok or high-edged skillet, sauté pork cubes in oil until lightly browned and cooked through. Remove from pan. Add onion and stir-fry until onion is translucent. Add garlic, carrots, and mushrooms; cook 2 minutes. Add this mixture to cooked pork. Remove all ingredients from wok and set aside.

2. In wok, stir-fry egg (if using) and cook until set. Break up pieces using spatula. Add rice and all cooked ingredients to wok. Add soy sauce, green onions, snow peas, bean sprouts, oil, salt, and pepper. Stir to combine and bring to serving temperature. Serve immediately. Serves 4.

Calories	Fat	Protein	Carb	Chol	Sodium	Fiber
330	15g	17g	35g	86mg	890mg	3g

~ Pork Medallions with Cherry Sauce ~

2 lb. pork tenderloin
1 tsp. black pepper
1 cup dried tart cherries
1 cup port wine or red grape juice

1 tsp. unsalted butter
 or canola oil
¼ cup balsamic vinegar
½ tsp. dried marjoram leaves

1. Season pork chops with pepper. Roast in 325° oven until thermometer registers 160°. (About 25 minutes per lb.)

2. In small pan over medium heat, combine cherries and ⅓ cup port wine. Bring to simmer. Turn off heat; let cherries soak 15 minutes. Return mixture and remaining port wine to medium heat. Add remaining ingredients; boil to thicken. Serve on sliced pork. Serves 6.

Calories	Fat	Protein	Carb	Chol	Sodium	Fiber
360	8g	43g	21g	122mg	91mg	1g

~ Thai Pork Noodle Bowl ~

½ lb. pork (½-inch cubes)
¼ cup chopped green onions
1 garlic clove, minced
1 Tbsp. cooking oil
½ cup chopped red bell pepper
¼ cup rice vinegar
3 Tbsp. gf tamari soy sauce
6 Tbsp. brown sugar

4 tsp. paprika
1 tsp. Reese's anchovy paste
¾ tsp. cayenne pepper
¼ cup chopped fresh cilantro
2 cups mung bean sprouts
12 oz. rice noodles, cooked
¼ cup cashews (optional)

1. In large, heavy skillet over medium heat, sauté pork, onions, and garlic in oil until pork is done.

2. Add pepper, vinegar, soy sauce, sugar, paprika, anchovy paste, and cayenne pepper to skillet and toss, along with cilantro, until hot.

3. Place bean sprouts and cooked noodles plate on plate. Top with meat mixture. Garnish with chopped cashews. Serves 6.

Calories	Fat	Protein	Carb	Chol	Sodium	Fiber
262	7g	25g	27g	67mg	487mg	1g

~ Pork Tenderloin with Ginger Sauce ~

Fruit and ginger complement pork, so this sauce greatly enhances the pork tenderloin.

1 lb. pork tenderloin
½ tsp. salt
½ tsp. black pepper
1 Tbsp. olive oil
1 clove garlic, minced
¼ cup fresh grated onion or
   1 tsp. onion powder
1 inch fresh ginger, grated or
   1 tsp. ground ginger

¼ tsp. curry powder
1 Tbsp. honey or sugar
1 ¼ cups apple juice
⅓ cup dried tart cherries or apricots
¼ tsp. salt
¼ tsp. black pepper
1 tsp. cornstarch
2 Tbsp. water

1. Cut pork tenderloin into medallions; sprinkle with salt and pepper. Brown medallions in olive oil in large skillet over medium heat. Transfer to plate and keep warm while preparing sauce.

2. In same skillet, add garlic, onion, ginger, and curry powder and sauté for one minute. Add honey, apple juice, cherries, and ¼ tsp. salt and pepper— scraping up browned bits. Bring to boil, reduce to low and simmer, uncovered, until mixture is reduced by half (about 5 minutes).

3. Stir cornstarch into 2 Tbsp. water until smooth and gradually stir into mixture. Increase heat to medium and stir until mixture thickens slightly. Serve sauce over pork tenderloins. Serves 4.

Calories	Fat	Protein	Carb	Chol	Sodium	Fiber
262	7g	25g	26g	67mg	487mg	1g

~ Bayou Red Beans & Rice ~

A crock pot is an ideal way to cook the beans. Assemble the ingredients in the morning and cook all day. You'll be greeted with a wonderful aroma when you arrive home from work.

1 celery stalk, chopped	2 tsp. salt
1 small yellow onion, chopped	1 tsp. black pepper
3 garlic cloves, minced	2 Tbsp. brown sugar
1 tsp. olive oil	⅛ tsp. cayenne pepper
1 lb. dried red beans (not kidney)	2 bay leaves
1 tsp. dried basil leaves	¼ lb. Canadian bacon, chopped
1 tsp. crushed dried rosemary	Water to cover beans
½ tsp. dried oregano leaves	4 cups hot cooked white rice
½ tsp. dried thyme leaves	1 Tbsp. parsley (optional)

1. In large, heavy saucepan over medium heat, sauté celery, onion, and garlic in olive oil until translucent.

2. Rinse and pick over beans to remove stones or debris. Add to saucepan along with basil, rosemary, oregano, thyme, salt, black pepper, sugar, cayenne pepper, bay leaves, and Canadian bacon.

3. Add enough water to cover beans and simmer over medium heat for 2 hours— or until beans are done. Serve over cooked rice. Garnish with parsley, if desired. Serves 8.

Calories	Fat	Protein	Carb	Chol	Sodium	Fiber
220	2g	9g	40g	7mg	910mg	6g

Rice contributes 22 of the total 40g of carbohydrates per serving.

~ Sweet-and-Sour Pork ~

This is an old standby, but a real favorite. It makes a great answer to "Let's eat Chinese tonight." For the prettiest effect, be sure to vary the shapes of the vegetables. Cut the carrots into ¼-inch ridge diagonals, the bell peppers into ¼-inch long slices, and the onions into quarters.

Marinade & Pork
1 Tbsp. gf tamari soy sauce
1 tsp. ground ginger
1 Tbsp. cornstarch
1 garlic clove, minced
1 Tbsp. pineapple juice
1 lb. pork, cubed

Vegetables & Sauce
1 small onion, coarsely chopped
1 carrot, cut in ¼-inch thick slices
½ cup chopped red bell pepper
1 small green bell pepper, chopped
1 Tbsp. cooking oil
1 can (8 oz) pineapple chunks in juice
2 Tbsp. brown or maple sugar
3 Tbsp. cider vinegar
1 Tbsp. grated fresh ginger
2 Tbsp. gf tamari soy sauce
⅛ tsp. white pepper
1 Tbsp. tapioca flour
1 Tbsp. water
4 cups hot cooked white rice

Marinade & Pork
Combine first 5 ingredients in bowl and add pork cubes to marinate.

Vegetables & Sauce
1. In heavy skillet over medium heat, brown onion, carrots, and pork cubes in oil until lightly browned, stirring frequently. Remove from skillet. Sauté red and green bell peppers 3 minutes, stirring frequently. Remove from skillet. Set aside.

2. To skillet, add pineapple chunks (including juice and water to equal ⅔ cup liquid), sugar, vinegar, ginger, soy sauce, and pepper over medium heat. Stir tapioca flour with 1 Tbsp. water until paste forms. Stir slowly into skillet, continuing to stir until mixture thickens slightly.

3. Return pork, onions, and carrots to skillet. Cover and simmer gently for minutes. Add red and green bell peppers and bring to serving temperature. Serve over hot cooked rice. Serves 6.

Calories	Fat	Protein	Carb	Chol	Sodium	Fiber
390	14g	18g	47g	52mg	553mg	2g

Rice contributes 25g of the total 47g of carbohydrates per serving.

~ Coconut Shrimp with Orange Marmalade ~

If eggs are inappropriate, dip shrimp in flour mixture only.

1 lb. jumbo shrimp
½ cup cornstarch
½ cup shredded coconut
½ tsp. garlic powder
½ tsp. onion powder

½ tsp. baking powder
½ tsp. salt
¼ tsp. cayenne pepper
2 large egg whites, beaten to foam
Oil for frying
Orange Marmalade (see below)

1. Peel and clean shrimp, removing intestinal vein. To butterfly shrimp, use paring knife to open shrimp down the back without cutting all the way through. Press each shrimp flat. Set aside.

2. In bowl, whisk together cornstarch, coconut, garlic and onion powders, baking powder, salt, and cayenne pepper.

3. In large bowl, whisk egg whites until they reach foamy texture. Heat enough cooking oil to cover shrimp in deep fryer or deep, heavy pot. Dip each shrimp in eggs, then in coconut-flour mixture. Fry shrimp in small batches, turning twice to ensure even browning. Drain on paper towels. Continue with remaining shrimp. Serve with Orange Marmalade as dip. Serves 4.

Calories	Fat	Protein	Carb	Chol	Sodium	Fiber
287	7g	19g	40g	188mg	525mg	2g

~ Orange Marmalade ~

1 large thin-skinned orange, seeded   ½ cup sugar (or more)

1. Chop orange (peel and pulp) coarsely. Pulverize in food processor. Measure mixture in glass measuring bowl; add equal amount of sugar.

2. Microwave on high, covered, 2 minutes. Stir. Microwave again 2 minutes. Stir again. Continue to microwave for 1 minute periods, stirring at each interval, until mixture thickens. Cool. Refrigerate in glass jar, covered, for up to 1 week. Serves 16 (1 Tbsp. each).

Calories	Fat	Protein	Carb	Chol	Sodium	Fiber
28	0g	1g	7g	0mg	0mg	.2g

~ Salmon in Parchment ~

4 salmon fillets (1 ¼ lb)
1 tsp. dried dill weed
1 tsp. dried thyme
½ tsp. salt
¼ tsp. black pepper
1 small carrot, julienne
(cut in matchsticks)

1 small red bell pepper, julienne
1 small zucchini, julienne
1 Tbsp. grated fresh onion
2 tsp. grated lemon peel
1 Tbsp. olive oil
Parchment paper or aluminum foil

1. Preheat oven to 425°. Cut parchment paper (or foil) into four 13-inch squares. Lay a salmon fillet on each square.
2. Combine remaining ingredients and distribute evenly on each salmon fillet. Fold parchment paper together, twisting ends tightly to seal. Spray with cooking spray (not foil).
3. Bake 15-20 minutes or until packages puff and are lightly browned. Open carefully to avoid steam burns. Serves 4.

Calories	Fat	Protein	Carb	Chol	Sodium	Fiber
211	.5g	29g	4g	74mg	393mg	1g

~ Red Snapper in Parchment ~

4 red snapper fillets (1 ¼ lb)
¼ cup chopped sun-dried tomatoes
2 Tbsp. fresh lemon juice
2 tsp. grated lemon peel
2 tsp. crushed dried rosemary

1 small garlic clove, minced
½ tsp. salt
¼ cup black pepper
Parchment paper or
    aluminum foil

1. Preheat oven to 425°. Cut parchment paper (or foil) into four 13-inch squares. Lay fillet on each square.
2. Combine remaining ingredients; divide among fillets. Fold parchment paper together. Fold edges; twist ends tightly to seal. Spray with cooking spray (parchment paper only).
3. Bake about 15-20 minutes or until packages puff and are lightly browned. Cut open carefully to avoid steam burns. Serves 4.

Calories	Fat	Protein	Carb	Chol	Sodium	Fiber
110	2g	20g	3g	35mg	405mg	1g

~ Shrimp Creole ~

This dish makes an excellent buffet dish since the sauce can be served in a crock pot or chafing dish. The rice and vegetables can be arranged in a molded pan for a very pretty presentation.

1 Tbsp. olive oil
½ cup chopped onion
1 garlic clove, minced
½ cup chopped celery
1 can (16 oz) peeled tomatoes
1 can (8 oz) tomato sauce
1 Tbsp. Worcestershire sauce
   (Lea & Perrins)
1 tsp. salt
1 tsp. sugar

½ tsp. celery salt
¾ tsp. chili powder
⅛ tsp. cayenne pepper
2 tsp. cornstarch
1 Tbsp. cold water
1 lb. shrimp (peeled, deveined)
½ cup chopped green bell pepper
4 cups hot cooked white rice
¼ cup fresh chopped parsley

1. In large, heavy Dutch oven, sauté onion, garlic, and celery in olive oil until tender, but not brown. Add tomatoes, tomato sauce, Worcestershire sauce, salt, sugar, chili powder, and cayenne pepper. Simmer, uncovered, 30 minutes.

2. Mix cornstarch with cold water until smooth. Stir into sauce. Cook, stirring until bubbly. Add shrimp and green bell pepper. Cover and simmer another 5 minutes.

3. To mold cooked rice, spray Bundt pan or other decoratively shaped pan with cooking spray. Pack hot cooked rice in pan. It works better to fill pan all the way to the top, rather than using a larger pan that you only fill halfway. Turn out on serving place. 4. For an even more décorative presentation, serve a colorful vegetable such as hot cooked green peas in the center hole (if using Bundt pan). Serve immediately. Serves 4.

Calories	Fat	Protein	Carb	Chol	Sodium	Fiber
430	7g	30g	62g	170mg	13mg	4g

Rice contributes 45g of total 62g of carbohydrates per serving

~ Paella ~

All you need with this dish is a tossed salad and bread. Serve it in a large, attractive dish—perhaps the one you cook it in. I cook mine in a large, flat copper pan that goes from oven to tabletop. It makes a great centerpiece.

3 lb. chicken drumsticks
2 Tbsp. olive oil
¼ lb. gf Sausage (p. 47)
½ cup chopped onions
½ lb. medium tomatoes (chopped)
½ lb. shrimp (peeled, deveined)
1 pkg. (9 oz) frozen artichoke
   hearts or 1 can (16 oz) artichoke
   hearts
1 clove garlic
¼ cup chopped parsley or
   1 Tbsp. dried parsley

1 tsp. paprika
1 tsp. Beau Monde seasoning
½ tsp. crushed saffron
1 tsp. salt
¼ tsp. black pepper
3 cups low-sodium gf chicken
   broth
1 ½ cups uncooked white rice
3 oz. pimientos (optional)
1 dozen mussels or clams
½ lb. fish fillets (cod, perch)
1 cup green peas

1. In large skillet, brown chicken on all sides in olive oil. Remove. Add sausage, onions, and tomatoes and cook until onion is lightly browned.

2. Return chicken to pan, add shrimp and remaining ingredients, except green peas. Cover and simmer 30 minutes. (If using an ovenproof skillet, you may also place skillet in oven to cook). Uncover, add green peas and cook another 5 minutes. Serves 6.

Calories	Fat	Protein	Carb	Chol	Sodium	Fiber
676	23g	59g	55g	195mg	999mg	6g

~ Poached Salmon ~

Serve this atop a bed of mixed greens. Arrange several spears of cooked, chilled asparagus alongside the salmon and drizzle your favorite salad dressing over the whole dish. Very refreshing on a hot summer day!

4 salmon steaks (1 ¼ lb)
4 cups gf vegetable
 stock (p. 213)
1 tsp. salt
2 Tbsp. lemon juice
10 whole black peppercorns
6 whole dill seeds
2 whole cloves
1 bay leaf

1 small garlic clove
1 Tbsp. chopped fresh parsley or
 1 tsp. dried parsley
1 Tbsp. fresh thyme or 1 tsp.
 dried thyme leaves
1 Tbsp. fresh tarragon or 1
 tsp. dried tarragon leaves
Fresh herb sprigs for garnish
Vinegar-Free Herb Dressing (p. 165)

1. In large, deep pan or skillet place stock through tarragon and bring to boil. Reduce heat and bring liquid to simmer. Add as many salmon steaks as will comfortably fit in single layer. Cover, and simmer 5-10 minutes or until thoroughly cooked— depending on thickness of steak. Check to make sure salmon is thoroughly cooked before removing from poaching liquid.

2. Remove from liquid with large spatula or slotted spoon. Chill before serving. Serve garnished with fresh herbs and dollop of Vinegar-Free Herb Dressing. Serves 4.

Calories	Fat	Protein	Carb	Chol	Sodium	Fiber
200	5g	35g	2g	74mg	685mg	.5g

~ Spicy Shrimp & Pasta ~

This beautiful dish is especially appropriate for guests. It is very attractive and colorful, with the contrast of the snow peas and red bell peppers against the pasta. If you like extra-spicy foods, increase the cayenne pepper a bit. Also, if you prefer not to use wine, you may use the same amount of chicken broth instead.

1 Tbsp. cooking oil
8 oz. snow peas (fresh or frozen)
1 red bell pepper (¼-inch strips)
1 medium garlic clove, minced
1 Tbsp. tapioca flour
1 cup low-sodium gf chicken broth
½ cup dry white wine
½ tsp. dried basil
½ tsp. paprika
½ tsp. dried thyme leaves
¼ tsp. cayenne pepper

¼ tsp. black pepper
¼ tsp. crushed red peppers
1 lb. medium-size shrimp
4 cups cooked gf fettuccini or spaghetti
½ cup Parmesan cheese (cow, rice, soy) for garnish
1 Tbsp. chopped fresh parsley, divided
1 tsp. grated lemon peel, divided

1. Place oil in large, heavy skillet. Over low-medium heat, sauté peas, red bell pepper, and minced garlic until vegetables are crisp-tender— about 3 minutes. Remove vegetables and set aside.

2. In same skillet, combine tapioca flour with two tablespoons of the chicken broth to form smooth paste. Then add paste, along with wine and remaining chicken broth. Stir in basil, paprika, thyme, cayenne pepper, black pepper, and crushed red peppers. Bring mixture to boil until slightly thickened.

3. Add shrimp. Reduce heat; cook five minutes or until shrimp are pink and curled. Return vegetables to skillet and cook one minute longer. Keep warm.

4. To serve, divide cooked pasta among four serving plates. Garnish with fresh parsley and sprinkle of grated Parmesan cheese. Just before serving, toss shrimp mixture with remaining lemon peel and chopped parsley. Serve over hot noodles. Sprinkle with more Parmesan cheese, if desired. Serves 4.

Calories	Fat	Protein	Carb	Chol	Sodium	Fiber
427	10g	33g	47g	171mg	790mg	5g

~ Tuna Burgers with Grilled Pineapple Slices ~

These burgers are an interesting change from hamburgers. Grilled pineapple slices add flavor, color, variety, and nutrients to any meal. If you're not using the outdoor barbecue grill, try using a ridged skillet on top of the range.

Oriental Sauce
1 cup pineapple or apple juice
½ cup rice vinegar
1 tsp. ground ginger
¼ cup gf tamari soy sauce
¼ cup brown sugar
¼ cup fresh lemon juice
1 tsp. white pepper
⅛ tsp. ground allspice
½ tsp. cornstarch
1 Tbsp. cold water

Tuna Burgers
1 lb. fresh tuna steaks or 3
   cans (6 oz. each) gf tuna
½ cup gf bread crumbs
1 large egg or ¼ cup flax mix (p. 211)
1 tsp. dry mustard*
½ tsp. dried thyme leaves
½ tsp. salt
1 Tbsp. gf tamari soy sauce
½ tsp. black pepper
Paprika for garnish
Grind mustard seeds with small coffee grinder

Grilled Pineapple Slices
8 pineapple slices (16 oz. can)
1 tsp. cooking oil

Oriental Sauce
1. Combine all ingredients in small saucepan. Bring to boil over medium heat, reduce to low and simmer until liquid is reduced by half. Just before serving, stir ½ tsp. cornstarch with 1 Tbsp. water until smooth. Add to sauce, stirring until mixture thickens slightly. Set aside.

Tuna Burgers
1. While sauce cooks, grind tuna in food processor or use 3 cans— 6 oz. each— of tuna in spring water, drained. Combine with burger ingredients and shape into 4 patties. In large cast-iron skillet, nonstick skillet, or barbecue grill, cook tuna burgers on both sides. Serve burgers with sauce and pineapple slices. Garnish with dash of paprika.

Grilled Pineapple Slices
1. Coat pineapple slices with oil. Then grill 3-5 minutes, turning when grill marks are visible on underside. Handle carefully so slices don't slip through grate or use metal basket specially designed for grilling. Serves 4.

Calories	Fat	Protein	Carb	Chol	Sodium	Fiber
390	9g	33g	44g	96mg	999mg	2g

~ Walnut Shrimp Salad ~

This fabulous dish is best eaten immediately after it's prepared. Unfortunately, the dish loses a lot of flavor without the sour cream, so . . . it is not dairy-free.

2 lb. medium shrimp (peeled, cooked)
1 Tbsp. gf tamari soy sauce
1 cup walnut halves
1 cup diagonally sliced celery
½ cup green onions (sliced diagonally)
1 can (8 oz) water chestnuts, sliced

1 cup mandarin oranges
6 red-leaf lettuce leaves
1 cup sour cream
2 Tbsp. apple cider vinegar
½ tsp. salt
Dash paprika for garnish

1. Toss shrimp with soy sauce. Add walnuts, celery, onions, drained oranges, and water chestnuts and mix well. Arrange on 6 serving plates lined with lettuce leaves.

2. To make dressing, combine sour cream, vinegar, and salt. Drizzle over each salad plate. Garnish with paprika. Serves 6.

Calories	Fat	Protein	Carb	Chol	Sodium	Fiber
361	22g	28g	15g	232mg	653mg	3g

~ Lamb Chops with Rosemary Marinade ~

3 lb. lamb chops (½-inch thick)
¾ cup orange juice
2 Tbsp. olive oil
3 Tbsp. gf tamari soy sauce
2 tsp. crushed dried rosemary

¼ tsp. cayenne pepper
¼ tsp. salt
⅛ tsp. black pepper
1 tsp. cornstarch
2 tsp. water

1. Arrange chops in single layer in shallow glass dish. Add remaining ingredients (except cornstarch and water) Chill 4 hours.

2. Grill lamb chops over grill or ridged skillet until done.

3. Meanwhile, in small saucepan over medium heat, bring remaining marinade to boil. Stir cornstarch into water to form paste and stir paste into marinade. Reduce heat to medium and whisk until mixture thickens. Serve with chops. Serves 4.

Calories	Fat	Protein	Carb	Chol	Sodium	Fiber
563	30g	60g	8g	200mg	880mg	.5g

~ Chorizo (Mexican Sausage) ~

1 lb. ground round
2 lb. ground pork
1 Tbsp. paprika
⅓ cup apple cider vinegar
1 tsp. salt
1 tsp. crushed red peppers

2 tsp. dried oregano leaves
3 garlic cloves, minced
1 tsp. ground coriander
1 tsp. ground cumin
½ tsp. ground cloves

1. In large bowl, mix ground meats together. Add remaining ingredients. Mix thoroughly. Shape into large ball or log. Chill.

2. Shape meat mixture into 12 patties, ½-inch thick and two inches in diameter or 12 links, 3 inches long and ¾-inch wide.

3. In non-stick pan coated with cooking spray, fry patties until nicely browned on both sides. Makes 12 patties.

Calories	Fat	Protein	Carb	Chol	Sodium	Fiber
230	15g	22g	1g	64mg	260mg	<1g

~ Sausage ~

1 lb. ground round
1 lb. ground pork
1 lb. ground turkey
4 garlic cloves, minced
½ cup finely chopped onion
½ cup finely minced green
  bell pepper
½ cup finely minced red
  bell pepper

2 tsp. chopped fresh cilantro
2 tsp. ground cumin
2 tsp. dried thyme leaves
2 tsp. fennel seed
¼ tsp. ground nutmeg
½ tsp. crushed red peppers
1 tsp. salt

In large bowl, mix together all ingredients with your hands or large spatula. Shape meat into large ball or log. Refrigerate for 4 hours. Shape mixture in patties or meatballs. Brown on baking sheet in 350° oven for 20-25 minutes. Serves 12.

Calories	Fat	Protein	Carb	Chol	Sodium	Fiber
215	13g	22g	2g	66mg	270mg	.5g

~ Corned Beef & Cabbage ~

On a trip to Ireland, I couldn't find this dish on Irish menus. The reason? It's like our turkey dinners at Thanksgiving— reserved for special occasions only. But, it sure makes a great St. Patrick's Day dinner. Serve this with Colcannon (p. 184) and Irish Griddle Cakes (p. 68).

1 lean corned beef brisket (4 lb)
2 medium onions, peeled
6 whole cloves
4 whole allspice berries
6 whole black peppercorns
½ tsp. whole mustard seeds
Water to cover beef
1 lb. carrots (peeled, 2-inch pieces)

2 garlic cloves, peeled
16 small new red potatoes
1 small head cabbage, quartered
1 3-inch strip orange peel
½ cup chopped fresh parsley
Salt and pepper to taste
Additional parsley for garnish

1. Wash and pat beef dry. Place in large ovenproof casserole dish that has been sprayed with cooking spray. Add onions, cloves, allspice, peppercorns, and mustard seeds. Cover with water and bake, covered, in 325° oven about 3 hours, or until meat is tender. Remove beef and keep warm.

2. Strain the liquid and discard the solids. Return beef and liquid to casserole dish along with remaining ingredients. Cover and bake another 30-45 minutes, or until vegetables are fork-tender.

3. Place beef on serving platter, surrounded by cooked vegetables. Garnish with additional fresh parsley. Strain liquid, ladle some over platter, and serve remainder in a gravy boat. Serve with your favorite sauces or condiments. Serves 8.

Calories	Fat	Protein	Carb	Chol	Sodium	Fiber
563	34g	37g	25g	122mg	362mg	7g

~ Orange Beef Stir Fry ~

Looking for a change of pace for your next dinner? This dish is different, easy to prepare, and looks great on your plate. Your family and your guests will love it.

1 cup orange juice
¼ cup grated orange peel
1 Tbsp. molasses
¼ cup gf tamari soy sauce
1 Tbsp. rice vinegar
2 Tbsp. cornstarch
1 lb. lean beef (cut in ¼-inch diagonal slices)

1 Tbsp. canola oil
1 large garlic clove, minced
1 Tbsp. grated fresh ginger
½ tsp. crushed red peppers
½ lb. broccoli florets, sliced
1 small red bell pepper, chopped
½ cup sliced green onions
4 cups hot cooked white rice

1. Combine orange juice, orange peel, molasses, soy sauce, rice vinegar, and cornstarch and set aside.

2. Slice beef diagonally into ¼-inch thick slices. (For easier slicing, freeze meat for 30 minutes before slicing). In large, heavy skillet or wok, brown meat in oil until lightly seared and no longer pink. Remove from pan and keep warm.

3. In same pan, add garlic, ginger, crushed red peppers, broccoli florets, and red bell pepper and stir over medium heat 1 minute. Cover and cook for 1 more minute. Remove cover and add orange juice mixture to pan, stirring until mixture thickens. Return beef to pan, add chopped green onions, and bring to serving temperature. Serve over rice. Serves 4.

Calories	Fat	Protein	Carb	Chol	Sodium	Fiber
500	10g	35g	67g	77mg	999mg	4g

Rice contributes 44g of total 67g of carbohydrates per serving.

~ Spaghetti Sauce & Meatballs ~

I've been making this low-fat sauce for nearly 25 years and, even though we've tried several others, it remains our favorite. A crock pot works best.

1 can (48 oz) tomato juice
3 cans (6 oz each) tomato paste
3 Tbsp. dried parsley
2 Tbsp. dried basil leaves
1 Tbsp. dried rosemary leaves
2 bay leaves
2 tsp. dried oregano leaves

1 tsp. black pepper
3 Tbsp. sugar
2 tsp. salt
¼ cup Romano or Parmesan
  cheese (optional)
½ lb. sausage meatballs (p.47)

In large crock pot, combine all ingredients. Mix well. Cook all day on low-medium heat. Stir occasionally. Makes about 8 cups of sauce. Serve with meatballs and your favorite pasta. Serves 12 (¾ cup each).

Calories	Fat	Protein	Carb	Chol	Sodium	Fiber
118	5g	5g	17g	9mg	553mg	3g

~ Fresh Tomato Basil Sauce with Pasta ~

Choose the most flavorful tomatoes you can find for this easy, fresh-tasting sauce.

4 cups plum tomatoes
2 large garlic cloves, minced
¼ cup extra virgin olive oil,
  divided
½ tsp. salt

¼ tsp. black pepper
½ cup chopped fresh basil
  or 2 Tbsp. dried basil
4 cups hot cooked pasta
¼ cup Parmesan cheese for garnish

1. Dip tomatoes in boiling water. Peel, quarter, seed tomatoes.

2. In large bowl, crush tomatoes with potato masher. Drain again and reserve juice for another use.

3. In medium-sized, nonreactive pan sauté garlic in 1 Tbsp. oil for 2 minutes. Add tomatoes, salt, pepper, basil, and remaining oil. Simmer gently for 15 minutes, uncovered. Serve with pasta and Parmesan cheese. Serves 4.

Calories	Fat	Protein	Carb	Chol	Sodium	Fiber
190	16g	4g	9g	5mg	423mg	2g

~ Pad Thai ~

This dish sounds difficult, but it's actually quite easy. Egg-sensitive people can simply omit the eggs. To julienne means to cut into thin, matchstick shapes.

8 oz. rice noodles, uncooked
2 qt. water
2 tsp. salt
¼ cup lemon or lime juice
1 Tbsp. gf fish sauce (optional)
¼ cup gf tamari soy sauce
1 Tbsp. brown sugar
¼ tsp. crushed red peppers
1 Tbsp. sesame oil or olive oil

1 lb. shrimp (peeled, deveined)
1 cup snow peas
¼ cup red bell pepper, julienne
½ cup green onions
2 large garlic cloves, minced
2 large eggs, lightly beaten
   (optional)
2 cups bean sprouts
¼ cup cashews
½ cup fresh cilantro, divided

1. This dish cooks quickly, so have all ingredients assembled beforehand. Cook rice noodles in boiling water with 2 tsp. salt. Drain thoroughly.

2. Meanwhile, while noodles are cooking combine lemon juice, fish sauce, soy sauce, sugar, and crushed red peppers. Set aside.

3. Heat oil in wok or heavy skillet. Sauté shrimp, snow peas, red bell pepper, green onions, and garlic cloves 2-4 minutes over medium heat until shrimp turn pink. Add eggs, if using, and continue stirring until eggs are cooked. Add cooked noodles and lemon juice mixture and heat, stirring constantly, another 2-3 minutes.

4. Just before serving, stir in bean sprouts, cashews, and half of the cilantro. Garnish with additional nuts and remaining cilantro, if desired. Serves 4.

Calories	Fat	Protein	Carb	Chol	Sodium	Fiber
294	10g	26g	26g	240mg	999mg	3g

~ Veal (Pork) Scaloppini ~

For a dairy-free version, omit butter and use ½ tsp. arrowroot mixed in 2 tsp. water to form paste. Stir into reduced liquid until mixture thickens slightly.

4 veal or pork cutlets (1 ¼ lb)
Salt and pepper to taste
2 Tbsp. olive oil
2 Tbsp. lemon juice
½ cup low sodium gf chicken
    broth or white wine

2 Tbsp. butter or margarine
2 Tbsp. gf capers
1 Tbsp. dried parsley or ¼ cup
    chopped fresh parsley
⅛ tsp. ground nutmeg

1. Season veal (or pork) with salt and pepper. Pound to ¼-inch thick. In large, heavy skillet brown meat in batches in oil— about 2 minutes on each side. Remove from skillet; keep warm.

2. Increase heat to high; add lemon juice and broth to skillet. Continue cooking until reduced by half. Add chilled butter and whisk until thoroughly melted. Or, use arrowroot mixture (see above.) Add capers, parsley, and nutmeg and serve over meat. Serves 4.

Calories	Fat	Protein	Carb	Chol	Sodium	Fiber
238	18g	17g	1g	64mg	234mg	.5g

~ Pasta Salad ~

2 cups penne pasta (uncooked)
¼ cup red wine vinegar
2 Tbsp. lemon juice
1 Tbsp. dried basil leaves
1 tsp. Dijonnaise mustard
1 small garlic clove, minced
¼ tsp. each salt and pepper

¼ cup olive oil
1 cup snow peas (blanched)
1 cup broccoli flowerets (blanched)
1 small red bell pepper
¼ cup black olives, halved
¼ cup toasted pine nuts
¼ cup Parmesan cheese
    (optional)

1. Cook pasta in boiling, salted water. Drain; chill. Meanwhile, whisk together vinegar, lemon juice, basil, mustard, garlic, salt, pepper, and olive oil. Combine remaining ingredients in large bowl. Add cooked pasta. Toss with dressing. Chill. Serves 4.

Calories	Fat	Protein	Carb	Chol	Sodium	Fiber
494	22g	10g	65g	5mg	402mg	2.5g

~ Pizza Crust & Pizza Sauce ~

Pizza Crust
1 Tbsp. active dry yeast
⅔ cup brown rice flour
1/2 cup tapioca flour
2 tsp. xanthan gum
½ tsp. salt
1 tsp. unflavored gelatin powder
1 tsp. Italian herb seasoning
⅔ cup warm milk (110°)
   (cow, rice, soy)
½ tsp. sugar
1 tsp. olive oil
1 tsp. cider vinegar
Extra rice flour for sprinkling

Pizza Sauce
8 oz. tomato sauce
½ tsp. dried oregano leaves
½ tsp. dried basil leaves
½ tsp. crushed dried rosemary
½ tsp. fennel seeds
¼ tsp. garlic powder
2 tsp. sugar
½ tsp. salt
Toppings of your choice

Sauce
1. Combine all ingredients in small saucepan. Bring to boil over medium heat. Reduce heat to low; simmer 15 minutes while Pizza Crust is being assembled. Makes about 1 cup.

Crust
1. Preheat oven to 425°. In medium mixer bowl using regular beaters (not dough hooks), blend yeast, flours, xanthan gum, salt, gelatin powder, and Italian seasoning on low speed. Add warm milk, sugar, oil, and vinegar.

2. Beat on high speed 2 minutes. Dough will resemble soft bread dough. Put mixture on greased 12-inch pizza pan or baking sheet (for thin, crispy crust). Liberally sprinkle rice flour onto dough, then press dough into pan, continuing to sprinkle dough with flour to prevent sticking to your hands. Make edges thicker to hold toppings.

3. Bake pizza crust 10 minutes. Remove from oven. Top Pizza Crust with sauce and your preferred toppings. Bake another 20-25 minutes or until top is nicely browned. Serves 6 (1 slice per serving).

Calories	Fat	Protein	Carb	Chol	Sodium	Fiber
153	1.5g	4g	33g	1mg	635mg	3g

~ Spice Rub for Meat ~

Spice rubs are one of the hottest food trends. This is a great one to keep on hand. When I'm not sure about what to fix for dinner, I simply sprinkle this on the meat we're having and presto— we have flavor!

1 Tbsp. paprika
1 tsp. garlic powder
1 tsp. salt
¾ tsp. black pepper
¼ tsp. cayenne pepper

¾ tsp. onion powder
½ tsp. dried oregano leaves
½ tsp. dried thyme leaves
⅛ tsp. ground allspice

1. Combine in glass, airtight container. Use about 2 Tbsp. per lb. of meat. Store in dark, dry place up to 1 month. Makes less than ¼ cup.

~ Spicy Fettuccini with Basil ~

So very simple to make and so impressive and tasty. The perfect entrée for a meatless meal. If you absolutely must have meat, try adding shrimp or cubed chicken.

½ cup extra virgin olive oil
2 large garlic cloves, minced
½ tsp. crushed red peppers
3 cups gf fettuccini, uncooked
6 quarts boiling, salted water
2 tsp. dried basil

⅓ cup gf bread crumbs (toasted)
½ cup grated Parmesan cheese
  (cow, rice, soy)
4 plum tomatoes, finely chopped
1 lemon cut into 4 wedges
¼ cup chopped fresh parsley

1. Heat 1 Tbsp. of oil in medium skillet over low heat. Sauté garlic and crushed red peppers for 2-3 minutes, stirring frequently. Set aside.

2. Cook pasta in 6 quarts boiling, salted water until al dente— about 2-3 minutes. Drain, leaving ⅓ cup hot water in pot. Return pasta to pot; remove pot from heat. Add garlic-pepper mixture, remaining oil, basil, bread crumbs, and Parmesan cheese and toss gently. Garnish with chopped tomatoes, parsley, and a squeeze of lemon juice. Serve immediately. Serves 4.

Calories	Fat	Protein	Carb	Chol	Sodium	Fiber
500	32g	8g	47g	10mg	333mg	3g

~ Asparagus Soup ~

Spring-time green, smooth, and creamy—a wonderful choice for a spring luncheon.

1 ½ lb. fresh asparagus spears
1 small onion (finely chopped)
1 large garlic clove
1 peeled carrot (1-inch pieces)
½ tsp. dried basil leaves
1 tsp. dried tarragon leaves
1 tsp. dried parsley

1 tsp. dried thyme
½ tsp. salt
¼ tsp. black pepper
⅛ Tbsp. cayenne pepper
3 cups low-sodium gf chicken broth
½ cup sour cream or soft silken tofu
¼ tsp. paprika for garnish

1. Wash and trim woody ends from asparagus. Cut stalks into 1-inch pieces. Reserve tips and add later.

2. Place all ingredients (except sour cream, if using) asparagus tips, and paprika) in heavy, large saucepan and cook, covered tightly, 30-40 minutes or until done. Remove soup from heat and cool.

3. Place mixture in food processor and process until very smooth. Strain soup through medium-size sieve to remove woody fibers.

4. Return soup to saucepan and add asparagus tips. Simmer until tips are done, about 10 minutes. Just before serving, stir in all but 2 Tbsp. of sour cream (if using) and heat to serving temperature.

5. To serve, ladle soup into serving bowls. Top with dollop of the remaining sour cream or tofu and a sprinkle of paprika. Serves 4.

Calories	Fat	Protein	Carb	Chol	Sodium	Fiber
100	3g	8g	13g	0mg	999mg	4g

Sour cream adds additional 45 calories, 12mg cholesterol, and 5g fat.

~ Chinese Hot-Sour Soup ~

If you don't use the egg, the soup might not be quite as thick. But it will still be delicious. To julienne means to cut into thin matchsticks.

4 cups low sodium gf beef broth
2 green onions (thinly sliced)
1 small carrot, julienne
1 Tbsp. grated fresh ginger
½ tsp. white pepper
1 tsp. cooking oil
1 cup fresh, sliced mushrooms

½ cup tofu, (¼-inch cubes)
1 cup turkey dark meat, diced
⅛ tsp. cayenne pepper
1 tsp. fish sauce (optional)
1 Tbsp. cornstarch or arrowroot
2 Tbsp. rice vinegar
1 egg white, well-beaten (optional)

1. In large saucepan, combine beef broth, green onions (reserve 2 Tbsp. for garnish), carrot, ginger, and white pepper. Bring to boil over high heat, simmering for 15 minutes.

2. In medium skillet, sauté mushrooms in cooking oil over high heat about 1 minute. To beef stock, add mushrooms plus tofu, turkey meat, cayenne, and fish sauce (if using).

3. In small bowl, dissolve cornstarch in vinegar. Add to soup and stir until thickened, about 1 minute.

4. Remove soup from heat and, stirring constantly, slowly pour in the beaten egg white (if using). Cook until egg is done. Taste and adjust seasonings, adding more vinegar or white pepper. Ladle soup into four serving bowls. Garnish with sliced green onions. Serves 4.

Calories	Fat	Protein	Carb	Chol	Sodium	Fiber
154	5g	17g	12g	30mg	999mg	2g

~ Colorado Chili ~

Cook in a crock pot and let guests help themselves as they wish. If the chili thickens too much as it cooks, add a bit of water.

1 lb. ground round
1 cup finely chopped onions
1 can (15 oz) pinto or kidney beans
1 can (15 oz) canned tomatoes
2 tsp. chili powder
½ tsp. ground allspice

½ tsp. ground cumin
½ tsp. ground coriander
¼ tsp. ground cloves
¼ tsp. ground cinnamon
1 tsp. salt
Water (if too thick)

In large Dutch oven or skillet, combine ground round and chopped onion. Brown over medium heat. Add remaining ingredients, cover, and simmer on low 2 hours. Or, cook in crock pot 4-6 hours. Serve with crackers and various garnishes— green onions, shredded cheese, chopped cilantro. Serves 6.

Calories	Fat	Protein	Carb	Chol	Sodium	Fiber
210	7g	20%	16g	28mg	466mg	5g

~ Green Chile Stew ~

For easy entertaining, cook and serve this in a crock pot.

1 lb. lean pork (1-inch pieces)
½ cup chopped onion
2 carrots (½-inch pieces)
1 Tbsp. olive oil
1 can (4 oz) diced green chiles
3 cups low-sodium beef broth
2 medium white potatoes, diced
4 plum tomatoes, diced

1 large garlic clove, minced
½ ground cumin
½ tsp. ground coriander
½ tsp. dried oregano leaves
½ tsp. salt
¼ tsp. black pepper
½ cup chopped fresh cilantro

In heavy Dutch oven, brown pork, onion, and carrots in olive oil over medium heat until lightly browned. Add remaining ingredients (except cilantro) and simmer, covered, one hour. Or, transfer mixture to a slow cooker (crock pot) and simmer all day on low. Add cilantro just before serving. Serves 4.

Calories	Fat	Protein	Carb	Chol	Sodium	Fiber
340	16g	26g	25g	72mg	480mg	4g

~ Notes ~

~ BREADS ~

Hearty, flavorful breads complement any meal. They add wonderful flavor, help "fill you up", and provide a very important tactile element (they're fun to chew). Think of breads as the "rising stars" at any meal.

Many of you have asked for gluten-free breads that also contain no dairy or eggs. So . . . I'm happy to introduce a new set of bread recipes in this section. Some are yeast-leavened; others are quick breads that use baking soda or baking powder (or a combination of cream of tartar and baking soda).

Easy directions for each gluten-free recipe show you how to make the bread with or without eggs and milk––so you leave out only the ingredients you don't want. Enjoy!

For additional breads without wheat, gluten, or dairy see *Gluten-Free 101: Easy, Basic Dishes without Wheat*, 2003, or *Wheat-Free Recipes & Menus: Delicious Dining without Wheat or Gluten*, 2002. For additional wheat and gluten-free bread recipes that can also be made without eggs, sugar, or yeast see *Special Diet Solutions: Healthy Cooking without Wheat, Gluten, Dairy, Eggs, Yeast, or Refined Sugar*, 2001.

~ "Cracked Wheat" Bread ~

Cracked brown rice imitates the texture of whole wheat bread. Crack rice in blender or coffee grinder until kernels are ¼ to ⅓ normal size.

Ingredients	1 lb.	1 ½ to 2 lb.
	Serves 10	Serves 16
Active dry yeast (hand)	1 ½ Tbsp.	2 ¼ Tbsp.
(machine)	1 ½ tsp.	2 ¼ tsp.
Brown rice flour	1 ¾ cups	2 ¼ cups
Potato starch	½ cup	¾ cup
Tapioca flour	¼ cup	⅓ cup
Whole brown rice	¼ cup	⅓ cup
Xanthan gum	1 tsp.	1 ½ tsp.
Salt	1 tsp.	1 ½ tsp.
Brown sugar	1 Tbsp.	2 Tbsp.
Ener-G® egg replacer	1 tsp.	1 ½ tsp.
Eggs	2 large eggs or ½ cup soft silken tofu	3 large eggs or ¾ cup soft silken tofu
Butter (melted) or oil	3 Tbsp.	⅓ cup
Apple cider vinegar	1 tsp.	2 tsp.
Milk (cow, rice, soy) 110°	1 cup	1 ½ cups
Pans	Three 5x3-inch pans or one 9x5-inch pan	Five 5x3-inch pans or two 8x4-inch pans

Hand: Combine yeast, sugar, and milk and set aside 5 minutes.
1. In large mixer bowl with electric beaters (not dough hooks), combine flours through egg replacer. In separate bowl, cream together eggs, butter, and vinegar until very smooth. With mixer on low, add egg mixture and yeast-milk mixture to dry ingredients and blend on high 2 minutes.
2. Divide dough among greased pans. Rise in warm place (75-80°) until dough is level with top of pan.
3. Preheat oven to 350°. Bake small loaves 25-30 minutes; large loaves 40-50 minutes— or until tops are nicely browned. Cool 5 minutes in pan. Remove from pan; cool on wire rack.
Machine: Spray pan with cooking spray. Add room temperature ingredients in order listed by manufacturer. Set controls and bake.

Calories	Fat	Protein	Carb	Chol	Sodium	Fiber
200	4g	4g	38g	1mg	290mg	2g

Eggs and butter add additional 52mg cholesterol per serving.

~ Focaccia ~

This is a great bread because it is a success— no matter how it turns out.

Bread
¾ cup warm water (110°)
1 tsp. sugar
2 large eggs*
2 Tbsp. olive oil
½ tsp. cider vinegar
1 ½ tsp. active dry yeast
1 cup brown rice flour
½ cup tapioca flour
1 tsp. unflavored gelatin powder

1 ½ tsp. xanthan gum
1 tsp. dried rosemary leaves
½ tsp. onion powder
¾ tsp. salt
Topping
1 ¼ tsp. Italian herb seasoning
¼ tsp. salt
1 Tbsp. olive oil
Parmesan cheese (cow, rice, soy)

Bread

1. Combine warm water, sugar, eggs, oil, and vinegar in medium mixer bowl. Beat dough with mixer (using regular beaters) until smooth. Add yeast, flours, gelatin, xanthan gum, rosemary, onion powder, and salt. Beat 2 minutes. Dough will be soft and sticky.

2. Transfer dough to greased 11 x 7-inch nonstick pan. Cover with foil; let rise in warm place 30 minutes or until desired height.

Topping

1. Preheat oven to 400°. Sprinkle Focaccia with Italian seasoning, salt, and oil (or to taste). Bake 15 minutes or until golden brown. Sprinkle Parmesan cheese on top. Serves 6.

Focaccia without Eggs: Omit eggs. Use ½ cup soft silken tofu.

Calories	Fat	Protein	Carb	Chol	Sodium	Fiber
215	8g	4g	32g	20mg	396mg	3g

Eggs add additional 42mg cholesterol per serving.

Additional Toppings

Herb: Combine ½ tsp. each dried rosemary, sage, and thyme, ¼ tsp. black pepper, and 2 Tbsp. Parmesan cheese (cow, rice, soy).
Sun-Dried Tomato & Olive: Sauté ¼ cup minced sun-dried tomatoes, ¼ cup sliced black olives, and ¼ cup chopped onion in 1 tsp. oil.
Pesto: Purée in food processor just until smooth, leaving bit of texture: 1 cup fresh basil leaves, 1 garlic clove, ½ cup pine nuts. With motor running, slowly add ¼ cup olive oil through feed tube. Add ¼ cup Parmesan cheese (cow, rice, soy) and dash of black pepper.

~ French Bread ~

This one is so easy— and it can be ready in a little over an hour.

1 ½ tsp. active dry yeast
1 tsp. sugar or honey
1 cup warm (110°) milk (cow, rice, soy)
1 tsp. cornmeal for pan (optional)
¼ cup soft silken tofu
2 Tbsp. melted butter or canola oil
1 tsp. apple cider vinegar

1 ¾ cups brown rice flour
½ cup potato starch
⅓ cup tapioca flour
1 tsp. xanthan gum
½ tsp. guar gum
¼ tsp. soy lecithin
1 tsp. salt

1. Dissolve yeast and sugar in warm milk. Let foam 5 minutes.

2. Grease baking pan or cookie sheet or French-loaf shaped pan. Lightly dust with cornmeal, if desired.

3. In bowl of food processor, purée the yeast mixture along with the tofu, butter (or oil), and vinegar until very, very smooth. Add flours, xanthan and guar gums, soy lecithin, and salt. Blend until thoroughly mixed. Mixture will be stiff.

4. Spoon onto prepared pan, smoothing top of dough with wet spatula. Cover and let rise in warm place until doubled in bulk, about 30-40 minutes. Spray with oil (or brush with milk or eggs) for glossier shine. (Beaten egg white makes glossiest sheen.)

5. Place bread in *cold* oven, turn heat to 425°. Bake approximately 30 minutes, or until bread is nicely browned. Remove bread from pans and cool on wire rack. Cool thoroughly before slicing. Makes 1 loaf. Serves 12.

Calories	Fat	Protein	Carb	Chol	Sodium	Fiber
140	2g	3g	28g	.5mg	229mg	1g

Garlic French Bread: Spread slices of French Bread with mixture of ½ cup softened butter or margarine and 1 garlic clove, minced. One Tbsp. butter adds 100 calories.

~ Italian Breadsticks ~

Breadsticks are one of the easiest ways to serve bread at any meal. For an attractive presentation, stand the sticks on end in a decorative pitcher or container.

1 Tbsp. active dry yeast
⅔ cup warm milk (110°)
  (cow, rice, soy)
½ tsp. sugar or honey
½ cup brown rice flour
½ cup + 1 Tbsp. tapioca flour
2 tsp. xanthan gum
½ cup grated Parmesan cheese
  (cow, rice, soy)

½ tsp. salt
1 tsp. onion powder
1 tsp. unflavored gelatin powder
1 Tbsp. olive oil
1 tsp. cider vinegar
1 large egg white, beaten to
  foam or cooking spray
1 tsp. Italian herb seasoning

1. Mix yeast, milk, and sugar in small bowl. Let foam 5 minutes.

2. Preheat oven to 400° 5 minutes, then turn off.

3. In medium-size mixer bowl, blend yeast-milk mixture, flours, xanthan gum, Parmesan cheese, salt, onion powder, gelatin, oil, and vinegar on low speed of electric mixer. Beat on high 3 minutes. Dough will be soft and sticky.

4. Place dough in large, heavy-duty plastic freezer bag with ½-inch opening cut diagonally on one corner. (This makes a 1-inch circle.) Grease large baking sheet. Squeeze dough out of plastic bag onto sheet in 10 strips, each 1-inch wide by 6 inches long. For best results, hold bag of dough upright as you squeeze, rather than at an angle. Also, hold bag with corners perpendicular, rather than horizontal, to baking sheet for more authentic-looking breadstick. Brush with beaten egg white or spray with cooking spray for crispier, shinier breadstick. Sprinkle with Italian Seasoning.

5. Let rise in warmed oven 20-30 minutes. While breadsticks remain in oven, turn oven to 400° and bake until golden brown, about 15-20 minutes. Rotate cookie sheet halfway through baking to assure even browning. Cool on wire rack. Serves 10.

Calories	Fat	Protein	Carb	Chol	Sodium	Fiber
100	3g	4g	15g	4mg	231mg	1.5g

~ Pumpernickel Bread ~

This bread is great for sandwiches such as a Reuben.

Ingredients	1 lb.	1 ½ to 2 lb.
	Serves 10	Serves 16
Active dry yeast (hand)	1 ½ Tbsp.	2 ¼ Tbsp.
(machine)	1 ½ tsp.	2 ¼ tsp.
Sorghum or brown rice flour	1 ¾ cups	2 cups
Potato starch	½ cup	¾ cup
Tapioca flour	¼ cup	⅓ cup
Xanthan gum	1 tsp.	1 ½ tsp.
Salt	1 tsp.	1 ½ tsp.
Brown sugar	1 Tbsp.	1 ½ Tbsp.
Ener-G egg replacer	1 tsp.	1 ½ tsp.
Caraway seeds	1 Tbsp.	1 ½ tsp.
Unsweetened cocoa	1 Tbsp.	1 ½ Tbsp.
Instant coffee powder	1 tsp.	1 ½ tsp.
Onion powder	½ tsp.	¾ tsp.
Eggs	2 large eggs or ½ cup soft silken tofu	3 large eggs or ¾ cup soft silken tofu
Melted butter or canola oil	2 Tbsp.	3 Tbsp.
Molasses	2 Tbsp.	3 Tbsp.
Apple cider vinegar	1 tsp.	1 ½ tsp.
Milk (cow, rice, soy) 110°	1 cup	1 ½ cups
Pans	Three 5x3-inch pans or one 9x5-inch pan	Five 5x3-inch pans or two 8x4-inch pans

Hand

1. Mix yeast, milk, and sugar in bowl to foam 5 minutes.
2. Combine remaining dry ingredients in large mixer bowl; blend on low speed. Add eggs, oil, molasses, vinegar, and yeast mixture to dry ingredients. Beat on high for two minutes.
3. Divide dough among greased pans. Rise in warm place (75-80°) until dough is level with top of pan.
4. Preheat oven to 350°. Bake in small loaves 25-30 minutes; large loaves 40-50 minutes.

Machine

1. Spray pan with cooking spray. Add room temperature ingredients in order listed by manufacturer. Set controls and bake.

Calories	Fat	Protein	Carb	Chol	Sodium	Fiber
160	4g	4g	27g	0mg	260mg	2g

Eggs and butter add additional 56mg cholesterol per serving.

~ Sandwich Bread ~

This dairy-free, egg-free bread will remind you of heavy, European breads.

Ingredients	1 lb.	1 ½ to 2 lb.
	Serves 10	Serves 16
Active dry yeast (hand)	1 ½ Tbsp.	2 ¼ Tbsp.
(machine)	1 ½ tsp.	2 ¼ tsp.
Sorghum or brown rice flour	1 ¾ cups	2 cups
Potato starch	½ cup	¾ cup
Tapioca flour	¼ cup	⅓ cup
Xanthan gum	1 tsp.	1 ½ tsp.
Salt	1 tsp.	1 ½ tsp.
Brown sugar	1 Tbsp.	2 Tbsp.
Ener-G® egg replacer	1 tsp.	1 ½ tsp.
Eggs	2 large eggs or ½ cup soft silken tofu	3 large eggs or ¾ cup soft silken tofu
Melted Butter or canola oil	3 Tbsp.	¼ cup
Apple cider vinegar	1 tsp.	2 tsp.
Milk (cow, rice, soy) 110°	1 cup	1 ½ cups
Pans	Three 5x3-inch pans or a 9x5-inch pan	Five 5x3-inch pans or two 8x4-inch pans

Hand

1. Mix yeast, sugar, and milk in bowl. Let foam 5 minutes.
2. In large mixer bowl using regular beaters, combine flour through egg-replacer. Add eggs, butter, vinegar, and yeast mixture.
3. Mix ingredients together on low speed, then beat on high 2 minutes, scraping sides of bowl with spatula.
4. Divide dough among greased pans. Rise in warm place (75-80°) until dough is level with top of pan.
5. Preheat oven to 350°. Bake small loaves 25-30 minutes; large loaves 40-50 minutes— or until tops are nicely browned. Cool 5 minutes in pan. Remove from pan; cool on wire rack.

Machine

1. Spray pan with cooking spray. Add room temperature ingredients in order listed by manufacturer. Set controls and bake.

Calories	Fat	Protein	Carb	Chol	Sodium	Fiber
180	3.5g	3.5g	35g	1mg	290mg	1g

Eggs and butter add additional 56mg cholesterol per serving.

~ Bacon Onion Muffins ~

These tasty muffins are best eaten right after they come out of the oven.

½ cup chopped cooked bacon
1 Tbsp. dried minced onions
1 ½ cups brown rice or sorghum flour
¾ cup potato starch
¾ cup tapioca flour
1 ½ tsp. unflavored gelatin powder
1 ½ tsp. xanthan gum

1 Tbsp. baking powder
1 Tbsp. sugar
1 tsp. salt
1 tsp. dried thyme
1 cup milk (cow, rice, soy)
⅓ cup cooking oil
3 large eggs, lightly beaten*

1. Preheat oven to 400°. Grease standard 12-muffin tin.

2. In medium mixer bowl, combine all dry ingredients. In another small bowl, whisk together milk, oil, and eggs until very smooth. Add bacon and onion to milk mixture.

3. Make well in center of dry ingredients. Add milk mixture all at once, stirring just until moistened. Divide evenly in 12-muffin tin, filling each tin to just below top.

4. Bake 20-25 minutes or until tops are golden brown and crusty. Serve immediately. Makes 12.

Calories	Fat	Protein	Carb	Chol	Sodium	Fiber
200	6g	4g	32g	4mg	430mg	1.5g

Eggs add additional 70mg cholesterol per serving.

*Egg Alternative: ¾ cup soft silken tofu in place of 3 large eggs. Muffins will be heavier and somewhat dense.

~ Corn Bread with Green Chiles ~

Some cornbread experts insist on baking cornbread in a pre-heated 9-inch cast-iron skillet. That method works fine with this recipe, producing a slightly crispy crust. If you are not accustomed to eating green chiles, you might reduce the amount to 2 Tbsp. the first time you make this corn bread.

1 can (4 oz) diced green chiles
2 Tbsp. chopped fresh cilantro
¼ cup brown rice flour
3 Tbsp. tapioca flour
3 Tbsp. potato starch
½ tsp. xanthan gum
½ cup yellow cornmeal
2 Tbsp. sugar

1 tsp. baking powder
½ tsp. baking soda
½ tsp. salt
1 large egg*
⅔ cup buttermilk or 1 Tbsp.
   cider vinegar and enough non-
   dairy milk to equal ⅔ cup
2 Tbsp. canola oil

1. Preheat oven to 375°. Grease 8 x 8-inch pan or 9-inch cast-iron skillet. Set aside.

2. In medium bowl, combine flour through salt. Make well in center.

3. In another bowl, beat egg, buttermilk, and oil until well blended. Add egg mixture all at once to dry mixture, stirring just until moistened. Gently stir in chiles and cilantro.

4. Bake 20-25 minutes or until top is firm and edges are lightly browned. Serve warm. Serves 6.

*Corn Bread without Eggs: Omit egg, add 2 tsp. Ener-G ® egg replacer and increase buttermilk to 1 cup. Bake 20-25 minutes or until top is firm and lightly browned.

Calories	Fat	Protein	Carb	Chol	Sodium	Fiber
150	4g	4g	25g	37mg	485mg	2g

Eggs add additional 36mg cholesterol per serving.

~ Irish Griddle Cakes ~

This is a great way to use up left over mashed potatoes and it provides a great way to have crispy, chewy bread in relatively little time.

1 cup mashed potatoes
¼ cup brown rice flour
¼ cup potato starch
¼ cup tapioca flour
½ tsp. xanthan gum
½ tsp. salt

½ tsp. crushed dried rosemary
½ tsp. onion powder
½ tsp. baking powder
1 Tbsp. cooking oil
1 Tbsp. milk (cow, rice, soy)
1 Tbsp. canola oil for frying

1. Combine all ingredients (except oil for frying) in food processor until thoroughly mixed. Roll out between sheets of waxed paper into ¼-inch thick circle. Dust with additional rice flour to prevent sticking.

2. With sharp knife, cut circle in half, then cut each half into three wedges.

3. Heat griddle or cast-iron skillet until medium-hot. Add oil and fry cakes for 5-7 minutes on each side or until golden brown, turning once. Serve hot. Serves 6.

Calories	Fat	Protein	Carb	Chol	Sodium	Fiber
115	3g	1g	21g	1mg	390mg	1g

~ Irish Soda Bread with Dried Cherries ~

Serve this bread with your favorite Irish meal. It is also great just on its own. The dried tart cherries are not traditional, but provide a contemporary touch.

1 cup brown rice flour
⅔ cup potato starch
⅓ cup tapioca flour
2 tsp. sugar
1 tsp. xanthan gum
¾ tsp. salt
½ tsp. unflavored gelatin powder
½ tsp. cream of tartar

½ tsp. baking soda
1 large egg*
1 ⅓ cups low-fat yogurt or
    1 cup milk
2 Tbsp. canola oil
1 Tbsp. caraway seed
½ cup chopped dried cherries

1. Preheat oven to 350°.Grease two 5 x 3-inch nonstick pans or 8 x 8-inch nonstick pan.

2. Combine dry ingredients in large mixing bowl and mix well. With electric mixer on low, add egg, yogurt, oil, and caraway seeds. Blend on medium speed 2 minutes. Stir in dried cherries.

3. Spoon into prepared pans. Smooth tops with wet spatula (if necessary) and bake small pans for 45-50 minutes, large pan for 50-55 minutes or until top is deeply browned and loaf sounds hollow when tapped. Cool on wire rack. Slice with serrated knife or electric knife when bread reaches room temperature. Serves 8.

*Irish Soda Bread without Eggs: Omit egg. Add 1 Tbsp. Ener-G ®️ egg replacer and ¼ cup water. Bake as directed. Bread will be heavy and dense.

Calories	Fat	Protein	Carb	Chol	Sodium	Fiber
200	4g	4g	40g	2mg	365mg	2g

Egg adds additional 27mg cholesterol per serving.

~ Notes ~

~ BREAKFAST & BRUNCH ~

S pecial occasions take on a different atmosphere when they're celebrated in the morning, at breakfast, or mid-day— such as a brunch. I especially love to use brunch as an occasion to celebrate with friends or family.

In fact, brunch is probably my favorite way to entertain. When guests enter my home, I want them to be greeted with the aroma of freshly-brewed coffee, fresh-baked muffins or scones––piping hot from the oven, pleasant music, and table decorations to complete the ambience. Nothing terribly fancy— but I like to use lots of color to set the mood. It's just a great way to begin the day!

For a wide variety of additional wheat, gluten, and dairy-free breakfast dishes, see *Gluten-Free 101: Easy, Basic Dishes without Wheat*, 2003; *Wheat-Free Recipes & Menus: Delicious Dining Without Wheat or Gluten*, 2002, or *Special Diet Solutions: Healthy Cooking without Wheat, Gluten, Dairy, Eggs, Yeast, or Refined Sugar*, 2001.

~ Blueberry Muffins with Lemon Curd ~

These delightful muffins are perfect for everyday— or special breakfasts or brunches. Use the tangy lemon curd as you would use butter— it adds a delightful twist. See egg-free version on next page.

Muffins
1 cup brown rice flour
⅔ cup potato starch
⅔ cup tapioca flour
1 tsp. xanthan gum
1 tsp. unflavored gelatin powder
2 ½ tsp. baking powder
½ cup sugar
1 tsp. salt
1 cup milk (cow, rice, soy)
¼ cup canola oil
2 large eggs

1 tsp. vanilla extract
1 Tbsp. grated lemon peel
1 cup blueberries (fresh or frozen)

Lemon Curd
1 cup thawed pure white grape
  juice frozen concentrate
¾ cup orange juice
¼ cup lemon juice
¼ cup cornstarch or arrowroot
¼ tsp. salt
1 Tbsp. grated lemon peel
1 tsp. vanilla extract

Muffins

1. Preheat oven to 400°. Grease 12-cup nonstick muffin tin.

2. Stir together flours, xanthan gum, gelatin, baking powder, sugar, and salt in large bowl. Make well in center.

3. In another bowl, combine milk, oil, eggs, vanilla extract, and lemon peel. Pour into well of flour mixture. Stir just until ingredients are moistened. Add blueberries and gently stir in. (If the blueberries are frozen, add 5 minutes baking time.)

4. Divide batter among muffin tins. Bake 20-25 minutes— or until tops of muffins are lightly browned. Remove from oven. Cool.

Lemon Curd: Combine all ingredients in blender. Process until very smooth. Place in small, heavy saucepan. Cook over medium heat, stirring constantly, until thick— about 3-5 minutes. Cover, chill.

Per muffin

Calories	Fat	Protein	Carb	Chol	Sodium	Fiber
182	4g	3g	34g	36mg	367mg	1g

Per 2 ½ Tbsp. Lemon Curd

Calories	Fat	Protein	Carb	Chol	Sodium	Fiber
64	<1g	<1g	16g	0mg	50mg	0g

~ Blueberry Muffins without Eggs ~

If you love Blueberry Muffins but not eggs—this is the recipe for you. These muffins will be somewhat heavier than those on the previous page, but they'll taste fabulous! They're best warm from the oven.

Muffins
1 cups brown rice flour
⅔ cup potato starch
⅔ cup tapioca flour
1 tsp. unflavored gelatin powder
1 ½ tsp. xanthan gum
1 Tbsp. baking powder
1 tsp. salt
½ cup sugar
1 cup milk (cow, rice, soy, nut)
½ cup soft silken tofu

¼ cup canola oil
1 Tbsp. grated lemon peel
1 tsp. vanilla extract
1 cup blueberries (fresh or frozen)

Streusel Topping
2 Tbsp. brown rice flour
¼ cup brown sugar
½ tsp. ground cinnamon
¼ cup chopped pecans
1 Tbsp. canola oil

Muffins
1. Preheat oven to 375°. Grease 12-cup muffin pan.

2. In large mixing bowl, combine flours, gelatin, xanthan gum, baking powder, salt, and sugar. Make well in center. Set aside.

3. In medium bowl with electric mixer, beat milk, tofu, oil, vanilla, and lemon peel until smooth. Beat liquid mixture into dry ingredients. Gently fold blueberries into batter, which will be consistency of thick cake batter. Distribute batter evenly in pan.

Streusel Topping
1. Combine ingredients thoroughly. Sprinkle topping evenly on muffins. Bake 20-25 minutes or until toothpick inserted in center comes out clean. Remove from oven. Serves 12.

Per Muffin

Calories	Fat	Protein	Carb	Chol	Sodium	Fiber
233	7g	5g	39g	1mg	452mg	2g

~ Cappuccino Chocolate Chip Muffins ~

These delicious muffins combine two favorite flavors— coffee and chocolate. These muffins travel well and are sure to delight your chocoholic friends and family.

1 cup cocoa powder (not Dutch)
⅔ cup brown sugar
½ cup brown rice or sorghum flour
¼ cup potato starch
½ cup tapioca flour
1 ½ tsp. xanthan gum
½ tsp. baking soda
1 tsp. unflavored gelatin powder
1 tsp. instant coffee granules
 or espresso powder

1 tsp. ground cinnamon
1 tsp. salt
½ cup milk (cow, rice, soy)
½ cup (110°) brewed coffee
¼ cup canola oil
2 large eggs*
1 tsp. vanilla extract
½ cup gf/df chocolate chips
¼ cup finely chopped nuts

1. Preheat oven to 375°. Grease 12-cup muffin tin.

2. Stir together cocoa, sugar, flours, xanthan gum, baking soda, gelatin, coffee granules, cinnamon, and salt in large bowl. Make well in center.

3. In another bowl, whisk together milk, coffee, oil, eggs, and vanilla extract until very smooth. Pour into well of flour mixture. Stir just until ingredients are moistened. Gently stir in chocolate chips and nuts.

4. Divide batter among muffin pans. Bake 20-25 minutes— or until tops of muffins are very firm. Remove from oven. Serve slightly warm so chocolate chips are soft.

*Egg Alternative: Use ½ cup soft silken tofu in place of 2 eggs. Muffins will be heavier and more dense. For best results, use sorghum flour.

Calories	Fat	Protein	Carb	Chol	Sodium	Fiber
226	9g	5g	36g	1mg	336mg	4g

Egg adds additional 35mg cholesterol per muffin.

~ Bran Muffins ~

If you prefer a hearty muffin for breakfast, but one that isn't too sweet— this muffin is for you. If you like to bake only a few muffins at a time, this batter keeps in the refrigerator for up to 2 days.

1 cup brown rice or sorghum flour
⅔ cup potato starch
⅓ cup tapioca flour
3 Tbsp. rice bran or rice polish
1 ¼ tsp. xanthan gum
1 ¼ tsp. ground cinnamon
¾ tsp. baking soda
¾ tsp. salt
½ tsp. soy lecithin
½ tsp. ground ginger
½ tsp. ground allspice

¼ tsp. ground nutmeg
1 cup milk (cow, rice, soy)
3 Tbsp. cider vinegar
1 large egg*
3 Tbsp. canola oil
½ cup molasses
1 tsp. vanilla extract
⅔ cup raisins
⅓ cup chopped walnuts
1 Tbsp. grated orange peel

1. Preheat oven to 375°. Grease 12-cup muffin pan.

2. In large bowl, mix flours with other dry ingredients. In separate bowl, use electric mixer to combine milk, vinegar, egg, oil, molasses, and vanilla until very smooth. Stir into dry ingredients until moistened. Gently stir in raisins, nuts, and orange peel.

3. Distribute evenly into muffin pan. Bake 25-30 minutes or until tops are firm.

*Egg Alternative: ¼ cup soft silken tofu in place of 1 egg. Increase baking soda to 1 tsp. Muffins will be heavier and more dense For best results, use sorghum flour.

Calories	Fat	Protein	Carb	Chol	Sodium	Fiber
210	6g	3g	40g	1mg	344mg	2g

Egg adds additional 17mg cholesterol per muffin.

~ Pumpkin Doughnuts ~

Although the idea of pumpkin seems appropriate for fall and winter, you can make these doughnuts any time you like.

3 Tbsp. sugar
1 cup brown rice flour
½ cup potato starch
¼ cup tapioca flour
1 tsp. xanthan gum
2 ¼ tsp. ground cinnamon
½ tsp. ground nutmeg
1 ½ tsp. baking powder
1 ½ tsp. baking soda

½ tsp. salt
1 large egg*
1 cup buttermilk or 2 Tbsp.
   cider vinegar with enough
   non-dairy milk to equal 1 cup
¾ cup brown sugar
½ cup canned pumpkin
3 Tbsp. canola oil
1 tsp. grated lemon peel

1. Preheat oven to 400°. Grease 6-cup mini-Bundt pan. Sprinkle molds with 3 Tbsp. sugar, tapping out excess.

2. In large bowl, combine flours, xanthan gum, cinnamon, nutmeg, baking powder, baking soda, and salt. Set aside.

3. In another bowl, whisk together the egg, buttermilk, brown sugar, pumpkin, oil, and lemon peel until very smooth. Add dry ingredients and stir just until combined. Spoon ¼ cup batter into prepared molds.

4. Bake 15-18 minutes or until doughnuts brown around edges. Cool 2 minutes. Then loosen edges and invert doughnuts onto wire rack to cool. Repeat with remaining half of batter. Makes 12 doughnuts.

***Egg Alternative:** Use ¼ cup soft silken tofu in place of 1 large egg.

Calories	Fat	Protein	Carb	Chol	Sodium	Fiber
175	3g	2g	36g	1mg	385mg	1.5g

Egg adds 18mg cholesterol per doughnut.

~ Pumpkin Muffins ~

These muffins are perfect for a crisp, fall morning. The heavenly aroma makes your kitchen a very appealing place! You can make the batter, refrigerate (covered), and bake the next morning.

¾ cup canned pumpkin
½ cup pure maple syrup
2 Tbsp. molasses
⅓ cup canola oil
2 large eggs*
1 tsp. cider vinegar
¾ cup brown rice or sorghum flour
½ cup potato starch
⅓ cup tapioca flour

1 tsp. xanthan gum
½ tsp. salt
1 ½ tsp. baking powder
1 ½ tsp. baking soda
2 tsp. pumpkin pie spice
½ tsp. ground allspice
½ cup chopped nuts (optional)
½ cup raisins

1. Preheat oven to 350°. Grease 12-muffin pan.

2. Combine pumpkin, maple syrup, molasses, oil, egg, and vinegar in large mixing bowl. Beat on low until very smooth— about 1 minute.

3. Combine remaining ingredients (except nuts and raisins) and add to pumpkin mixture. Blend at low speed until moistened. Stir in nuts and raisins. Transfer batter to prepared pan (use spring-action ice cream scoop for uniformly-sized muffins) and bake 25-30 minutes or until firm. Cool in pan on wire rack for 10 minutes. Remove from pan and cool on wire rack. Serves 12.

*Egg Alternative: Omit eggs. Use ½ cup soft silken tofu. For best results, use sorghum flour.

Calories	Fat	Protein	Carb	Chol	Sodium	Fiber
230	10g	3g	34g	0mg	330mg	2g

Eggs add 35mg cholesterol per muffin.

~ Sally Lunn (Soleil et Lune) Bread ~

Serve this bread with a dusting of powdered sugar or with Orange Marmalade (p. 39). If you wish, assemble the dough the night before and let rise, covered, in refrigerator all night. Next morning, remove from refrigerator and bake for an extra 10 minutes— or until done. Because eggs provide part of the leavening, this is not an egg-free bread.

Cake
1 Tbsp. active dry yeast
¼ cup sugar, divided
½ cup warm water (110°)
2 cups brown rice flour
1 cup potato starch
½ cup tapioca flour
2 tsp. xanthan gum
1 tsp. unflavored gelatin powder
1 ¼ tsp. salt
¾ tsp. ground mace

1 ½ Tbsp. grated orange peel
1 cup hot orange juice (115°)
6 Tbsp. butter or margarine or
    ¼ cup canola oil
3 large eggs (room temp)
3 tsp. vanilla extract

Glaze
3 Tbsp. orange juice
3 Tbsp. powdered sugar
2 Tbsp. grated orange peel

1. Dissolve yeast and 1 tsp. sugar in ½ cup warm water. Set aside until foamy.

2. Combine flours, remaining sugar, xanthan gum, gelatin, salt, and mace in large mixing bowl with electric mixer. Add orange peel, orange juice, butter, eggs, vanilla, and yeast mixture. Beat with regular beaters 3 minutes. Batter will be very soft and sticky.

3. Transfer dough to 10-inch greased Bundt pan. Cover loosely with oiled plastic wrap; let rise at room temperature (75-80°) until doubled in volume, 45 minutes to 1 hour.

4. Ten minutes before baking, preheat oven to 350°. Remove plastic wrap and bake bread 30-35 minutes, or until cake tester inserted into center comes out clean. Turn bread on to wire rack to cool.

5. In small saucepan (or in microwave oven), heat orange juice and sugar until sugar melts. Brush warm bread with glaze. Serves 12.

Calories	Fat	Protein	Carb	Chol	Sodium	Fiber
235	5g	4g	45g	53mg	260	0g

Butter adds additional 30 calories, 3g fat, and 15mg cholesterol per serving.

~ Scones with Citrus Butter ~

Scones are fool proof because any way you make them they're a success.

¼ cup butter or margarine
⅔ cup plain yogurt*
1 large egg, lightly beaten
1 ¼ cups brown rice flour
½ cup tapioca flour
1 ½ tsp. cream of tartar
¾ tsp. baking soda

1 tsp. xanthan gum
¼ tsp. soy lecithin (optional)
½ tsp. salt
2 Tbsp. sugar
½ cup currants
Citrus Butter (see below)

1. Preheat oven to 425°. Grease baking sheet or line with parchment paper.

2. In food processor, blend butter, yogurt, and egg until well mixed. Add flours, cream of tartar, baking soda, xanthan gum, lecithin, salt, and sugar. Blend just until mixed. Add currants and pulse a few times to incorporate. Dough will be soft.

3. Transfer dough to baking sheet; pat into 8-inch circle, ¾-inch thick. Bake 15-20 minutes or until deeply browned. For crispier, wedge-shaped pieces, cut into 8 wedges and return to oven for final 5 minutes of baking. Serves 8.

***Dairy Alternative:** ½ cup milk (rice, soy) instead of ⅔ cup yogurt

Calories	Fat	Protein	Carb	Chol	Sodium	Fiber
230	7g	4g	38mg	43mg	290mg	2g

~ Citrus Butter ~

1 Tbsp. grated orange peel
1 tsp. grated lemon peel
1 tsp. grated lime peel

1 Tbsp. orange juice
1 stick (½ cup) butter or margarine
⅛ tsp. salt

Bring butter to room temperature. With spatula, combine all ingredients thoroughly.. Chill until ready to serve. Serve at room temperature. Makes about ⅔ cup. Serves 8 (1 Tbsp. each).

Calories	Fat	Protein	Carb	Chol	Sodium	Fiber
100	11g	<1g	.5g	31mg	37mg	<1g

~ Scones with Ham ~

Hearty scones are almost a meal by themselves. For an egg-free version, see p. 81.

¼ cup butter or margarine
⅔ cup plain yogurt*
1 large egg, lightly beaten
1 ¼ cups brown rice flour
½ cup tapioca flour
1 ½ tsp. cream of tartar

¾ tsp. baking soda
1 tsp. xanthan gum
½ tsp. salt
2 Tbsp. sugar
1 ½ tsp. dried sage leaves
½ cup finely chopped ham

1. Preheat oven to 425°. Grease nonstick baking sheet or with line parchment paper.

2. In food processor, blend butter, yogurt, and egg together until well mixed. Add flours, cream of tartar, baking soda, xanthan gum, salt, sugar, and sage. Blend just until mixed. Remove bowl from stand and quickly stir in chopped ham. Dough will be soft.

3. Transfer dough to baking sheet, patting with spatula into 8-inch circle, ¾-inch thick. Bake 15-20 minutes or until deeply browned. For crispier, wedge-shaped pieces, cut into 8 wedges and return to oven for final 5 minutes of baking. Serves 8.

*Dairy Alternative: ½ cup milk (rice, soy) in place of ⅔ cup yogurt

Calories	Fat	Protein	Carb	Chol	Sodium	Fiber
210	8g	5g	31g	46mg	390mg	2g

Scones with Sun-Dried Tomatoes & Olives: Omit sage and chopped ham. Add 1 tsp. crushed rosemary leaves, ½ cup sun-dried tomatoes (see p. 214 for Oven-Dried Tomatoes) and ½ cup sliced black olives. Bake as directed as above.

Calories	Fat	Protein	Carb	Chol	Sodium	Fiber
220	8g	4g	33g	42mg	407mg	2g

~ Scones without Eggs ~

If you want this to be a sweeter scone, increase the sugar to ¼ cup. Use this recipe to make egg-free versions of the other scones in this chapter.

¼ cup butter or margarine
¾ cup milk (cow, rice, soy)
1 ¼ cups sorghum flour
½ cup tapioca flour
1 ½ tsp. cream of tartar
¾ tsp. baking soda

1 tsp. xanthan gum
¼ tsp. soy lecithin
½ tsp. salt
2 Tbsp. sugar
½ cup currants

1. Preheat oven to 425°. Grease nonstick baking sheet or line with parchment paper.

2. In food processor, blend butter, milk, flours, cream of tartar, baking soda, xanthan gum, lecithin, salt, and sugar. Blend just until mixed. Add currants and pulse a few times to incorporate. Work quickly so the leavening doesn't lose its power. Dough will be soft.

3. Transfer dough to baking sheet, patting with spatula into 8-inch circle, ¾-inch thick. Bake 15-20 minutes or until deeply browned. For crispier, wedge-shaped pieces, cut into 8 wedges and return to oven for final 5 minutes of baking. Serves 8.

Calories	Fat	Protein	Carb	Chol	Sodium	Fiber
220	8g	7g	33g	16mg	300mg	3g

~ Blueberry Apricot Coffee Cake ~

Cake

⅓ cup butter or margarine or
  ¼ cup canola oil
¾ cup sugar
2 large eggs*
1 Tbsp. grated orange peel
1 cup brown rice flour
6 Tbsp. potato starch
2 Tbsp. tapioca flour
1 tsp. xanthan gum

½ tsp. baking powder
½ tsp. baking soda
½ tsp. salt
2 Tbsp. cider vinegar
½ cup + 2 Tbsp. milk
  (cow, rice, soy)
1 tsp. vanilla extract
½ cup chopped dried blueberries
½ cup chopped dried apricots

Topping

¼ cup brown sugar
½ tsp. ground cinnamon
¼ tsp. ground nutmeg
2 Tbsp. canola oil

2 Tbsp. brown rice flour
¼ cup chopped nuts of choice
¼ cup rolled rice flakes*
*Available at health food stores or www.vitamincottage.com

1. Preheat oven to 350°. Grease 11 x 7-inch nonstick pan.

2. Using electric mixer and large mixer bowl, cream together oil, sugar, eggs, and orange peel on medium speed until smooth.

3. In medium bowl, combine flours, xanthan gum, baking powder, baking soda, and salt. In another medium bowl, combine vinegar, milk, and vanilla.

4. On low speed, beat dry ingredients into egg mixture, alternating with milk mixture, beginning and ending with dry ingredients. Mix just until combined. Stir in blueberries and apricots.

5. Spoon batter into pan. Mix topping ingredients and sprinkle on top. Bake 35 minutes or until top is golden brown and cake tester comes out clean. Serves 10.

*Egg Alternative: Omit eggs. Use ½ cup soft silken tofu. Increase baking powder and baking soda by ⅛ tsp. each. Cake will be heavier and more dense.

Calories	Fat	Protein	Carb	Chol	Sodium	Fiber
340	12g	5g	27g	60mg	264mg	3g

~ Breakfast Fruit Pizza ~

Surprise your children or your guests with this unique pizza.

Pizza
1 Tbsp. active dry yeast
⅔ cup brown rice flour
½ cup tapioca flour
2 tsp. xanthan gum
½ tsp. salt
1 tsp. unflavored gelatin powder
1 tsp. cinnamon
¼ tsp. ground mace (optional)
⅔ cup warm milk (110°-cow, rice, soy)
1 Tbsp. sugar
1 tsp. canola oil
1 tsp. cider vinegar
2 tsp. grated lemon peel

Topping
½ cup orange juice
2 Tbsp. sugar
1 Tbsp. cornstarch
¼ tsp. ground cinnamon
¼ tsp. salt
2 cups finely chopped fruit:
  apples, peaches, plums,
  blueberries, etc.
or use dried fruit:
  cherries, cranberries, apricots
1 cup chopped nuts (optional)

Pizza
1. Preheat oven to 425°. Grease 12-inch nonstick pizza.

2. In medium mixer bowl using regular beaters, blend yeast, flours, xanthan gum, salt, cinnamon, and gelatin powder on low speed. Add warm milk, sugar, oil, vinegar, and lemon peel.

3. Beat on high speed 2 minutes. Dough will resemble soft bread dough. Put mixture onto prepared pan. Liberally sprinkle rice flour onto dough; then press dough into pan, continuing to sprinkle dough with flour to prevent sticking. Make edges thicker to hold toppings. Bake crust 10 minutes. Remove from oven.

Topping
1. Combine orange juice, sugar, cornstarch, and cinnamon in small pan and cook over low-medium heat, continuing to stir until mixture thickens. Stir in fruit. Spread filling on baked pizza crust.

2. Return pizza to oven and bake another 10-15 minutes or until golden brown. Add nuts during last 5 minutes of baking. Cool 5 minutes before serving. Serves 6 (1 slice each).

Calories	Fat	Protein	Carb	Chol	Sodium	Fiber
320	14g	7g	47g	<1mg	320mg	5g

~ Caffee Borgia Coffee Cake ~

Borrowed from the chocolate-infused coffee drink that is also flavored with orange, this cake is perfect for brunch. If you're a coffee lover, be sure to try this one.

Cake

¾ cup brown sugar
¼ cup canola oil
2 large eggs*
2 Tbsp. grated orange peel
2 tsp. vanilla extract
½ cup brewed coffee
⅔ cup brown rice flour
½ cup potato starch

¼ cup tapioca flour
1 Tbsp. cocoa powder (not Dutch)
1 Tbsp. espresso powder or 2
   Tbsp. gf instant coffee powder
2 ¼ tsp. baking powder
½ tsp. xanthan gum
½ tsp. salt
1 tsp. ground cinnamon

Topping

1 tsp. cocoa powder
1 tsp. ground cinnamon
1 Tbsp. canola oil

¼ cup brown sugar
2 Tbsp. brown rice flour

Cake

1. Preheat oven to 350°. Grease 8 x 8-inch nonstick pan.

2. Using electric mixer and large mixer bowl, cream together sugar, oil, eggs, orange peel, vanilla extract, and coffee on medium speed until very smooth— about 1 minute. Add remaining cake ingredients and mix just until combined. Pour batter into pan.

Topping

1. Combine ingredients thoroughly with pastry blender or fork. Sprinkle topping on batter. Bake 25-30 minutes or until tester comes out clean. Serves 10.

*Egg Alternative: ½ cup soft silken tofu in place of 2 eggs.

Calories	Fat	Protein	Carb	Chol	Sodium	Fiber
230	8g	3.5g	38g	0mg	220mg	2g

Eggs add additional 44mg of cholesterol per serving.

~ Lemon Poppy Seed Raspberry Coffee Cake ~

Old-fashioned poppy seed cake is updated to include lemon and raspberry flavors.

Cake

¼ cup canola oil
¾ cup granulated sugar
2 large eggs*
3 Tbsp. grated lemon peel
1 cup brown rice flour
6 Tbsp. potato starch
2 Tbsp. tapioca flour
1 tsp. xanthan gum

½ tsp. baking powder
½ tsp. baking soda
½ tsp. salt
2 Tbsp. cider vinegar
⅔ cup milk (cow, rice, soy)
1 tsp. vanilla extract
⅓ cup poppy seeds
1 cup fresh raspberries

Topping

¼ cup brown sugar
½ tsp. ground cinnamon
2 tsp. poppy seeds

1 Tbsp. canola oil
2 Tbsp. brown rice flour

Cake

1. Preheat oven to 350°. Grease 11 x 7-inch nonstick pan.

2. With electric mixer and large mixer bowl, cream together oil, sugar, eggs, and lemon peel on medium speed until very smooth.

3. In medium bowl, combine flours through salt. In another medium bowl, combine vinegar, milk, and vanilla.

4. On low speed, beat dry ingredients into egg mixture, alternating with milk mixture, beginning and ending with dry ingredients.

5. Stir in poppy seeds. Spoon ⅔ of batter into pan. Arrange fresh raspberries in single layer on top of batter; then pour remaining batter over raspberries.

Topping

1. Combine ingredients thoroughly with pastry blender. Sprinkle on batter. Bake 35 minutes or until cake tester comes out clean. Serves 10.

*Egg Alternative: Omit eggs. Use ½ cup soft silken tofu.

Calories	Fat	Protein	Carb	Chol	Sodium	Fiber
250	7g	4g	44g	1mg	288mg	3g

Eggs add additional 42mg cholesterol per serving.

~ Banana-Pecan Waffles
with Maple Raisin Syrup ~

*Save those extra-ripe bananas and surprise your family or impress
your guests with this special breakfast dish.*

Waffles
1 cup brown rice flour
½ cup potato starch
¼ cup tapioca flour
2 tsp. baking powder
½ tsp. salt
1 Tbsp. sugar
2 large ripe bananas (mashed)
2 Tbsp. canola oil
1 Tbsp. cider vinegar
1 cup milk (cow, rice, soy)

1 tsp. vanilla extract
1 tsp. rum extract
⅓ cup finely chopped pecans

Maple Raisin Syrup
1 cup pure maple syrup
⅓ cup dark raisins
1 Tbsp. rum or 1 tsp. rum extract

Waffles
1. Heat waffle iron. Spray with cooking spray. Combine all waffle
ingredients in medium bowl; whisk thoroughly until very smooth.

2. Pour ¼ of batter onto heated waffle iron. Close and bake according
to manufacturer's instructions or until steaming stops, about 4-6
minutes. Repeat with remaining batter.

Maple Raisin Syrup
While waffles are baking, heat maple syrup, raisins, and rum in a small
saucepan over low heat. Simmer until ready to serve with waffles. Makes
4 waffles, each 9 inches.

Calories	Fat	Protein	Carb	Chol	Sodium	Fiber
690	16g	16g	125g	108mg	720mg	5g

~ Pancakes ~

1 large egg	½ tsp. baking soda
½ cup nonfat plain yogurt*	1 tsp. sugar
¼ cup brown rice flour	½ tsp. salt
2 Tbsp. potato starch	1 tsp. vanilla extract
2 Tbsp. tapioca flour	1 Tbsp. canola oil
1 tsp. baking powder	Additional oil for frying

1. Blend egg and yogurt in blender or whisk vigorously in bowl. Add remaining ingredients and blend, just until mixed.

2. Over medium heat, place large, nonstick skillet lightly coated with oil. Pour batter into skillet and cook until tops are bubbly (3-5 minutes). Turn and cook until golden brown (2-3 minutes). Makes eight 4-inch pancakes. Serves 4 (2 pancakes each).

*Dairy Alternative: ⅓ cup milk (cow, rice, soy) instead of ½ cup yogurt

Per 2 pancakes:

Calories	Fat	Protein	Carb	Chol	Sodium	Fiber
260	4g	4g	52g	55mg	646mg	.5g

~ Pancakes without Eggs ~

⅔ cup milk (cow, rice, soy)	1 tsp. sugar
2 tsp. Ener-G ® Egg Replacer powder	¾ tsp. baking soda
¼ cup brown rice flour	½ tsp. salt
¼ cup potato starch	1 tsp. vanilla extract
1 Tbsp. tapioca flour	1 Tbsp. canola oil
1 ¼ tsp. baking powder	Additional oil for frying

1. Blend milk and egg replacer in blender 1 minute. Blend in remaining ingredients. Over medium heat, place large, lightly oiled nonstick skillet. Pour batter into skillet and cook until tops are bubbly (2-3 minutes). Turn; cook until golden brown (1-2 minutes). Makes eight 4-inch pancakes. Serves 4 (2 each).

Per 2 pancakes:

Calories	Fat	Protein	Carb	Chol	Sodium	Fiber
110	3g	2g	20g	1mg	736mg	.5g

~ Sweet Potato Waffles ~

You're probably thinking "Sweet potatoes in waffles?" Remember— sweet potatoes are extremely nutritious and provide an excellent source of beta carotene, they're low-calorie and high in fiber, and they are one of the least allergenic foods on earth. They bind the ingredients in this recipe (no need for eggs) and are absolutely delicious. Try them!

1 cup brown rice flour
½ cup potato starch
¼ cup tapioca flour
1 Tbsp. sugar
2 tsp. baking powder
1 tsp. ground cinnamon
½ tsp. salt

½ tsp. xanthan gum
2 Tbsp. canola oil
1 medium cooked sweet potato,
   mashed to yield ½ to ¾ cup
1 ¼ cups milk (cow, rice, soy)
1 tsp. vanilla extract

1. Combine dry ingredients (flour through xanthan gum) in medium bowl. In separate bowl, whisk together oil, sweet potato, milk, and vanilla extract. Whisk liquid mixture into flour mixture just until combined.

2. Cook on waffle iron, according to manufacturer directions. Makes 4 waffles, depending on size of waffle iron.

Calories	Fat	Protein	Carb	Chol	Sodium	Fiber
340	7g	12g	58g	2g	684mg	5g

~ Waffles ~

This waffle recipe is so easy and dependable. See egg-free version below.

1 cup brown rice flour
½ cup potato starch
¼ cup tapioca flour
2 tsp. baking powder
½ tsp. salt
1 Tbsp. sugar

2 large eggs
2 Tbsp. canola oil
2 Tbsp. cider vinegar
1 ⅓ cups milk (cow, rice, soy)
1 tsp. vanilla extract

1. Combine dry ingredients (flour through sugar) in medium bowl. In separate bowl, whisk together eggs, oil, vinegar, milk, and vanilla. Whisk liquid mixture into flour mixture just until combined.

2. Cook on waffle iron, according to manufacturer instructions. Makes 4 waffles, depending on size of waffle iron.

Calories	Fat	Protein	Carb	Chol	Sodium	Fiber
350	10g	15g	51g	108mg	644mg	3g

~ Waffles without Eggs ~

Even without eggs, these waffles are crisp and delicious.

1 cup brown rice flour
½ cup potato starch
¼ cup tapioca flour
1 Tbsp. sugar
1 tsp. baking soda
½ tsp. salt

½ tsp. xanthan gum
2 Tbsp. canola oil
1 ¼ cups buttermilk or 1 Tbsp.
   cider vinegar with enough milk
   (cow, rice, soy) to equal 1 ¼ cups
1 tsp. vanilla extract

1. In small bowl, mix together flours, sugar, baking soda, salt, and xanthan gum. Whisk in oil, buttermilk, and vanilla.

2. Heat waffle iron. Pour ¼ of batter onto heated waffle iron. Follow manufacturer's directions for your waffle iron. Close and bake until steaming stops, about 4-6 minutes. Repeat with remaining batter. Makes 4 waffles, depending on size of waffle iron.

Per waffle:

Calories	Fat	Protein	Carb	Chol	Sodium	Fiber
325	9g	6g	58g	3mg	690mg	2g

~ Breakfast Sausage ~

If you love sausage in the "wurst" way, this recipe makes it easy to include this flavorful meat on your breakfast plate. If you want an even lower fat content, try using half ground turkey and half ground pork. You can either shape the meat into patties or links— or brown the meat in a crumbled fashion. You can sprinkle the crumbles onto your scrambled eggs or your favorite pizza. Yum!!!

1 lb. ground pork, turkey, or beef
1 tsp. rubbed sage
½ tsp. salt
½ tsp. dried thyme
½ tsp. ground cumin
½ tsp. dried savory

½ tsp. black pepper
½ tsp. fennel seed
¼ tsp. ground nutmeg
⅛ tsp. ground cloves
⅛ tsp. cayenne pepper

Blend all ingredients together in large bowl using your hands or large spatula. Form into patties or links (spray your hands with cooking spray first) and fry over medium heat until cooked through. Or, simply brown mixture in skillet in a crumbled fashion. Serves 12.

Calories	Fat	Protein	Carb	Chol	Sodium	Fiber
110	8g	10g	<1g	36mg	125mg	<1g

~ Breakfast Trifle ~

This dish looks pretty in individual, clear glass goblets or in a straight sided, glass serving dish. This allows the layers of ingredients to be visible from the side. Use whatever fruit you have available— blueberries, raspberries, sliced peaches, etc.

½ Basic Cake (p. 98-99) cut in
   1-inch cubes
4 small cartons (8 oz. each) flavored
   yogurt or 4 cups pudding of choice

2 small bananas, diced
2 cups sliced strawberries
Fresh mint for garnish

Layer ingredients in serving dish, starting and ending with yogurt. Garnish with few pieces of whole fruit and mint. Serve chilled. Serves 6.

Calories	Fat	Protein	Carb	Chol	Sodium	Fiber
450	10g	13g	80g	56mg	500mg	3g

~ Bircher-Muesli ~

I've always loved this cereal and now I have it frequently at home knowing it contains no wheat or gluten. You can assemble the rolled rice flakes, nuts, and spices the night before. Then add the fresh fruit and yogurt (or milk) just before serving. You can double this recipe for big groups. I've enjoyed this wonderful breakfast dish both cold and warm and I prefer the warm version.

2 cups rolled rice flakes*
2 tsp. grated lemon peel
1 Tbsp. grated orange peel
1 cup fresh orange juice
½ tsp. ground cinnamon
¼ cup dried tart cherries
¼ cup golden raisins
¼ cup dried apricots

¼ cup dried blueberries
½ cup nuts of your choice
1 apple, finely chopped
1 pear, finely chopped
1 banana, finely chopped
1 cup yogurt or ¾ cup milk
 (cow, rice, soy)
*Available at health food stores or
www.vitamincottage.com*

Combine all ingredients in large serving bowl. Heat to desired temperature or serve chilled. Makes about 8 cups. Serves 8 (about 1 cup each). (If mixture is too thick, add additional yogurt or milk to achieve desired consistency.)

Calories	Fat	Protein	Carb	Chol	Sodium	Fiber
210	6g	4g	40g	0mg	75mg	3g

~ Gourmet Granola ~

This makes a small recipe, but one that fits nicely in a fairly thin layer on a 15 x 10-inch jelly roll pan. If you have a very large oven and/or very large baking pans you can double the recipe. The sweetener you use will affect the flavor somewhat. You can vary the dried fruit as you wish in this morning treat. In fact, dried blueberries or dried peaches will also work nicely.

2 cups rolled rice flakes*
½ tsp. ground cinnamon
¼ cup sesame seeds
¼ cup sunflower or pumpkin seeds
¼ cup almond slivers
¼ cup unsweetened coconut flakes
1 tsp. vanilla extract

2 tsp. canola oil or spray
¼ tsp. salt
¼ cup honey
¼ cup golden raisins
¼ cup dried cranberries
¼ cup chopped dried apricots
Available at health food stores or www.vitamincottage.com

1. Combine all ingredients, except dried fruit (raisins, cherries, apricots). Shake all ingredients together in very large plastic container with tight fitting lid or in very large plastic bag. For lower-fat version, omit canola oil and spray mix with cooking spray each time you stir during browning process described below.

2. Spread granola on greased baking sheet. Bake 30-40 minutes at 300°, or until lightly browned. Stir every 10 minutes to assure even browning. Remove from oven and cool 15 minutes. Add dried fruit. Cool completely. Store in airtight container in dark, dry place. Makes about 4 cups. Serves 8 (½ cup each).

Calories	Fat	Protein	Carb	Chol	Sodium	Fiber
210	9g	4g	31g	<1mg	128mg	3g

~ Granola Bars ~

You can vary the fruits in this easy, but highly nutritious granola bar. For example, dates or dried blueberries or cranberries also work great. The potato flour (not potato starch) gives the bars a nice, chewy texture that more closely resembles granola bars made with oatmeal. This recipe makes a thin granola bar.

¼ cup applesauce
¼ cup honey
¼ cup golden raisins
¼ cup dried tart cherries
¼ cup chopped dried apricots
1 Tbsp. grated orange peel
1 tsp. vanilla extract
2 tsp. canola oil
¼ cup potato flour
2 cups rolled rice flakes*

1 tsp. xanthan gum
1 tsp. ground cinnamon
1 tsp. baking powder
¼ cup sesame seeds
¼ cup sunflower or pumpkin seeds
¼ cup almond slivers
¼ cup unsweetened coconut flakes
½ tsp. salt
*Available at health food stores or www.vitamincottage.com

1. Preheat oven to 325°. Grease 13 x 9-inch pan and line with waxed paper or parchment paper if you plan to invert pan. Grease again. Set aside.

2. Combine all ingredients in food processor. Pulse until mixture is thoroughly combined. A food processor is especially good for this recipe because it chops ingredients evenly, making for a more consistent granola bar.

3. Spread batter evenly in prepared pan. Bake 30-35 minutes or until mixture begins to brown around edges. Remove from oven and cool for 10 minutes. If inverting pan onto a cutting surface, do so now. Otherwise, let bars cool to room temperature before cutting. Makes 18 bars.

Calories	Fat	Protein	Carb	Chol	Sodium	Fiber
100	4g	2g	15g	<1mg	117mg	2g

~ Notes ~

~ DESSERTS ~

I like to think of dessert as the "grand finale" to a spectacular meal— similar to the surprise ending to a wonderful play. Dessert should be memorable, like the way you remember the encore performance of a talented entertainer.

Desserts also create an opportunity to establish rituals— such as baking that favorite birthday cake every year . . . or making an apple dish with the first hint of fall . . .or making homemade ice cream on July 4th. All the more memorable because of dessert!

Cakes
Applesauce Spice Cake 97
Basic Cake 98-99
Basic Chocolate Cake 100-101
Black Forest Brownie Torte 102
Caramelized Pear Torte 103
*Chocolate Cake & Espresso
Sauce/Orange Coulis 104*
Chocolate Cherry Cake 106
Chocolate Macaroon Tunnel Cake 107
Double Chocolate Cherry Torte 108
Ginger Pound Cake with Cardamom Glaze 109
*Heart Cake with
Chocolate Covered Strawberries 110*
Irish Apple Cake 111
Mexican Chocolate Cake 100
Pecan Nut Torte with Chocolate Ganache 112

Cookies & Bars
Celebration Cookies 152
Chocolate Cherry Almond Biscotti 151
Chocolate Cherry Cookies 152
Chocolate Ice Cream Sandwiches 153
Colorado Chocolate Chip Cookies 154
"Oatmeal" Cookies 155
Rocky Road Brownies 156
Basic (Cut-Out) Cookies 157

(More desserts on next page)

Birthday Cakes for Kids
Butterfly Cake 121
Candle Cake 123
Caterpillar Cake 125
Down on the Farm Cake 127
Halloween Spider Web Cake 128
How Old Are You? Cake 129
Indy 500 Race Track Cake 131

Cookies, Etc. for Kids
Basic (Cut-Out) Cookies 157
Bug Cookies 150
Cookie Monsters 150
Flower Pot Treats 146
Snakes 150
Spider Cookies 150

Desserts (continued)

Pies, Puddings, Etc.
Pumpkin Pie 141
Peach or Cherry Cobbler 143
Chocolate Covered Strawberries 144
Chocolate Dipped, Filled Strawberries 144
Chocolate Pots De Crème 140
Chocolate Mocha Fudge Trifle 145
Flower Pot Treats 146
Frozen Tiramisu 147
Panna Cotta 148
Peach Melba Ice Cream Pie 149

Wedding Cakes
Chocolate Raspberry Groom's Cake 113
Coconut Wedding Cake 114
Lemon Wedding Cake 115
Spice Wedding Cake 116-117
White Wedding Cake with Fruit Filling 118
Yellow Tiered Wedding Cake 119

Ice Cream, Etc.
Chocolate Cappuccino Ice Cream 158
Chocolate Sorbet 158
Lemon Sorbet 159
Peach Ice Cream 160
Raspberry Sherbet 160
Strawberry Sherbet 160
Vanilla Frozen Yogurt without Eggs 161
Vanilla Ice Cream with Eggs 161

Frostings, Toppings, Etc.
Apricot Filling 133
Caramel Sauce 134
Cherry Pie Filling 133
Chocolate Cinnamon Cream 135
Chocolate Ganache 135
Chocolate Syrup 136
Chocolate Frostings 136-137
Espresso Ganache 135
Raspberry Filling 138
Un-chocolate Frosting 138
Whipped Topping (Nut-based) 139
Whipped Topping (Soy-based) 139
White 7-Minute Frosting 140

For additional desserts without wheat, gluten, or dairy see *Gluten-Free 101: Easy, Basic Dishes without Wheat*, 2003; *Wheat-Free Recipes & Menus: Delicious Dining without Wheat or Gluten*, 2002; or *Special Diet Solutions: Healthy Cooking without Wheat, Gluten, Dairy, Eggs, Yeast, or Refined Sugar*, 2001.

~ Applesauce Spice Cake ~

Think of a crisp, fall day with the aroma of this cake in your kitchen.
Wonderful! This recipe is, perfect for the smaller (6 cup) Bundt pan.

½ cup brown rice flour
¼ cup potato starch
¼ cup tapioca flour
½ tsp. xanthan gum
1 tsp. unflavored gelatin powder
½ tsp. salt
1 ½ tsp. baking soda
1 ½ tsp. baking powder
1 tsp. ground cinnamon
½ tsp. ground cloves

¼ tsp. ground nutmeg
¼ tsp. ground allspice
½ cup chopped walnuts
½ cup currants or dark raisins
⅓ cup butter or margarine or
    ¼ cup canola oil
⅔ cup brown sugar
2 large eggs*
½ cup applesauce
1 Tbsp. apple cider vinegar

1. Preheat oven to 350°. Grease 6-cup nonstick Bundt cake pan.

2. Sift dry ingredients together (flour through allspice). Toss walnuts and currants with 2 Tbsp. of the dry ingredients.

3. In large mixing bowl, cream butter, sugar, egg, applesauce, and vinegar until thoroughly blended and very smooth. Slowly add dry ingredients, mixing just until combined. Fold in nuts and currants.

4. Transfer to prepared pan and bake for 25-30 minutes. Cool in pan 5-10 minutes. Remove cake to wire rack and cool completely. Serves 8.

Calories	Fat	Protein	Carb	Chol	Sodium	Fiber
300	13g	5g	43g	0mg	500mg	2g

Eggs and butter add additional 75mg cholesterol per serving.

*Egg Alternative: ½ cup soft silken tofu in place of 2 eggs. Cake will be heavy and dense.

~ Basic Cake ~

This is an all-purpose basic cake that you can use for many occasions. For a white cake, use 3 egg whites rather than 2 whole eggs. For an egg-free version, see next page.

⅓ cup butter or margarine or
   ¼ cup canola oil
1 cup sugar
2 large eggs (or 3 egg whites)
1 Tbsp. grated lemon peel
1 cup brown rice flour
⅓ cup potato starch
3 Tbsp. tapioca flour

1 tsp. xanthan gum
½ tsp. baking powder
½ tsp. baking soda
¼ tsp. salt
¾ cup buttermilk or 2 tsp.
   cider vinegar and enough
   non-dairy milk to equal ¾ cup
1 tsp. vanilla extract

1. Preheat oven to 325°. Grease two 8-inch round and line with parchment paper or waxed paper. Or, grease two 5 x 3-inch small cake pans.

2. Using electric mixer and large mixer bowl, cream butter and sugar on medium speed until thoroughly blended. Mix in eggs and grated lemon peel on low speed until blended.

3. In medium bowl, sift together flours, xanthan gum, baking powder, baking soda, and salt. In another medium bowl, combine buttermilk and vanilla extract.

4. On low speed, beat dry ingredients into butter mixture, alternating with buttermilk, beginning and ending with dry ingredients. Mix just until combined. Divide batter in prepared pans and smooth tops.

5. Bake 8-inch cakes about 30-35 minutes or small loaf pans for 30-40 minutes— or until tops are golden brown and a cake tester inserted in center comes out clean. Cool cake in pans 5 minutes, then remove from pan, remove paper, and cool on rack. Serves 12.

Calories	Fat	Protein	Carb	Chol	Sodium	Fiber
195	6g	2g	33g	35mg	144mg	1g

Butter adds additional 15mg cholesterol per serving.

~ Basic Cake without Eggs ~

This cake was designed for people who don't want to eat eggs. It can be baked as cupcakes, a layer cake, or used for any dessert requiring a basic cake.

1 cup brown rice flour
½ cup potato starch
¼ cup tapioca flour
½ tsp. xanthan gum
2 ¼ tsp. baking powder
¼ tsp. salt
¾ cup sugar

½ cup butter or margarine or
  ⅓ cup canola oil
2 tsp. vanilla extract
½ cup soft silken tofu
Grated lemon peel of 1 lemon
½ cup boiling water

1. Preheat oven to 350° and grease 11 x 7-inch nonstick pan (or two 5 x 3-inch pans— or other pan sizes, see below). (Cake rises better in smaller pans.) Sift together flours, xanthan gum, baking powder, and salt. Set aside.

2. In food processor, cream sugar, butter (at room temperature), vanilla, tofu, and lemon peel. Process on high until completely smooth and glossy. Add boiling water and process on high until completely mixed. Add flour mixture and process until smooth. Scrape down sides of bowl with spatula, if necessary.

3. Spoon batter into prepared pan(s) and bake 11 x 7-inch pan 25-30 minutes; small loaf pans 30-40 minutes or until tops are firm. Cake will not brown very much. Remove from oven and cool 10 minutes before removing from pan(s). Cool completely before cutting. Serves 12.

Calories	Fat	Protein	Carb	Chol	Sodium	Fiber
200	9g	4g	28g	0mg	154mg	<1g

Butter adds additional 20mg cholesterol per serving.

Cupcakes: Bake 12 standard-size cupcakes 20-25 minutes or until tops are firm.

Layer Cake: Grease, then line 8 or 9-inch round nonstick pan with waxed paper or parchment paper; grease again. Spread batter in pan; bake 35-40 minutes at 350° or until top is firm. Or, bake in two 8-inch round, nonstick pans 25-30 minutes or until tops are firm. Cool cake 10 minutes before removing from pan. Cool on wire rack.

~ Basic Chocolate Cake ~

This basic chocolate cake is extremely versatile and it will become one of your favorites. Though it makes a somewhat small cake, it is virtually fail-proof. For an egg-free version, see next page.

½ cup brown rice flour
½ cup potato starch
¼ cup tapioca flour
½ cup cocoa (not Dutch)
1 tsp. xanthan gum
1 tsp. baking soda
¾ tsp. salt

1 cup brown sugar
2 tsp. vanilla extract
½ cup milk (cow, rice, soy)
½ cup butter or margarine
1 large egg
¾ cup warm (110°) coffee or water

1. Preheat oven to 350°. Grease 9 x 9-inch round or square nonstick pan or 11 x 7-inch nonstick pan.

2. Place all ingredients, except coffee, in large bowl and blend with electric mixer. Add coffee and mix until thoroughly blended. Pour into prepared pan; bake 30-35 minutes or until toothpick placed in center of cake comes out clean. Serves 12.

Cupcakes: Bake 12 cupcakes 20-25 minutes or until toothpick comes out clean.

Layer Cake: Double recipe (increase baking soda to 1 ¼ tsp.) and bake in 9-inch round nonstick pan 35-40 minutes, or two 8-inch round nonstick pans 25-30 minutes or until toothpick inserted in center comes out clean. Grease pans and line with waxed paper or parchment paper; then grease again for easier cake removal.

Calories	Fat	Protein	Carb	Chol	Sodium	Fiber
210	9g	2g	33g	18mg	300mg	2g

Egg adds additional 20mg cholesterol per serving.

Mexican Chocolate Cake: Add 1 ½ tsp. almond extract and 1 Tbsp. ground cinnamon. Bake as directed.

~ Basic Chocolate Cake without Eggs ~

This version can be used just like the Chocolate Cake recipe on the previous page.
If you prefer a larger cake, double the recipe. For best results, use garbanzo/fava bean flour
or sorghum flour.

½ cup brown rice flour or
   garbanzo/fava bean flour
   or sorghum flour
½ cup potato starch
¼ cup tapioca flour
½ cup cocoa (not Dutch)
½ tsp. xanthan gum

2 ¼ tsp. baking powder
½ tsp. salt
¾ cup brown sugar*
¼ cup butter, margarine, or canola oil
½ cup soft silken tofu
2 tsp. vanilla extract
⅔ cup boiling hot coffee or water

1. Preheat oven to 350°. Grease 9-inch round or square nonstick pan. Combine flours, cocoa, xanthan gum, baking powder, and salt. Set aside.

2. In food processor, blend together sugar, butter (at room temperature), tofu, and vanilla extract until very smooth. Add boiling coffee (or water) and blend until completely mixed. Add flour mixture and blend at low speed until smooth.

3. Spoon batter into prepared pan. Bake 25-30 minutes or until top is firm and toothpick inserted in center comes out clean. Remove from oven. Cool 5 minutes before removing from pan. Serves 12.

Cupcakes: Bake 12 cupcakes 20-25 minutes or until toothpick comes out clean.

Layer Cake: Double recipe (use 1 Tbsp. baking powder) and bake in 9-inch round nonstick pan 30-35 minutes or two 8-inch round nonstick pans 25-30 minutes or until tooth-pick inserted in center comes out clean. Grease, then line pan(s) with waxed paper or parchment paper; then grease again for easier cake removal.

Calories	Fat	Protein	Carb	Chol	Sodium	Fiber
150	5 g	3g	10g	10mg	200 mg	2 g

Butter adds additional 10mg cholesterol per serving.

~ Black Forest Brownie Torte ~

If you love chocolate and cherry, you'll love this dessert. Commercial cherry pie filling may contain corn syrup and red food coloring (plus thickeners of unknown origin), so consider making your own using the recipe on p.133.

½ cup brown rice flour
½ cup potato starch
¼ cup tapioca flour
½ cup cocoa (not Dutch)
1 tsp. baking powder
½ tsp. salt
¼ tsp. xanthan gum
¼ cup butter or margarine
    or canola oil

½ cup sugar
½ cup brown sugar
1 large egg*
2 tsp. vanilla extract
¼ cup hot (115°) water or coffee
1 can (22 oz) cherry pie filling (p.133)
1 cup Chocolate Syrup (p. 136)

1. Preheat oven to 350°. Grease two 8-inch round, nonstick pans. Line with parchment paper or waxed paper. Grease again.

2. Stir together flours, cocoa, baking powder, salt, and xanthan gum. In large mixing bowl, beat butter and sugar with electric mixer on medium speed until well combined.

3. Add egg and vanilla; beat until well combined. With mixer on low speed, add dry ingredients and hot water. Mix together.

4. Divide batter between greased pans and bake 20-25 minutes or until toothpick inserted in center comes out almost clean. Cool brownies 10 minutes. Run knife around edges of pan to loosen brownies. Turn out onto cooling rack.

5. To assemble, place one brownie layer on serving plate. Top with ⅔ of cherry pie filling. Place second brownie layer on top of cherry pie filling. Top with remaining cherry pie filling. Serve with Whipped Topping (p. 139) and a drizzle (scant 1 Tbsp.) of Chocolate Syrup. Serves 10.

Calories	Fat	Protein	Carb	Chol	Sodium	Fiber
310	6g	3g	64g	12mg	200mg	3g

Butter and egg add additional 22mg cholesterol per serving.

*Black Forest Brownie Torte without Eggs: Omit egg and add 1 Tbsp. Ener-G ® egg replacer powder. Increase hot water or coffee to ½ cup. Bake as directed.

~ Caramelized Pear Torte ~

This is best made in a cast-iron skillet so you don't pour the caramel into another dish.

¾ cup brown sugar
2 Tbsp. water
3 firm ripe pears
⅓ cup butter or margarine
   or canola oil
1 cup sugar
2 large eggs*
1 Tbsp. grated lemon peel
1 cup brown rice flour
⅓ cup potato starch

3 Tbsp. tapioca flour
1 tsp. xanthan gum
½ tsp. baking powder
½ tsp. baking soda
¼ tsp. salt
½ cup buttermilk or 2 tsp.
   cider vinegar and enough
   non-dairy milk to equal ½ cup
1 tsp. vanilla extract

1. Preheat oven to 350°. In greased 10-inch cast iron skillet, combine sugar and water. Bring to simmer over low heat, swirling pan occasionally, until sugar dissolves. Cook another minute, gently swirling pan if sugar colors unevenly. Remove from heat. Cool 10 minutes.

2. Wash and peel pears. Cut in half, lengthwise; then in quarters. Remove core from each piece. Cut each quarter into 3 uniformly-sized wedges. Arrange pears in pin-wheel design in caramel.

3. Using electric mixer and large mixer bowl, cream together butter and sugar on medium speed until thoroughly blended. Mix in eggs and lemon peel on low speed until mixture is very smooth.

4. In medium bowl, sift together flours through salt. In another medium bowl, combine buttermilk and vanilla.

5. On low speed, beat dry ingredients into butter mixture, alternating with buttermilk. Mix well. Pour batter over pears.

6. Bake 30-35 minutes or until tester comes out clean. Cool 5 minutes. Loosen edges with knife. Using hot mitts, invert torte onto serving plate. Remove skillet. Cool to room temperature. Serves 12.

Calories	Fat	Protein	Carb	Chol	Sodium	Fiber
295	7.5g	2.5g	57g	36mg	150mg	2g

Butter adds additional 14mg cholesterol per serving.
***Caramelized Pear Torte without Eggs:** Use Basic Cake without Eggs on p. 99.

~ Chocolate Cake with
Espresso Sauce & Orange Coulis ~

This is absolutely, wonderfully decadent— combining the wonderful flavors of chocolate, orange, and coffee. As an alternative to the espresso beans, dissolve 3 Tbsp. espresso powder in milk or cream.

Cake
½ cup brown rice flour
½ cup potato starch
¼ cup tapioca flour
½ cup cocoa (not Dutch)
1 tsp. xanthan gum
1 ¼ tsp. baking soda
¾ tsp. salt
1 cup brown sugar
2 tsp. vanilla extract
½ cup milk (cow, rice, soy)
⅓ cup canola oil
1 tsp. flaxseed meal
1 Tbsp. grated orange peel
1 Tbsp. espresso powder
¾ cup warm (110°) coffee

Orange Coulis
¾ cup fresh orange juice
⅓ cup sugar
1 Tbsp. grated orange peel
1 tsp. cornstarch

Espresso Sauce
3 Tbsp. espresso powder
1 cup heavy cream or ¾ cup milk
  (cow, soy, rice)
⅓ cup brown sugar
6 oz. (1 pkg) gf/df chocolate chips
2 Tbsp. butter or margarine
  or 1 Tbsp. canola oil
1 tsp. vanilla extract
Grated orange peel for garnish

Cake
1. Preheat oven to 350°. Grease 9-inch nonstick springform pan.

2. Place all ingredients, except coffee, in large bowl and blend with electric mixer. Add coffee and mix until thoroughly blended. Pour into prepared pan and bake 35-40 minutes or until tester placed in center of cake comes out clean. Cool on wire rack.

Espresso Sauce
1. Combine espresso powder, cream, and sugar in saucepan. Bring to boil, remove from heat and stir in chocolate chips, butter, and vanilla. Stir until completely smooth.

Orange Coulis
1. While cake is baking, combine orange juice, sugar, and orange peel over low heat. Stir constantly until mixture is thick and syrupy and reduced by half— about 5-10 minutes. If mixture is not thick enough,

mix ½ tsp. cornstarch into tablespoon of water and stir into orange coulis until thickened. Set aside to cool.

2. When ready to serve, place small pool of orange coulis on each plate. Place espresso sauce in measuring cup with spout or in squeeze bottle (e.g., an empty ketchup bottle) and drizzle sauce in concentric circles over orange coulis, beginning in center and ending at edge of orange coulis pool.

3. Holding kitchen knife perpendicular to plate, draw it through sauce beginning at center and ending at edge of orange coulis. Repeat at even intervals around entire plate. This gives a radiating "star" design to sauce.

4. Cut cake into wedges and very carefully place wedge of cake in center of sauce. Top with dollop of remaining espresso sauce and additional grated orange peel, if desired. Serves 12.

Calories	Fat	Protein	Carb	Chol	Sodium	Fiber
340	13g	3g	57g	6mg	300mg	3g

~ Chocolate Cherry Cake ~

If you like the combination of chocolate and cherries, then try this recipe. For variety, try the sweeter Bing cherries. This produces a heavy, dense cake— especially if you use the tofu.

½ cup brown rice flour
½ cup potato starch
¼ cup tapioca flour
½ cup cocoa (not Dutch)
1 tsp. xanthan gum
1 ¼ tsp. baking soda
¾ tsp. salt
¾ cup brown sugar
2 tsp. vanilla extract

1 tsp. almond extract
½ cup milk (cow, rice, soy)
½ cup butter or margarine
  or ⅓ cup canola oil
1 large egg or ¼ cup soft silken tofu
½ cup warm (110°) coffee or water
1 can (16 oz) canned tart cherries,
  drained

1. Preheat oven to 350°. Grease 9-inch round or square nonstick pan. Combine flours, cocoa, xanthan gum, baking powder, and salt.

2. In food processor, blend together sugar, vanilla and almond extracts, butter (room temp), and egg until smooth. Add warm coffee and blend until very smooth. Add flour mixture and mix at low speed until smooth. Add cherries; pulse until incorporated.

3. Spoon batter into prepared pan and bake 25-30 minutes or until top is firm and tester inserted in center comes out clean. Remove from oven. Cool 5 minutes before removing from pan. Serves 12.

Cupcakes: Bake 12 cupcakes 20-25 minutes or until tester comes out clean.

Layer Cake: Bake in greased 9-inch round nonstick pan 30-35 minutes or two 8-inch round nonstick pans 25-30 minutes or until tester comes out clean. Line pan(s) with waxed paper or parchment paper and grease again for easier cake removal. Frost with desired frosting. (See frosting section.) Serves 12.

Calories	Fat	Protein	Carb	Chol	Sodium	Fiber
190	9g	3g	31g	0mg	150mg	2g

Butter and egg add additional 39mg cholesterol per serving.

~ Chocolate Macaroon Tunnel Cake ~

This cake combines two of the most wonderful flavors on earth— chocolate and coconut.

1 ¼ cups brown rice flour
⅔ cup potato starch
⅓ cup tapioca flour
1 ½ tsp. xanthan gum
1 ½ tsp. baking soda
1 tsp. salt
1 ¼ cups sugar
1 Tbsp. vanilla extract
1 tsp. coconut extract
2 large eggs*

½ cup canola oil
¾ cup buttermilk or 1 Tbsp.
    cider vinegar with enough
    non-dairy milk to equal ¾ cup
¾ cup warm (110°) water
½ cup shredded coconut
2 tsp. coconut extract
⅔ cup cocoa (not Dutch)
Additional coconut for garnish
Frosting of choice

1. Preheat oven to 350°. Grease 10 -inch nonstick Bundt pan. Combine flours, xanthan gum, baking soda, and salt in small bowl.

2. In large bowl, blend sugar, vanilla and coconut extracts, eggs, and oil with electric mixer until thoroughly blended. Add dry ingredients and buttermilk alternately, ending with dry ingredients. Add warm water and mix until thoroughly blended. Remove ⅔ cup batter and combine with coconut and coconut flavoring.

3. To remaining batter, beat in cocoa with electric mixer until thoroughly mixed. Pour half of chocolate batter into pan, spreading evenly. Carefully spoon coconut batter over center of chocolate batter to form uniformly-sized ring, making sure not to let coconut batter touch sides of pan.

4. Carefully pour remaining chocolate batter into prepared pan, taking care not to disturb coconut ring. Gently spread chocolate batter to edges of pan as evenly as possible.

5. Bake 40-45 minutes or until tester placed in center of cake comes out clean. Serves 12.

Calories	Fat	Protein	Carb	Chol	Sodium	Fiber
310	13g	4g	47g	32mg	382mg	3g

*Chocolate Macaroon Tunnel Cake without Eggs: Use Basic Chocolate Cake without Eggs recipe on p. 101.

~ Double Chocolate Cherry Torte ~

You can use tart red cherries or Bing cherries in this flavorful desert.

Cake

1 can (16 oz) canned cherries
(drain, reserve ¼ cup juice)
⅓ cup brown rice flour
¼ cup potato starch
¼ cup tapioca flour
½ cup cocoa (not Dutch)
1 tsp. xanthan gum
1 tsp. baking soda
½ tsp. baking powder

¾ tsp. salt
1 cup brown sugar
⅓ cup canola oil
2 tsp. vanilla extract
1 tsp. almond extract
½ cup sliced almonds
2 tsp. water
2 large eggs or ½ cup soft
silken tofu

Sauce

¼ cup reserved cherry juice
¼ cup cocoa (not Dutch)
2 Tbsp. canola oil
⅓ cup honey

Filling

¼ cup milk (cow, rice, soy)
½ cup gf/df chocolate chips

Filling

1. In small saucepan, combine milk and chocolate chips over low heat and stir until smooth.

Cake

1. Preheat oven to 325°. In blender, purée drained cherries. Discard juice. Grease 8-inch nonstick springform pan.
2. In large bowl, mix dry ingredients (flour through sugar); then blend in oil, vanilla, and almond extracts. Set aside ½ cup of mixture, which will be dry and crumbly.
3. To remaining dry cake mixture, mix in puréed cherries and eggs. Spread batter in pan; top with filling. Stir nuts and water into ½ cup reserved dry cake mixture and sprinkle over filling.
4. Bake 50 minutes or until top of cake is firm. Cool in pan on wire rack 10 minutes. Remove from pan. Cool.
Sauce: Combine ingredients in blender until completely smooth. Drizzle over each serving. Serves 12.

Calories	Fat	Protein	Carb	Chol	Sodium	Fiber
375	15g	5g	71g	0mg	300mg	5g

Eggs add additional 44mg cholesterol per serving.

~ Ginger Pound Cake with Cardamom Glaze ~

Delightfully different, this cake will have your guests clamoring for more.

Cake
⅓ cup butter or margarine
   or ¼ cup canola oil
1 cup sugar
2 large eggs, or ½ cup
   soft silken tofu
1 tsp. grated lemon peel
1 cup brown rice flour
⅓ cup potato starch
2 Tbsp. tapioca flour
1 tsp. xanthan gum
½ tsp. baking powder
½ tsp. baking soda

¼ tsp. salt
1 Tbsp. ground ginger
⅔ cup buttermilk or 2 tsp. cider
   vinegar and enough non-dairy
   milk to equal ⅔ cup
1 Tbsp. grated fresh ginger
1 tsp. vanilla extract

Glaze
¼ cup water
⅓ cup sugar
1 tsp. ground cardamom
6 whole black peppercorns
1 slice fresh ginger root (½-inch)

Cake
1. Preheat oven to 325°. Grease 6 or 10-cup nonstick Bundt cake pan. Dust with rice flour; shake out excess.

2. Using electric mixer and large mixer bowl, cream together butter, sugar, eggs, and lemon peel on medium speed 1 minute.

3. In medium bowl, sift together flours through ginger. In another medium bowl, combine buttermilk, ginger, lemon peel, and vanilla. On low speed, beat dry ingredients into butter mixture, alternating with buttermilk. Mix just until combined and put in prepared pan.

4. Bake cake about 50-60 minutes or until top is golden brown and tester inserted in center comes out clean. Cool cake in pan 5 minutes, then remove from pan and cool on rack.

Glaze
1. Combine ingredients in small, heavy saucepan. Stir over medium heat until sugar dissolves. Remove from heat, cover. Let stand 10 minutes. Strain syrup through sieve into small bowl. Brush syrup over warm cake. Cool. Sprinkle with powdered sugar or garnish with fruit. Serves 12.

Calories	Fat	Protein	Carb	Chol	Sodium	Fiber
215	7g	2g	39g	16mg	148mg	1g

Eggs and butter add additional 56mg cholesterol.

~ Heart Cake with Chocolate Covered Strawberries ~

Perfect for Valentine's Day or that special occasion requiring a little romance.

Cake
1 prepared Basic Chocolate
   Cake (p. 100-101) or
   Basic Cake (p. 98-99)

Frosting
Seven-minute frosting (p. 140)
   or your favorite white frosting

Chocolate Drizzle
1 cup gf/df chocolate chips
1 Tbsp. butter or margarine

Chocolate Covered Strawberries
   (p. 144) or Chocolate Dipped,
   Filled Strawberries (p. 144)

Cake
1. Prepare batter as directed in recipe. Grease 8 x 2-inch heart-shaped cake pan. Line bottom with waxed paper or parchment paper; grease again.

2. Pour batter into prepared pan. Bake as directed in recipe. Cool in pan on wire rack 10 minutes. Invert on rack, peel off paper, and cool completely. Put cake on serving platter. Tuck strips of waxed paper under edges of cake to catch frosting.

Frosting
1. Prepare frosting. Frost top and sides of cake. Remove waxed paper strips.

Drizzle
2. Melt chocolate chips and butter together. Place in small heavy-duty plastic freezer bag and cut off ⅛ -inch diagonally on one corner. Drizzle chocolate in back and forth across cake.

Strawberries
Just before serving, arrange strawberries decoratively in center of cake. Serves 10.

See each individual recipe for nutritional content. Chocolate Drizzle adds 44 calories per serving.

~ Irish Apple Cake ~

This is an Irish version of the familiar apple cake. If nuts aren't appropriate for your diet, use raisins instead.

2 small Granny Smith apples
1 Tbsp. fresh lemon juice
¾ cup butter or margarine or
   canola oil
1 Tbsp. grated lemon peel
1 cup brown sugar
3 large eggs*
1 cup brown rice flour
½ cup potato starch

¼ cup tapioca flour
1 tsp. xanthan gum
1 tsp. baking powder
½ tsp. baking soda
½ tsp. salt
1 tsp. ground cinnamon
⅓ cup raisins or currants
¼ cup chopped pecans
2 Tbsp. powdered sugar

1. Preheat oven to 350°. Grease 9-inch springform pan Peel, core, and thinly slice apples. Sprinkle with lemon juice. Set aside.

2. Cream butter, lemon peel, and sugar. Add eggs, one at a time, and beat thoroughly after each addition. (If using tofu, add all at once and beat until very smooth.) Add flours, xanthan gum, baking powder, baking soda, salt, and cinnamon. Beat thoroughly.

3. Spoon half of mixture into prepared cake pan. Arrange apple slices on top. Scatter raisins and nuts on top of apples. Spread remaining batter over raisins and nuts.

4. Bake 40-45 minutes, or until tester inserted in cake comes out clean. Cool in pan 15 minutes, then remove sides. Dust with powdered sugar before serving. Serves 12.

Calories	Fat	Protein	Carb	Chol	Sodium	Fiber
325	15g	5g	42g	0mg	228mg	2g

Butter and eggs add additional 84mg cholesterol.

Irish Apple Cake without Eggs: Omit eggs. Use ¾ cup soft silken tofu.

~ Pecan Nut Torte with Chocolate Ganache ~

Since this cake relies on eggs for leavening, it obviously isn't egg-free.

Torte
1 ½ cups pecan meal
3 Tbsp. brown rice flour
1 tsp. xanthan gum
1 tsp. baking powder
¼ tsp. salt
5 large eggs, separated (room temp)
½ cup brown sugar, divided
1 tsp. vanilla extract
12 whole pecans for garnish

Filling
½ cup pecan meal
½ cup Chocolate Ganache
  (p.135)

Frosting
Chocolate Ganache (p. 135)

Torte
1. Heat oven to 350°. Grease three 8-inch round, nonstick pans. Line with waxed paper or parchment paper. Grease again.
2. In small bowl, combine dry ingredients (pecan meal to salt).
3. In medium bowl, beat egg whites with electric mixer on medium speed until foamy. Increase speed to high, gradually add ¼ cup of the sugar, and beat until stiff. Set aside.
4. In small bowl, beat egg yolks, remaining ¼ cup sugar, and vanilla until thick and pale. Whisk yolk mixture into nut mixture; combine thoroughly. Mixture will be fairly thick. Gently whisk nut-egg yolk mixture into egg whites until thoroughly combined. Spread evenly in prepared pans.
5. Bake 20-25 minutes or until tops spring back when touched lightly. Place on wire rack to cool completely.

Filling
1. Combine pecan meal and ½ cup Chocolate Ganache. To assemble cake, place first layer on serving plate. Top with ½ of the filling and use spatula or knife to spread filling to edges of cake. Repeat with second layer. Place top layer (top side up) on filling.

Frosting
1. Use Chocolate Ganache. Spread frosting over top of cake. If mixture is too thick, add water— 1 tsp. at a time to desired consistency. Garnish with reserved whole pecans, placing them toward edge. Serve within 30 minutes or ganache will harden and lose its sheen. Serves 12.

Calories	Fat	Protein	Carb	Chol	Sodium	Fiber
450	30g	9g	44g	88mg	140mg	3g

~ Chocolate Raspberry Groom's Cake ~

This cake makes an excellent bridegroom's cake as well as a wonderful wedding cake for those who prefer chocolate instead of the traditional white wedding cake.

1 cup brown rice flour
1 cup potato starch
½ cup tapioca flour
1 cup cocoa (not Dutch)
2 tsp. xanthan gum
2 ½ tsp. baking soda
1 ½ tsp. salt
2 cups brown sugar
1 Tbsp. vanilla extract

1 cup milk (cow, rice, soy)
1 cup butter or margarine
2 large eggs*
¼ cup warm (110º) coffee or water
1 cup thoroughly crushed raspberries
Raspberry Filling (p. 138)
½ cup raspberry jam (fruit-only
   version, slightly warmed)
Chocolate Frosting (p. 136-137)

1. Preheat oven to 350º. Grease two 9-inch nonstick cake pans. Line with waxed paper. Grease again.

2. Blend all ingredients, except coffee and raspberries, in large bowl with electric mixer. Add coffee and raspberries and mix until thoroughly blended. Pour into prepared pans. Bake two layers 35-40 minutes; four layers 20 minutes— or until tester placed in center of cake comes out clean. Cool 5 minutes. Turn cakes out of pans onto rack and remove paper. Cool thoroughly.

3. Slice each layer in half horizontally. Brush away excess crumbs.

4. Have Raspberry Filling and Chocolate Frosting ready. To assemble, place first layer on cake stand. Brush with thin layer of raspberry jam. Spread thin layer of Raspberry Filling on top of jam. Top with next cake layer. Chill cake 30 minutes.

5. Frost with desired chocolate frosting. Decorate with fresh flowers and fresh raspberries sprinkled around cake. Serves 16.

Calories	Fat	Protein	Carb	Chol	Sodium	Fiber
380	13g	3.5g	66g	58mg	450mg	5g

Butter adds additional 30mg cholesterol per serving.

*Chocolate Raspberry Groom's Cake without Eggs: Use Basic Chocolate Cake without Eggs (p. 101). Double recipe. Add raspberries with other liquid ingredients.

~ Coconut Wedding Cake ~

For large groups, make multiple batches of this small cake instead of doubling it.

⅓ cup butter or margarine
1 cup sugar
2 large eggs*
1 cup brown rice flour
⅓ cup potato starch
2 Tbsp. tapioca flour
1 tsp. xanthan gum
½ tsp. baking powder
½ tsp. baking soda
¼ tsp. salt
¼ cup shredded coconut

¾ cup buttermilk or 1 Tbsp.
  cider vinegar with enough
  non-dairy milk to equal ¾ cup
1 tsp. vanilla extract
1 tsp. coconut extract
1 tsp. almond extract
White 7-Minute Frosting (p. 140) or
  your favorite frosting
¼ cup shredded coconut
1 cup lightly toasted coconut flakes

1. Preheat oven to 325°. Grease two 8-inch round pans and line with waxed paper.

2. With electric mixer and large bowl, cream together butter and sugar on medium speed until light and fluffy. Mix in eggs.

3. In medium bowl, sift together dry ingredients (flours to salt). In another medium bowl, combine coconut, buttermilk and extracts. On low speed, beat dry ingredients into butter mixture, alternating with buttermilk. Spoon batter into prepared pans.

4. Bake cakes for about 30 minutes or until tops are golden brown and a cake tester inserted in center comes out clean. Let cakes cool in pans for 5 minutes, then remove from pan, remove parchment paper, and cool on rack.

5. Prepare white frosting of choice. To make coconut filling, stir ¼ cup shredded coconut into ½ cup frosting. Assemble cakes by placing layer on cake stand. Using spatula, spread coconut filling on cake, working from center out to edges. Add second layer and frost top and edges of cake with wide knife. Sprinkle toasted coconut on cake. Serves 12.

Calories	Fat	Protein	Carb	Chol	Sodium	Fiber
365	10g	4g	67g	52mg	235mg	2g

Butter adds additional 16mg of cholesterol per serving.

*Coconut Wedding Cake without Eggs: Use Basic Cake on p. 99.

~ Lemon Wedding Cake ~

Wonderfully lemony, this cake makes a wonderful choice for that special day.

½ cup butter, margarine
   or ⅓ cup canola oil
2 cups sugar
4 large eggs*
½ cup grated lemon peel
2 cups brown rice flour
⅔ cup potato starch
¼ cup tapioca flour
1 ½ tsp. xanthan gum
½ tsp. baking powder
½ tsp. baking soda

½ tsp. salt
1 ½ cups buttermilk or 1 Tbsp.
   cider vinegar with enough
   non-dairy milk to equal 1 ½ cups
2 tsp. vanilla extract
White 7-Minute Frosting (p. 140)
   or white frosting of choice
¼ cup grated lemon peel
Orange Marmalade (p. 39)
Fresh mint leaves for garnish
Fresh flowers for garnish

1. Preheat oven to 325°. Grease two 9-inch round, nonstick cake pans. Line with waxed paper; grease again.

2. Using electric mixer and large mixer bowl, cream together butter and sugar on medium speed. Mix in eggs and lemon peel.

3. In medium bowl, sift together dry ingredients (flours to salt). In another medium bowl, combine buttermilk and vanilla. On low speed, beat dry ingredients into butter mixture, alternating with buttermilk. Spoon batter into prepared pans; smooth tops.

4. Bake 30 minutes––or until tops are golden brown and cake tester inserted in center comes out clean. Cool cakes in pans 5 minutes. Remove from pan and cool on rack.

5. Slice cakes in half horizontally. Place layer on cake stand; brush on thin glaze of marmalade. Repeat with remaining layer. Chill.

6. Stir lemon peel into frosting. Frost cake with wide spatula using dips and swirls to create decorative effect. Garnish. Serves 16.

Calories	Fat	Protein	Carb	Chol	Sodium	Fiber
430	9g	5g	87g	54mg	245mg	1.5g

Butter adds additional 16mg of cholesterol per serving.

*Lemon Wedding Cake without Eggs: Use Basic Cake without Eggs on p. 99. Double recipe.

~ Spice Wedding Cake ~

A spice cake makes a wonderful bridegroom's cake. See egg-free version on next page.

1 ½ cups brown rice flour
1 cup potato starch
½ cup tapioca flour
1 tsp. xanthan gum
2 tsp. baking soda
1 tsp. salt
1 ½ Tbsp. ground ginger
3 tsp. ground cinnamon
¾ tsp. ground nutmeg
¼ tsp. ground cloves
2 ¼ cups milk (cow, rice, soy)

2 ¼ cups brown sugar, packed
½ cup cooking oil
½ cup molasses
1 ½ tsp. vanilla extract
3 large eggs
White 7-Minute Frosting (p. 140)
 or white frosting of choice
1 Tbsp. instant coffee powder
Garnishes of shaved chocolate,
 Dutch cocoa powder, or
 chopped nuts

1. Preheat oven to 325°. Grease two round, nonstick cake pans. Line bottom with wax paper; grease again.

2. Sift together dry ingredients (flours to cloves) in large bowl.

3. Bring milk and sugar to boil in heavy saucepan over medium heat. Remove from heat. Add oil, molasses, and vanilla extract.

4. Add milk mixture to flour mixture in mixing bowl and mix until thoroughly blended. Add eggs and mix until blended. Pour batter into prepared pans.

5. Bake cakes 35-40 minutes— or until tester inserted in center of cake comes out clean. Cool cakes in pans 5 minutes. Invert cakes onto plate or rack to finish cooling. Remove paper.

6. Slice each layer in half horizontally. Brush excess crumbs away.

7. Prepare frosting; add 1 Tbsp. instant coffee powder dissolved in 1 Tbsp. hot water. Place one layer on serving plate. Spread thin layer of frosting on bottom half. Repeat with remaining layers. Frost sides and top with deep swirls in decorative manner. Garnish. Serves 16.

Without frosting

Calories	Fat	Protein	Carb	Chol	Sodium	Fiber
420	12g	4g	73g	370mg	545mg	1g

~ Spice Wedding Cake without Eggs ~

For an interesting taste, try using brewed coffee as the liquid for the frosting. If you're using it as a wedding cake, make multiple batches rather than doubling recipe.

1 ½ cup brown rice flour
1 cup potato starch
3 Tbsp. tapioca flour
1 ½ tsp. xanthan gum
1 ½ tsp. baking powder
1 tsp. baking soda
1 tsp. salt
1 Tbsp. ground ginger
1 Tbsp. ground cinnamon
½ tsp. ground nutmeg
½ tsp. ground cloves

1 ½ cups boiling water, divided
1 cup brown sugar, packed*
¾ cup soft silken tofu
¾ cup molasses
1 ½ tsp. vanilla extract
½ cup cooking oil
White 7-Minute Frosting (p. 140)
   or frosting of choice
1 Tbsp. instant coffee powder
Garnishes of shaved chocolate, Dutch
   cocoa powder, or chopped nuts

1. Preheat oven to 325°. Grease two round nonstick pans. Line with waxed paper. Grease again.

2. In large bowl, sift together dry ingredients (flours to cloves). Dissolve sugar in 1 cup boiling water (reserve remaining water).

3. In large bowl with electric mixer, blend tofu, dissolved sugar/ water mixture, molasses, and vanilla until very smooth. Add flour mixture and process just until mixed. Add remaining boiling water and oil. Blend again, scraping sides of food processor bowl with spatula. Batter will be somewhat thick. Pour batter into pans.

4. Bake 30-35 minutes— or until toothpick inserted into center comes out clean. Remove from oven. Cool 10 minutes. Remove from pan, remove paper, and cool on wire rack.

5. Prepare frosting of choice, adding 1 Tbsp. instant coffee powder dissolved in 1 Tbsp. hot water. Place first layer on serving plate and spread with ½ cup frosting. Add top layer and frost sides and top with spatula using deep, decorative swirls. Garnish. Serves 16.

Without frosting

Calories	Fat	Protein	Carb	Chol	Sodium	Fiber
350	8g	4.5g	67g	0mg	475mg	2g

~ White Wedding Cake with Fruit Filling ~

This cake is especially pretty with the colorful raspberry and apricot layers. It is a small cake, but you can always bake several to feed a larger group.

⅓ cup butter or margarine or
   ¼ cup cooking oil
1 cup granulated sugar
3 large egg whites*
1 cup white rice flour
⅓ cup potato starch
3 Tbsp. tapioca flour
1 tsp. xanthan gum
½ tsp. baking powder
½ tsp. baking soda
¼ tsp. salt

¾ cup buttermilk or 2 tsp.
   cider vinegar with enough
   non-dairy milk to equal ¾ cup
1 tsp. vanilla extract
1 tsp. almond extract
Raspberry Filling (p. 138)
Apricot Filling (p. 133)
White 7-Minute Frosting (p. 140)
   or preferred frosting
Fresh raspberries, dried apricot
   slivers, or fresh mint (garnish)

1. Preheat oven to 325°. Grease three 8-inch round nonstick pans. Line with waxed paper. Grease again.

2. Using electric mixer and large bowl, cream together butter and sugar on medium speed until blended. Mix in egg whites.

3. In medium bowl, sift together dry ingredients (flours to salt). In another medium bowl, combine buttermilk and vanilla and almond extracts. On low speed, beat dry ingredients into butter mixture, alternating with buttermilk. Spoon batter into pans.

4. Bake cakes about 25-30 minutes or until tops are golden brown and tester inserted in center comes out clean. Cool cakes in pans 5 minutes. Then remove from pan, remove paper, and cool on rack.

5. Place one layer on plate. Spread Raspberry Filling with spatula, working from center to edges. Repeat process for next tier, using Apricot Filling. Place third tier on top. Chill cake.

6. Frost top layer and edges of cake with wide knife, using swirls and dips for a decorative effect. Garnish. Serves 12.

Calories	Fat	Protein	Carb	Chol	Sodium	Fiber
288	6g	3g	57g	1mg	150mg	2.5g

Butter adds additional 14mg cholesterol per serving.

*White Wedding Cake without Eggs: Use Basic Cake without Eggs on p. 99. See Raspberry Filling and Apricot Filling for nutrient content.

~ Yellow Tiered Wedding Cake ~

This is meant to resemble the traditional tiered wedding cake. However, the use of square rather than round tiers lends a more contemporary note.

1 cup butter or margarine
   or ¾ cup canola oil
3 cups sugar
6 large eggs*
3 Tbsp. grated lemon peel
3 cup white rice flour
1 cup potato starch
½ cup tapioca flour
1 Tbsp. xanthan gum
¾ tsp. baking powder

¾ tsp. baking soda
1 tsp. salt
2 ¼ cups buttermilk or 3 Tbsp.
   cider vinegar with enough
   non-dairy milk to equal 2 ¼ cups
1 Tbsp. vanilla extract
White 7-Minute Frosting (p. 140)
   or preferred white frosting
Fresh flowers for decoration

1. Preheat oven to 325°. Grease two 8 x 8 x 2-inch square pans. Line with waxed paper; grease again.

2. Using electric mixer and large bowl, cream together butter and granulated sugar on medium speed until light and fluffy. Mix in eggs on low speed until blended. Add grated lemon peel.

3. In medium bowl, sift together dry ingredients (flours to salt). In another medium bowl, combine buttermilk and vanilla. On low speed, beat dry ingredients into butter mixture, alternating with buttermilk. Spoon batter into prepared pans and smooth tops.

4. Bake cake about 50 minutes or until top is golden brown and tester inserted in center comes out clean. Cool cake in pan 5 minutes. Remove from pan, remove waxed paper, and cool on rack.

5. If not assembling cake on sturdy base such as a large cake stand, you'll need a firm base. Make one by cutting 12-inch square of cardboard or foam board (available in art-supply stores) and cover in aluminum foil.

6. To make wedding cake, cut one of the cakes into 6 x 6-inch square. Use leftover cake for another purpose (see Breakfast Trifle, p. 90). Place cake on prepared board.

7. Cut second cake into 2 smaller squares, one 3 ¾ x 3 ¾-inches and the other 2 ¼ x 2 ¼-inches. Once again, reserve leftover cake for another use.

8. With pastry brush, brush excess crumbs from all three pieces. Using spatula, frost top of 6-inch square cake with thin layer of frosting. Work from center to edges, then spread frosting around sides of cake. To smooth frosting, dip wide knife in hot water and dry it before spreading the frosting.

9. Repeat the process for remaining tiers. Chill cakes 30 minutes. Assemble cake by putting two remaining tiers on top of one another in descending order of size. Give entire cake another coating of frosting, again dipping wide knife in hot water then drying it before spreading the frosting.

10. Once final coat of frosting sets, (up to 1 hour), fill pastry bag with reserved frosting. Fit it with #3 pastry tip and pipe decorative border along edges of each tier. Decorate with fresh flowers as desired. Serves 36. (For more detailed directions on cake decorating, consult a cake decorating book.)

Calories	Fat	Protein	Carb	Chol	Sodium	Fiber
246	7g	3g	44g	36mg	156mg	1g

Butter adds additional 15mg cholesterol per serving.

*Yellow Tiered Wedding Cake without Eggs: Use yellow cake version of Basic Cake without Eggs on p. 99. Make 3 recipes to equal 36 servings.

~ Butterfly Cake ~

Perfect for a little girl's birthday party or a spring luncheon, this pretty cake will delight everyone.

⅓ cup butter or margarine
  or ¼ cup canola oil
1 cup sugar
2 large eggs*
1 cup brown rice flour
⅓ cup potato starch
3 Tbsp. tapioca flour
1 tsp. xanthan gum
½ tsp. baking powder
½ tsp. baking soda
¼ tsp. salt
½ cup buttermilk or 1 tsp.
  cider vinegar and enough
  non-dairy milk to equal ½ cup
1 tsp. vanilla extract
1 tsp. almond extract
Frosting of choice
Fruit leather or Jelly Belly® beans

1. Preheat oven to 325°. Grease two 8-inch round pans and line with waxed paper; grease again.

2. Using electric mixer and large bowl, cream together butter and granulated sugar on medium speed until completely blended. Mix in eggs on low speed until thoroughly blended.

3. In medium bowl, sift together dry ingredients (flours to salt). In another medium bowl, combine buttermilk and vanilla and almond extracts. On low speed, beat dry ingredients into butter mixture, alternating with buttermilk. Spoon batter into pans.

4. Bake cakes about 30-35 minutes or until tops are golden brown and tester inserted in center comes out clean. Cool cakes in pans 5 minutes, then remove from pan, remove paper, and cool on rack.

5. From each cake, cut 2-inch triangle and on opposite side of each cake, cut 1-inch wedge. Place the two circles together (straight sides together). Put triangle shapes on either side of "wings" butterfly body. (See next page.) Frost with frosting of choice. Decorate with halved jelly beans. Use strips of fruit leather for butterfly "antennae". Serves 12.

Without frosting

Calories	Fat	Protein	Carb	Chol	Sodium	Fiber
200	6g	2g	32g	50mg	144mg	1g

Butter adds additional 14mg of cholesterol per serving.

Butterfly Cake without Eggs: Use Basic Cake without Eggs on p. 99.

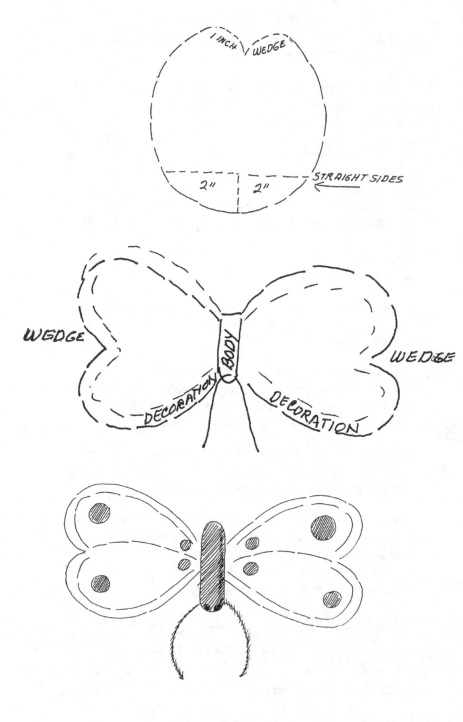

STRAIGHT SIDES

WEDGE

WEDGE

BODY

DECORATION

DECORATION

122

~ Candle Cake ~

This pretty cake is extremely simple to make and appropriate for any age group. It can be a birthday cake or a first anniversary cake.

⅓ cup butter or margarine or
    ¼ cup cooking oil
1 cup sugar
2 large eggs*
1 cup brown rice flour
⅓ cup potato starch
3 Tbsp. tapioca flour
1 tsp. xanthan gum
½ tsp. baking powder

½ tsp. baking soda
¼ tsp. salt
½ cup buttermilk or 2 tsp.
    cider vinegar and enough
    non-dairy milk to make ½ cup
1 tsp. vanilla extract
White Frosting (3-4 cups)
Fruit leather in dark color

1. Preheat oven to 325°. Grease 13 x 9-inch nonstick pan. Line with waxed paper; grease again. Dust with rice flour. Set aside.

2. Using electric mixer and large bowl, cream together butter and granulated sugar on medium speed until light and fluffy. Mix in eggs on low speed until blended.

3. In medium bowl, sift together flours through salt. In another medium bowl, combine buttermilk and vanilla extract. On low speed, beat dry ingredients into butter mixture, alternating with buttermilk. Spoon batter into prepared pan and smooth top.

4. Bake cake about 30-35 minutes or until top is golden brown and tester inserted in center comes out clean. Cool cake in pan 5-10 minutes, then invert onto piece of large cardboard covered with aluminum foil.

5. To make candle, cut cake in half (as shown in diagram on next page) down center of cake. Stack two pieces together, using ½ cup frosting between layers to hold them together. Slice off top right corner, as shown in diagram.

6. Cut piece into trimmed oval shape to resemble flame. Set flame aside. (Discard scraps of cake or make them disappear with quick taste-test!)

7. Tint 1 ½ to 2 cups of frosting into equal amounts of either light pink, light blue, or light green using commercial food colorings.

8. Frost entire cake. Put 1 cup white frosting into pastry bag fitted with basket-weave tip. Or, put frosting in plastic, freezer bag and cut ⅛-inch off one corner. Pipe frosting in diagonal stripes across candle. With remaining white frosting, arrange on top of candle to resemble melted wax.

9. Tint remaining frosting with yellow coloring and frost flame-shaped piece of cake. Place flame approximately ½ to 1-inch from cake and connect with a piece of dark-colored fruit leather (such as grape, raspberry, etc.) to resemble wick. Serves 12.

Calories	Fat	Protein	Carb	Chol	Sodium	Fiber
200	6g	2g	32g	50mg	144mg	1g

Butter adds additional 14mg of cholesterol per serving.

*Candle Cake without Eggs: Use Basic Cake without Eggs on p. 99.

~ Caterpillar Cake ~

Kids seem to love creepy, crawly things so they'll love this cute little caterpillar.

⅓ cup butter or margarine
   or ¼ cup canola oil
1 cup sugar
2 large eggs, lightly beaten*
1 cup brown rice flour
⅓ cup potato starch
3 Tbsp. tapioca flour
1 tsp. xanthan gum
½ tsp. baking powder
½ tsp. baking soda

¼ tsp. salt
½ cup buttermilk or 2 tsp.
   cider vinegar and enough
   non-dairy milk to make ½ cup
1 tsp. vanilla extract
Frosting of choice (tinted green)
Fruit leather
Jelly Belly® jelly beans
Coconut
Kraft Jet-Puff® miniature
   marshmallows

1. Preheat oven to 325°. Grease 6 or 10 cup non-stick Bundt pan.

2. Using electric mixer and large bowl, cream together butter and granulated sugar on medium speed until light and fluffy. Mix in eggs on low speed until blended.

3. In medium bowl, sift together flours, xanthan gum, baking powder, baking soda, and salt. In another medium bowl, combine buttermilk, and vanilla. On low speed, beat dry ingredients into butter mixture, alternating with buttermilk.

4. Spoon batter into prepared pan and smooth top, if necessary. Bake cake 50-55 minutes or until top is golden brown and tester inserted in center comes out clean. Cool cake in pan 5-10 minutes; then remove from pan, invert, and cool on rack.

5. To make caterpillar, trim bottom of cake (the top when it's baked) with sharp, serrated knife so it sits level, without wobbling. Cut into thirds. Arrange on large baking sheet or on cardboard covered with foil (trimmed side down), as shown in diagram on next page.

6. To make green frosting, add drops of green food coloring to your favorite white frosting. Frost caterpillar, placing frosting between cut ends. Fill in crevasses with frosting to hold them together. Use knife or spoon dipped in hot water to smooth "stripes" across caterpillar's body.

7. For the head, use small orange or lemon sliced in half, lengthwise and covered with frosting and shredded coconut. Take a strip of fruit leather, cut in semi-circle, and cut jags across top to form "ruff". (See diagram on next page.) Attach with frosting to neck of caterpillar. Use jelly beans for feet, or oblongs of fruit leather, or cut Kraft Jet-Puff® marshmallows. Serves 12.

Calories	Fat	Protein	Carb	Chol	Sodium	Fiber
200	6g	2g	32g	50mg	144mg	1g

Butter adds additional 14mg of cholesterol per serving.

*Caterpillar Cake without Eggs: Use Basic Cake without Eggs on p. 99.

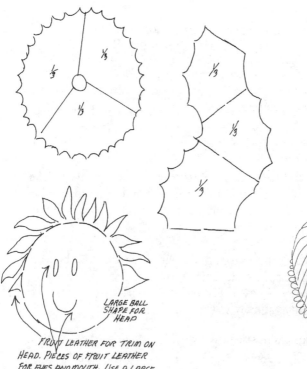

LARGE BALL SHAPE FOR HEAD

FRUIT LEATHER FOR TRIM ON HEAD. PIECES OF FRUIT LEATHER FOR EYES AND MOUTH. USE A LARGE SLICE OF LEMON OR SMALL ORANGE FOR HEAD. USE JELLY BELLIES FOR FEET, OR CUT MARSHMALLOWS OR OBLONGS OF FRUIT LEATHER.

~ Down on the Farm Cake ~

You'll need a few more "props" with this cake than with some of the others in this section, but if you have them on hand the effect is really worth it.

½ cup brown rice flour
½ cup potato starch
¼ cup tapioca flour
½ cup cocoa (not Dutch)
1 tsp. xanthan gum
1 ¼ tsp. baking soda
¾ tsp. salt
1 cup brown sugar
2 tsp. vanilla extract
½ cup milk (cow, rice, soy)

½ cup butter or margarine or
⅓ cup canola oil
1 large egg*
¾ cup warm (110°) coffee or water
Shredded coconut
Green food coloring
Cookies (see Basic Cookie, p. 157)
Gf (Glutano) pretzels or rice crackers
Toy farm animals and tractors

1. Preheat oven to 350°. Grease 11 x 7-inch nonstick pan. Line with waxed paper; grease again.

2. Place all ingredients, except coffee, in large bowl and blend with electric mixer. Add water and mix until thoroughly blended. Pour into prepared pan. Bake 30-35 minutes or until tester placed in center of cake comes out clean. Cool thoroughly. Invert cake onto platter or piece of cardboard covered with aluminum foil.

3. To make farm, tint frosting green for grass, and color coconut with green coloring and lay in "furrows". The dark chocolate of cake becomes the soil. Use clumps of frosting for grass to anchor fence posts. Use pretzels to make fence or use rice crackers lined up end to end as fence.

4. Make "cow" or "sheep" cookies or other animals using Basic Cookie recipe on page 157. Serves 12.

Calories	Fat	Protein	Carb	Chol	Sodium	Fiber
210	9g	2g	33g	39mg	300mg	2g

Butter adds additional 20mg cholesterol per serving.

*Down on the Farm Cake without Eggs: Use Basic Chocolate Cake without Eggs on p. 99.

~ Halloween Spider Web Cake ~

This cake is so easy and so much fun that the kids can join in the decorating.

½ cup brown rice flour
½ cup potato starch
¼ cup tapioca flour
½ cup cocoa (not Dutch)
1 tsp. xanthan gum
1 ¼ tsp. baking soda
¾ tsp. salt
1 cup brown sugar

2 tsp. vanilla extract
½ cup milk (cow, soy, rice)
½ cup butter or margarine or
    ⅓ cup canola oil
1 large egg*
¾ cup hot (110°) coffee or water
Frosting, divided (see below)

Cake

1. Preheat oven to 350°. Grease 12-inch round nonstick pizza pan.

2. Place all ingredients, except coffee, in large bowl and blend with electric mixer. Add coffee and blend thoroughly. Pour into prepared pan; bake 30-35 minutes or until tester comes out clean.

Frosting

1. Use your favorite white frosting recipe and tint with combination of red and yellow food coloring. Reserve ¼ of frosting and stir in enough cocoa powder to make brown colored frosting. Set brown frosting aside.

2. Frost cake with orange frosting. Place brown frosting in small, heavy-duty freezer bag (with ¼-inch opening cut on corner). Pipe concentric circles around cake, each circle about 1 to 2 inches from the next. Imagine that the cake is a clock. To create spider web, draw line with knife from noon to center circle, 1:30 to center circle, 3:00 and so on. Serves 12. (See diagram below.)

Without frosting

Calories	Fat	Protein	Carb	Chol	Sodium	Fiber
210	9g	2g	33g	39mg	300mg	2g

Butter adds additional 20mg of cholesterol per serving.

*Halloween Spider Web Cake without Eggs: Use Basic Chocolate Cake without Eggs on p. 101.

~ How Old Are You? Birthday Cake ~

Sometimes a simple cake in the shape of a child's age is the perfect answer for a birthday party. Directions are given here for ages 1 through 3. Now that you see how simple this is, use your imagination to devise cakes for older age groups.

⅓ cup butter or margarine or
    ¼ cup cooking oil
1 cup sugar
2 large eggs, lightly beaten*
1 cup brown rice flour
⅓ cup potato starch
3 Tbsp. tapioca flour
1 tsp. xanthan gum
½ tsp. baking powder
½ tsp. baking soda
¼ tsp. salt
½ cup buttermilk or 2 tsp.
    cider vinegar with enough
    non-dairy milk to make ½ cup
1 tsp. gf vanilla extract
White frosting of choice
Fruit leather
Jelly Belly ® jelly beans

1. Preheat oven to 325°. Grease appropriate pan (see "Ages" below). Line with waxed paper; grease again.

2. Using electric mixer and large bowl, cream together butter and sugar on medium speed until light and fluffy. Mix in eggs on low speed until blended.

3. In medium bowl, sift together flours, xanthan gum, baking powder, baking soda, and salt. In another medium bowl, combine buttermilk and vanilla extract. On low speed, beat dry ingredients into butter mixture, alternating with buttermilk. Serves 12.

Age One: Grease, then line 13 x 9-inch pan with waxed paper. Pour batter into pan. Bake 20-25 minutes or until cake tester inserted into center comes out clean. Cool cake in pan 5-10 minutes, then invert onto large baking sheet or piece of cardboard covered with aluminum foil.

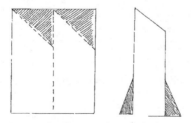

Cut in half down center of cake. Stack one layer on the other. Cut upper right hand corner off with diagonal cut, as shown in diagram. Cut diagonal piece in half, as shown in diagram below, and place each piece on opposite sides at base of cake. Frost as desired.

Age Two: Spread batter in 11 x 7-inch nonstick pan coated with cooking spray lined with parchment paper or waxed paper, then sprayed again. Bake for 30-35 minutes or until cake tester inserted into center comes out clean. Let cake cool in pan for 5-10 minutes, then invert onto a large baking sheet or piece of cardboard covered with aluminum foil. Used sharp, serrated knife to carve the number two, following diagram below. Frost.

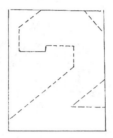

Age Three: Spread batter in greased 6 or 10-cup Bundt pan. Bake 45-50 minutes or until cake tester comes out clean. Cut cake in half, crosswise, at opposite sides. Cut off end of one piece so that the two pieces fit closer together as shown below. Frost as desired.

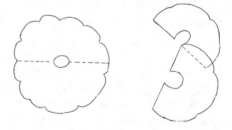

Calories	Fat	Protein	Carb	Chol	Sodium	Fiber
200	6g	2g	33g	35mg	144mg	1

Butter adds additional 15mg cholesterol per serving.

*How Old Are You? Birthday Cake without Eggs: Use Basic Cake without Eggs on p. 99.

~ Indy 500 Race Track Cake ~

This fabulous cake is sure to delight that youngster with a passion for cars.

Cake

½ cup brown rice flour
½ cup potato starch
¼ cup tapioca flour
½ cup cocoa (not Dutch)
1 tsp. xanthan gum
1 ¼ tsp. baking soda
¾ tsp. salt
1 cup brown sugar
2 tsp. vanilla extract
½ cup milk (cow, rice, soy)
½ cup butter or margarine or
⅓ cup cooking oil
1 large egg*
¾ cup brewed coffee or hot water

Decorations

2 ½ to 3 cups frosting
Cooked gf spaghetti
Glutino® gf pretzels
Rice crackers
Cocoa or carob powder
Gf crackers (p. 202)
Coconut for grass
Miniature flags, cars for
race track

Cake

1. Preheat oven to 350°. Grease two 8-inch round cake pans. Line with waxed paper; grease again. Place all cake ingredients, except coffee, in large bowl and blend with electric mixer. Add coffee and mix until thoroughly blended. Pour into prepared pans and bake 30-35 minutes or until toothpick placed in center of cake comes out clean.

2. To assemble cake: Cut 1-inch off one side of both cakes. Place both cakes, cut sides together, to form figure 8 on large jelly-roll pan (or place on large piece of cardboard that has been covered with aluminum foil).

3. Prepare frosting. Tint ½ cup frosting brown with 1 Tbsp. cocoa or carob powder. Spread frosting in 2-inch wide strip in figure 8 design around top of cake to form track.

4. Place cooked spaghetti strands on center of track to form lanes, either in single strands or in 1-inch pieces to resemble center line on highway. Tint remaining frosting green and frost edges of cake and center of each cake (inside race track). Place pretzels, around edge of cakes to form fence. Or, use brown rice crackers (dusted with cocoa or carob powder) stood on end around edge of cake. (continued on next page)

5. Tint ½ cup shredded coconut with green food coloring and sprinkle on centers of race track to resemble grass. Decorate cake with miniature flags and cars. Serves 12.

Without frosting

Calories	Fat	Protein	Carb	Chol	Sodium	Fiber
210	9g	33g	39mg	300mg	2g	2g

Butter adds additional 20mg cholesterol per serving.

*Indy 500 Race Track Cake without Eggs: Use Basic Chocolate Cake without Eggs on p. 101.

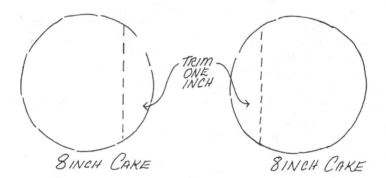

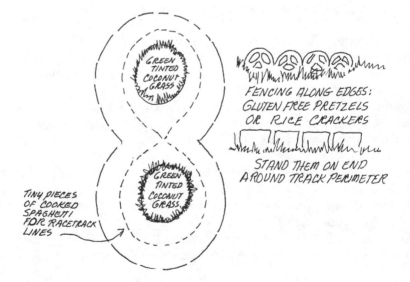

~ Apricot Filling ~

Use this tasty, colorful filling in layer cakes, such as the White Wedding Cake with Fruit Filling on p. 118.

⅔ cup dried apricots
½ cup fresh orange juice

⅛ tsp. ground cardamom or nutmeg
¼ cup sugar

1. Chop dried apricots and combine with orange juice, and cardamom in 4-cup glass microwave-safe bowl. Bring to boil in microwave, reduce heat, and simmer 10 minutes, covered, on low power— or until apricots are tender. Stir in sugar and simmer 8-10 minutes more on low power.

2. Mash mixture with potato masher or fork until smooth. Cover. Chill for 2 hours. Makes about ⅔ cup— enough to cover one layer of cake that serves 12.

Calories	Fat	Protein	Carb	Chol	Sodium	Fiber
45	<1g	<1g	11g	0mg	<1g	<1g

~ Cherry Pie Filling ~

Use this easy recipe when you don't want to use the commercial cherry pie filling, which contains corn syrup, modified food starch, and red food coloring.

1 can (16 oz) canned tart cherries
1 Tbsp. tapioca flour
⅓ cup sugar
¼ tsp. salt

1 tsp. vanilla extract
1 tsp. almond extract
Dash red food coloring
(optional)

1. Drain cherries, reserving ¼ cup juice. Combine reserved juice with tapioca flour until thoroughly blended.

2. Place tapioca-cherry juice mixture, cherries, sugar, and salt in glass or ceramic saucepan. Cook over medium heat until mixture thickens, stirring constantly. Remove from heat; stir in vanilla and almond extracts and red food coloring. Cool before using. Makes about 2 cups. Serves 12 (one layer of 12-serving cake).

Calories	Fat	Protein	Carb	Chol	Sodium	Fiber
45	<1g	<1g	11g	0mg	50mg	1g

~ Caramel Sauce ~

Use this smooth, creamy caramel sauce on your favorite ice cream, drizzled over chocolate cake or brownies, or on fresh fruit.

1 cup sugar	**½ cup milk** (cow, rice, soy)
¼ cup water	**1 tsp. vanilla extract**
1 Tbsp. butter or margarine	**⅛ tsp. salt**

1. Combine sugar and water in medium-sized, heavy saucepan. Dissolve sugar in water over low-heat. Do not stir. When sugar is completely dissolved, cover saucepan with lid and increase heat to medium. Bring to boil and boil 1 minute. This dissolves any sugar crystals clinging to edge of pan. (Undissolved sugar crystals may crystallize the entire mixture.)

2. Remove lid and continue to boil, uncovered, over medium heat. Do not stir. It may take up to 8 minutes for any color change to occur. Watch mixture very carefully because it can darken quickly and taste burned.

3. Continue boiling until mixture becomes amber or golden. Re-move from heat. Let stand for one minute. Carefully add butter or oleo with a long-handled wooden spoon. (I wear hot pad mitts to protect my hands because hot mixture may bubble and spatter.) Gradually add milk, stir-ring with long-handled wooden spoon. Mixture will harden and clump on spoon.

4. Place pan back on medium heat, stirring constantly until caramel sauce is smooth— about three minutes. Stir in vanilla and salt. Makes 1 ¼ cups. Store in refrigerator in sealed container. May need to warm slightly before serving. Serves 10 (2 Tbsp. per serving).

Calories	Fat	Protein	Carb	Chol	Sodium	Fiber
95	1g	<1g	21g	<1mg	36mg	0g

~ Chocolate Cinnamon Cream ~

Very easy to make and a wonderful dessert topping.

1 Tbsp. cocoa powder
¼ cup sour cream or soft silken tofu
¼ tsp. ground cinnamon
¼ cup pure maple syrup

1 tsp. vanilla extract
1 tsp. butter-flavored
    extract (optional)

Place all ingredients in blender or small bowl of food processor. Purée until very smooth. Add water if too thick, 1 Tbsp. at a time. Makes ½ cup. Serves 4 (2 Tbsp. each).

Calories	Fat	Protein	Carb	Chol	Sodium	Fiber
70	1g	1g	16g	0mg	3mg	1g

Sour cream adds additional 20 calories, 2g fat, and 6mg cholesterol.

~ Chocolate Ganache ~

You've seen the lovely, shiny finish on gourmet cakes. Make your own with this easy recipe.

12 oz. gf/df bittersweet chocolate
½ cup milk (cow, rice, soy)

1 Tbsp. butter or canola oil
1 Tbsp. espresso powder
    (see below)

Break chocolate into pieces and place in heatproof bowl. In small saucepan, heat milk and butter until bubbles appear around the edge. Remove from heat. (Add espresso, if using— see Espresso Ganache below— and stir to dissolve.) Pour hot milk over chocolate. Let stand 1 minute. Stir until melted and smooth. Let stand at room temperature 10 minutes before using. Pour over cake or dessert while lukewarm and spread with spatula. Serve within 30 minutes before ganache hardens and loses its sheen.

Calories	Fat	Protein	Carb	Chol	Sodium	Fiber
150	8g	2g	20g	3mg	13mg	<1g

Espresso Ganache: Add 1 tsp. instant espresso powder.

~ Chocolate Syrup ~

Use this syrup whenever the recipe calls for chocolate syrup. It is great drizzled on cakes when you don't want to use frosting.

3 Tbsp. milk (cow, rice, soy)   ¼ cup cocoa (not Dutch)
2 Tbsp. butter or margarine   5 Tbsp. honey

Combine in blender and blend until completely smooth. Refrigerate, covered. Serves 8 (about 1 ½ Tbsp. per serving).

Calories	Fat	Protein	Carb	Chol	Sodium	Fiber
66	3g	1g	11g	<1mg	5mg	1g

~ Chocolate Chip Frosting ~

A very simple frosting that's sure to please your guests.

2 cups gf/df chocolate chips   1 Tbsp. butter or margarine
¼ cup honey   or nut butter (almond or cashew)
¼ cup milk (cow, rice, soy)   1 tsp. vanilla extract

Place all ingredients in glass bowl and microwave on medium power for 2 minutes, stopping and stirring after a minute. If you prefer smooth frosting, process in food processor until very, very smooth— adding additional milk to reach spreading consistency. Otherwise, use frosting immediately or it will begin to harden. Frosts one double-layer cake to serve 12.

Calories	Fat	Protein	Carb	Chol	Sodium	Fiber
165	9g	1g	22g	3mg	6mg	2g

~ Chocolate Frosting ~

Another yummy chocolate frosting!

⅔ cup Chocolate Syrup (p. 136)   ¼ cup rice milk
1 Tbsp. arrowroot powder

1. Place chocolate syrup in small, heavy saucepan. Dissolve arrowroot powder in milk; then stir mixture into chocolate syrup.

2. Heat mixture over low-medium setting, stirring occasionally, until it starts to thicken— about 8-10 minutes. Remove from heat and cool slightly. Mixture will thicken as it cools.

3. Frost your favorite single-layer cake to serve 12— or 12 cupcakes. For larger cakes, double or triple the recipe. If frosting thickens too much, stir in a table-spoon of milk at a time to reach desired consistency.

Calories	Fat	Protein	Carb	Chol	Sodium	Fiber
50	2g	.5g	12g	0mg	10mg	.5g

~ Chocolate Tofu Frosting ~

This frosting has a very rich, bold chocolate flavor with a very creamy texture.

⅓ cup (3 oz) extra-firm silken tofu   2 cups cocoa (not Dutch)
2 cups pure maple syrup   1 Tbsp. vanilla extract

In food processor or blender, blend tofu with maple syrup until completely smooth. Add cocoa and vanilla and blend until very, very smooth. Refrigerate frosting 15 minutes before using. Frosts double layer cake that serves 12.

Calories	Fat	Protein	Carb	Chol	Sodium	Fiber
180	2g	3g	44g	0mg	8mg	5g

~ Un-chocolate Frosting ~

Use this frosting when you don't want to use the traditional powdered sugar frosting— and you want something other than chocolate. Add flavored extracts (e.g. almond or coconut) for additional interest.

12 oz. (1 pkg) extra-firm silken tofu 1 tsp. butter-flavored extract
¼ cup sugar ¼ tsp. salt
1 tsp. fresh lemon juice ¼ tsp. xanthan gum
1 tsp. butter or margarine
1 tsp. vanilla extract

Drain tofu thoroughly in mesh sieve. Discard liquid. Combine all ingredients in food processor. Process until very smooth, scraping down sides with spatula. Use immediately. Makes about 1 ¼ cups frosting. Frosts 8 x 8-inch single layer cake. Serves 12.

Calories	Fat	Protein	Carb	Chol	Sodium	Fiber
35	1g	1g	5g	0mg	50mg	0g

~ Raspberry Filling ~

This is a lovely filling for a white layer cake, but it is also delicious used in chocolate layer cakes.

2 cups fresh raspberries 2 Tbsp. cornstarch
½ cup sugar 1 tsp. vanilla

1. Mash fresh raspberries in small bowl until thoroughly crushed. Press mixture through sieve and discard seeds. Place crushed raspberries and sugar in small saucepan and whisk in cornstarch. Place pan over medium heat, stirring until mixture thickens. Cook and stir two minutes more. Remove from heat. Stir in vanilla.

2. Transfer filling to small bowl, cover, and refrigerate for at least two hours. Makes about ½ to ⅔ cup, which is enough filling for one layer cake in a two-layer cake that serves 12. Double recipe if you wish to put this filling between two layers. Triple it for cakes with 3 or 4 layers.

Calories	Fat	Protein	Carb	Chol	Sodium	Fiber
45	<1g	<1g	11g	0mg	<1mg	1g

~ Whipped Topping (Soy-based) ~

Tofu makes this topping smooth and creamy. Use like any dairy whipped topping.

½ cup soft silken tofu
2 Tbsp. honey
½ tsp. vanilla extract

¼ tsp. butter-flavored extract
⅛ tsp. salt

Combine all ingredients in blender or mini-food processor and blend thoroughly until very smooth. Makes about ½ cup. Serves 4 (2 Tbsp. each).

Calories	Fat	Protein	Carb	Chol	Sodium	Fiber
45	1g	1.5g	8g	0mg	75mg	0g

~ Whipped Topping (Nut-Based) ~

Unlike the previous topping, this one uses no soy products. But it does contain nuts.

¾ cup raw cashews or almonds
¼ cup honey
2 tsp. vanilla extract

½ tsp. butter-flavored extract
¼ cup water
¼ tsp. salt

Place nuts on baking sheet and toast in 350° oven 5-8 minutes or until lightly toasted, but not browned. In blender, grind nuts finely. Add honey, vanilla and butter extracts, water, and salt. Process again until very smooth— about 5-8 minutes. Refrigerate until ready to use. Makes 1 cup. Serves 8 (2 Tbsp. each).

Calories	Fat	Protein	Carb	Chol	Sodium	Fiber
110	5g	2g	17g	0mg	118mg	.5g

~ White 7-Minute Frosting ~

This traditional frosting is usually off-limits for many with food sensitivities because it contains eggs and cane sugar. However, for many of you it will be just fine so use it if you can. If you require an egg-free, cane sugar-free frosting see p. 139.

3 large egg whites	¼ tsp. cream of tartar
1 ¼ cups sugar	3 Tbsp. cold water
	1 tsp. vanilla extract

In double boiler over boiling water, combine egg whites, sugar, cream of tartar, and cold water. Beat with portable electric mixer 5-7 minutes until glossy and mixture reaches desired spreading consistency. Use immediately. Makes enough frosting to frost a double-layer cake for 12.

Calories	Fat	Protein	Carb	Chol	Sodium	Fiber
100	0g	1g	25g	0mg	17mg	0g

~ Chocolate Pots de Créme ~

This is a very simple, yet elegant dessert. Top with a dollop of whipped topping, a dusting of cinnamon, or fresh strawberries. If using rice milk, increase cornstarch to 3 Tbsp.

2 Tbsp. cocoa (not Dutch)	2 cups milk (cow, rice, soy)
½ cup brown sugar	1 oz. gf/df bittersweet chocolate
2 Tbsp. + 1 tsp. cornstarch	¼ tsp. salt
1 tsp. instant coffee or espresso powder	1 tsp. vanilla extract

1. Combine cocoa, sugar, cornstarch, and espresso in medium saucepan. Over medium heat, add milk, chocolate, and salt. Whisk constantly until chocolate melts and mixture thickens, about 5-8 minutes.

2. Remove from heat; add vanilla extract. Pour into individual dessert bowls. Chill until firm. Serves 4 (½ cup each).

Calories	Fat	Protein	Carb	Chol	Sodium	Fiber
200	2g	5g	43g	2mg	222mg	1g

~ Pumpkin Pie ~

This pie crust makes two pies and rolls out beautifully. With a little practice, you'll be a pro!

Pie Crust

1 cup Bob's Red Mill All-
    Purpose GF Flour
¾ cup tapioca flour
½ cup sweet rice flour
1 Tbsp. sugar
1 tsp. xanthan gum
1 tsp. guar gum
½ tsp. salt
½ cup shortening*
2 Tbsp. butter or margarine
    (non-diet)
¼ cup milk (cow, rice, soy)
Egg wash (optional)

*Non-hydrogenated shortenings, made by
Spectrum ® or Smart Balance ®, are available
at health food stores.*

Pumpkin Filling

2 cans (15 oz each) pure pumpkin
1 ½ cup sugar
4 tsp. pumpkin pie spice
2 tsp. cinnamon
1 ½ tsp. salt
4 eggs
2 cups milk (cow, rice, soy)

1. Place dry ingredients, shortening, and butter in food processor. Mix well. Add milk and blend until dough forms ball.

2. Flatten dough to circular disk, wrap tightly, and chill 1 hour so liquids are well distributed throughout dough.

3. Massage dough between hands until warm and pliable, making crust easier to handle. Roll half of dough to 10-inch circle between two pieces of heavy-duty plastic wrap dusted with rice flour. (Keep remaining half wrapped tightly to avoid drying out.) Use damp paper towel on counter-top to anchor plastic. Be sure to move rolling pin from center of dough to outer edge, moving around the circle in clockwise fashion to assure uniform thickness.

4. Remove top plastic wrap and invert crust, centering it over pie plate. Remove remaining plastic wrap and press into place. If dough is hard to handle, press entire bottom crust in place with your fingers. Repeat with remaining dough and place in second pie pan. Freeze 15 minutes.

5. Meanwhile, beat together pumpkin pie filling with electric mixer until

smooth. Pour into two prepared pastry shells. Place pies on nonstick baking sheet(s). Bake 15 minutes in preheated 425° oven on lower rack. Move pies to center rack; reduce heat to 350° and bake 40-50 minutes or until knife inserted near the center comes out clean. Cover edges of crust with foil if they start to brown too much. Cool 2 hours on wire rack. Serve immediately or refrigerate. Makes two pies. Serves 12 (6 slices per pie).

Pumpkin Pie Filling Only:

Calories	Fat	Protein	Carb	Chol	Sodium	Fiber
345	13g	5g	54g	80mg	435mg	1g

Bottom Crust only (double for double-crust pie)

Calories	Fat	Protein	Carb	Chol	Sodium	Fiber
375	22g	2g	44g	11mg	200mg	<1g

Directions for Double-Crust Pie

1. Follow steps 1 through 4, placing pie crust in a 9-inch pie plate. Place filling in pie crust.

2. Roll remaining dough to 10-inch circle between floured plastic wrap. Invert and center on filled crust. Don't remove top plastic wrap until dough is centered. Shape decorative ridge around rim of pie plate. Prick crust several times with fork to allow steam to escape. Freeze 15 minutes. Brush with beaten egg, if desired, for prettier crust. Sprinkle with sugar. Place on nonstick baking sheet.

3. Bake pie in preheated 375° oven 15 minutes on lower oven rack to brown bottom crust. Move to next higher oven rack and bake another 25-35 minutes--or until crust is nicely browned. Cover loosely with foil if edges brown too much. Cool completely on wire rack before cutting. Serves 6.

~ Peach or Cherry Cobbler ~

Substitute your own favorite fruit— perhaps cherries or blueberries— in this family favorite. Be sure to shake the buttermilk thoroughly before measuring.

½ cup brown rice flour
¼ cup potato starch
¼ cup tapioca flour
½ cup sugar
1 tsp. baking powder
½ tsp. xanthan gum
¼ tsp. salt

¼ cup cold butter or margarine
⅓ cup buttermilk*
1 large egg*
1 tsp. grated lemon peel
1 tsp. vanilla extract
1 tsp. sugar (to sprinkle
   on top of crust)

Topping

1. Preheat oven to 375°. Combine dry ingredients; cut in butter. Whisk together buttermilk, egg, lemon peel, and vanilla. Stir into dry ingredients until just mixed. Drop by tablespoonfuls on filling, which will spread out as it bakes. Sprinkle with sugar. Bake 35-40 minutes in middle of oven or until nicely browned.

Peach Cobbler

Grease 11 x 7-inch pan. In large bowl, combine 3 cups (about 3 large) sliced fresh peaches and 1 Tbsp. sugar. Let stand 30 minutes. Drain. Combine ½ cup sugar, 2 Tbsp. potato starch, and ¼ tsp. each cinnamon, nutmeg, and salt. Toss with drained peaches and 1 tsp. almond extract. Place in prepared pan. Add cobbler topping. Bake as directed above. Serves 6.

Calories 345, Fat 9g, Protein 3g, Carbohydrates 66g, Sodium 162mg, Cholesterol 56mg, Fiber 2g

Cherry Cobbler

Grease 8 x 8-inch pan. Combine 2 cans (about 14.5 oz. each) drained tart red cherries, ¼ cup of the cherry juice, ⅔ cup sugar, 1 Tbsp. quick-cooking tapioca, and 1 tsp. almond extract in pan. Let stand while preparing cobbler topping. Add cobbler topping; bake as directed above. Serves 6.

Calories 395, Fat 9g, Protein 4g, Carbohydrates 77g, Sodium 167mg, Cholesterol 56mg, Fiber 3g

*Cobbler without Eggs or Dairy: Use ¼ cup soft silken tofu in place of 1 large egg. Instead of buttermilk, add 1 tsp. lemon juice or cider vinegar to ⅓ cup rice, soy, or nut milk. Bake as directed.

~ Chocolate Covered Strawberries ~

For both of these desserts, choose big strawberries with stems intact.

**1 cup gf/df chocolate chips or
crushed chocolate squares**

**1 tsp. butter or margarine
1 pint large strawberries**

1. Melt chocolate chips (or chocolate squares) and butter in microwave or small saucepan over low heat, stirring often. Line cookie sheet or large plate with waxed paper. Dip each whole strawberry into melted chocolate, twist while removing strawberry from chocolate, and place on waxed paper— strawberry bottom down. Refrigerate until chocolate sets. Serves 4 (about 2 to 4 strawberries per serving).

Calories	Fat	Protein	Carb	Chol	Sodium	Fiber
230	14g	2g	32g	0mg	5mg	4g

~ Chocolate Dipped, Filled Strawberries ~

**1 pint large strawberries
1 cup gf/df chocolate chips or
crushed chocolate squares**

**1 tsp. butter or margarine
1 recipe Apricot Filling (p. 133)**

1. Wash and thoroughly pat strawberries dry with paper towel. With sharp knife, trim strawberries to make stem end level. Gently hollow out centers, leaving about ¼-inch-thick shells. Set aside.

2. Melt chocolate and butter in microwave or small saucepan over low heat, stirring often. (Or use a double boiler.)

3. Line cookie sheet or large plate with waxed paper. Dip pointed end of each whole strawberry into melted chocolate, twist while removing the strawberry from the chocolate, and place on waxed paper. Refrigerate until chocolate sets.

4. Using small spoon or knife tip, carefully fill each strawberry with Apricot Filling. Return strawberries to refrigerate until ready to serve. Serves 2 to 4, depending on size of strawberries.

Calories	Fat	Protein	Carb	Chol	Sodium	Fiber
365	14g	3g	64g	0mg	7mg	6g

~ Chocolate Mocha Fudge Trifle ~

This recipe is wonderful for a party because 1) it can be prepared ahead of time 2) it looks fabulous on a buffet table with the multi-layered effect, and 3) it is wickedly decadent, especially if you're a chocoholic! For large groups, this recipe can be doubled and even tripled. Just be sure to choose an appropriate-sized container. For this recipe, a 1 ½ quart container is required. If doubling the recipe, choose a 3 to 4-quart container. Tripling requires a 6-quart container.

1 recipe Basic Chocolate Cake
  (p. 100-101)
½ cup hot (115°) espresso or
  strong brewed coffee
2 ounces gf/df chocolate chips
  or chocolate squares

2 recipes Chocolate Pots de Crème
  with 1 tsp. gf instant coffee powder
  added to each recipe.(p. 140)
Grated chocolate for garnish
Fresh strawberries for garnish

1. Cut Chocolate Cake into large strips. Set aside. Melt chocolate in hot coffee. Brush each side of strip with coffee-chocolate mixture. Cut into 1-inch cubes and divide into 3 piles, each pile to be used for a layer. Place first layer of cake cubes in bottom of straight-sided, glass serving bowl that is at least 3 inches deep and 7 to 8 inches in diameter.

2. Spread ⅓ of Chocolate Pots de Crème over cake. Add second layer of cake cubes. Top with ⅓ of the Chocolate Pots de Crème. Add third layer of cake cubes. Top with final ⅓ of Chocolate Pots de Crème.

3. Place in refrigerator. Meanwhile, shave chocolate bar of choice with potato peeler. Place on top of Chocolate Mocha Fudge Trifle. Chill until serving time. To serve, garnish with fresh strawberries. Serves 6.

Calories	Fat	Protein	Carb	Chol	Sodium	Fiber
490	12g	10g	91g	38mg	666mg	3g

~ Flower Pot Treats ~

This is a delightful treat for children. They love to find the hidden treats inside the pudding. And, for some strange reason, children love the idea of eating dirt! One caveat: if using rice milk, increase cornstarch to 3 Tbsp.

2 Tbsp. cocoa (not Dutch)
½ cup brown sugar
2 Tbsp. cornstarch
2 cups milk (cow, soy, rice: see above)
¼ tsp. salt

1 ounce gf/df bittersweet
  chocolate
1 tsp. vanilla extract
1 cup crushed Chocolate
  Wafers (p. 153)
4 small terra cotta or plastic
  flower pots

1. Combine cocoa, sugar, and cornstarch in medium saucepan. Over medium heat, add milk and salt. Whisk constantly until mixture thickens, about 5-8 minutes.

2. Remove from heat and add bittersweet chocolate and vanilla, stirring until chocolate melts. Chill thoroughly in refrigerator.

3. Assemble flowerpots (which have been cleaned thoroughly.) Lay piece of aluminum foil over hole in bottom.

4. Layer pudding and crushed chocolate wafers, ending with layer of crushed cookies. You can hide edible surprises inside such as gf gummy worms, fruit leather cut in the shapes of worms, raisins, etc. Just make sure these items are safe for your diet. Serves 4.

Calories	Fat	Protein	Carb	Chol	Sodium	Fiber
315	6g	7g	62g	4mg	406mg	2g

~ Frozen Tiramisu ~

This is a great way to use leftover cake. You can slice it in any shape you want as long as it is about 1-inch thick. The amount of ice cream is a matter of personal choice. Some people like lots of ice cream and just a little cake. The overall flavor of the dessert will vary depending on whether you use the espresso coffee or orange juice, but both versions are equally delicious. For maximum flavor, use both!

1 cup brown sugar
1 ½ cups strong, brewed
   espresso or orange juice
2 Tbsp. cocoa
1 recipe Basic Chocolate Cake
   (p. 100-101)
2 pints Chocolate Cappuccino
   Ice Cream (p. 158)

¼ cup finely ground espresso or
   grated orange peel
¼ cup Dutch cocoa
Garnish of grated chocolate or
   crushed gf/df chocolate chips
   or Chocolate Cinnamon Cream
   (p. 135)

1. Dissolve sugar in freshly brewed espresso (or very strongly brewed coffee.) Bring to boil, reduce heat, and simmer for 1 minute to make espresso syrup. If using orange juice, follow same procedure but boil until mixture is reduced by ⅓, or about 1 cup. Remove from heat and cool.

2. Slice cake into 1-inch thick pieces with serrated knife. Place one layer in bottom of 9 x 9-inch pan sprayed with cooking spray. Brush cake with espresso or orange syrup. Sprinkle 2 Tbsp. of ground espresso over cake. Spread half of softened ice cream over cake. Top with second layer of cake. Brush with remaining syrup.

3. Sprinkle with remaining 2 Tbsp. espresso powder or orange peel. Top with remaining ice cream, creating decorative dips and swirls with back of spatula.

4. Return to freezer until completely frozen. At serving time, dust with Dutch cocoa and top with grated chocolate or crushed chocolate chips or Chocolate Cinnamon Cream (p. 135). Let stand at room temperature for a few minutes before serving. Serves 12.

Calories	Fat	Protein	Carb	Chol	Sodium	Fiber
400	15g	6g	68g	35mg	412mg	3g

Excludes garnishes

~ Panna Cotta ~

Panna Cotta is considered a rather trendy dessert these days but it's actually just creamy gelatin with an Italian name. Of course, the original version is made with heavy cream. Try to use the heaviest, thickest non-dairy milk you can find. Or, perhaps stir in non-dairy milk powder to the liquid milk you're using to boost its density.

1 Tbsp. unflavored gelatin powder
2 cups milk (cow, rice, soy), divided
1 tsp. vanilla or 1 vanilla bean
¼ cup honey

1 tsp. almond extract
⅛ tsp. salt
1 cup fresh strawberries or raspberries
Fresh mint for garnish

1. In small, heavy saucepan sprinkle gelatin powder over ¼ cup of the milk to soften, 3-5 minutes. Heat gently over very low heat.

2. Meanwhile, in another saucepan, heat remaining milk and vanilla bean (opened and scraped) until tiny bubbles form around edges of pan (do not boil.) Remove from heat, remove vanilla bean, and stir in gelatin mixture, honey, vanilla and almond extracts, and salt until thoroughly mixed. (If you're not using vanilla bean, stir in vanilla extract now.)

3. Pour into 5-cup, decorative ring mold and refrigerate 6 hours or overnight, until firm. (If you don't have such a mold, a Bundt cake pan will also work.)

4. Before unmolding panna cotta, hull and slice strawberries.

5. To serve, dip mold in lukewarm water and then dry bottom. Loosen edges with knife. Unmold onto serving platter. Spoon sliced strawberries in center of ring and garnish with fresh mint. Serve immediately. Serves 4.

Calories	Fat	Protein	Carb	Chol	Sodium	Fiber
130	<1g	6g	26g	2mg	140mg	1g

~ Peach Melba Ice Cream Pie ~

For extra peach flavor and additional texture in the pie, stir in a cup of chopped peaches to the softened peach ice cream before spreading it in the pie plate. For variation, substitute a portion of the coconut— perhaps ¼ cup— with ground nuts such as pecans, walnuts, or hazelnuts.

Crust
1 ½ cups shredded coconut
1 Tbsp. sweet rice flour
¼ tsp. salt
1 tsp. vanilla extract
2 Tbsp. butter or margarine

Pie Filling
1 pint Peach Ice Cream, softened
  (p. 160)
Topping
1 cup fresh raspberries
2 Tbsp. honey
2 medium ripe peaches, sliced
Fresh mint for garnish

Crust

1. Grease 9-inch pie plate. Combine ingredients thoroughly and press onto bottom and up sides. Bake at 325° until lightly toasted, approximately 10-15 minutes. Watch carefully so crust doesn't burn. Cool thoroughly.

Pie Filling

1. Spread softened Peach Ice Cream in crust. Return to freezer for about 4 hours or until firm. Remove from freezer about 15 minutes before serving.

Topping

1. Wash and pick over fresh raspberries. Combine with sliced peaches and toss with honey. Top each serving with 1 Tbsp. of peach-raspberry mixture. Garnish with sprig of fresh mint. Serves 10.

Calories	Fat	Protein	Carb	Chol	Sodium	Fiber
210	9g	2g	30g	9mg	161mg	3g

~ Theme Cookies for Kids ~

Perfect for birthday parties, school treats, or as a rainy-day activity, these cute little creatures are easy and fun to make.

Cookie Monsters: Two Basic Cookies (p. 157) or other gf cookies propped open with miniature Kraft Jet-Puff® marsh-mallows. Face can be sliced off Jelly Belly® licorice jelly beans for eyes or pure fruit leather cut in facial features.

Spider Cookies: Use large Kraft Jet-Puff® marshmallow decorated with pieces of pure fruit leather for body and use uncooked gf spaghetti strands for legs. For dark legs, spray legs with cooking spray and roll in cocoa powder or carob powder. Or, use small strands of dark-colored fruit leather.

Bug Cookies: Use Basic Cookie (p.157) or other gf cookie for body, with legs made from thin strands of gf spaghetti— or use fruit leather to cut strips.

Snakes: 5 Basic Cookies (p. 157) or other gf cookie with M&M's, or sliced Jelly Belly® jelly beans, or circles cut from fruit leather for eyes. Fangs of snake can be pasta strands.

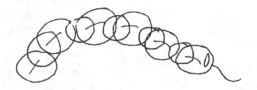

~ Chocolate Cherry Almond Biscotti ~

Biscotti are an elegant treat . . . meant for after-dinner dipping into hot coffee or tea, with morning coffee, or as a treat with cappuccino served any time. Though baked twice, they extremely easy to make— especially if you mix them in a food processor.

1 cup brown rice flour
½ cup potato starch
⅓ cup tapioca flour
1 ½ tsp. xanthan gum
2 tsp. baking powder
½ tsp. salt
½ cup cocoa (not Dutch)
1 tsp. instant coffee powder

¾ cup brown sugar
2 large eggs or ½ cup flax mix
   (p. 211)
⅓ cup canola oil
1 tsp. vanilla extract
½ tsp. almond extract
¾ cup dried tart cherries
¼ cup gf/df chocolate chips

1. Preheat oven to 350°. Grease baking sheet or line with parchment paper.

2. In food processor, combine flours, xanthan gum, baking powder, salt, cocoa, coffee, and sugar. Whirl until thoroughly mixed. Add eggs, oil, vanilla, and almond extract. Process until dough forms ball. Break ball into several pieces, add cherries; process until dough forms ball again.

3. Divide dough in half. On baking sheet, shape each half into log measuring two inches wide by 12 inches long by ½-inch thick. Bake 20 minutes. Remove from oven, but leave oven on.

4. Place each log on cutting board. (If using parchment paper, carefully slide parchment paper— logs and all— onto cutting board.) With electric knife or sharp, serrated knife diagonally cut each log into ¾ to 1-inch slices. Place each slice on cut side. Return to oven, reduce heat to 275°; bake 10 minutes. Turn slices over and bake another 10 minutes.

5. To further crisp biscotti, turn oven off but leave baking sheet in oven for another 10-15 minutes with oven door closed.

6. For chocolate-dipped biscotti, melt chocolate in double boiler or heavy saucepan. Dip each piece halfway into melted chocolate. Dip end of each biscotti into chocolate. Place on waxed paper to cool. Store in airtight container. Makes 24.

Calories	Fat	Protein	Carb	Chol	Sodium	Fiber
130	5g	2g	24g	1mg	99mg	1.5g

Eggs add additional 17mg cholesterol per cookie.

~ Chocolate Cherry Cookies ~

Use cranberries instead of dried tart cherries for a different flavor twist.

½ cup brown rice flour
¼ cup potato starch
2 Tbsp. tapioca flour
1 tsp. xanthan gum
½ cup cocoa (not Dutch)
1 tsp. baking soda
¼ tsp. salt
½ cup butter or margarine

½ cup sugar
⅓ cup brown sugar
1 large egg or ¼ cup flax mix
  (p. 211)
1 tsp. vanilla extract
½ cup gf/df chocolate chips
¼ cup dried tart cherries or
  cranberries

1. Preheat oven to 350°. In medium bowl, combine dry ingredients (brown rice flour through salt).

2. With electric mixer, cream butter (room temp), sugars, egg, and vanilla until well combined. Add dry ingredients gradually; mix only until moistened. Don't over mix. Fold in chocolate chips and cherries.

3. 3With small ice-cream scoop, place balls of dough (about 2 Tbsp. each) on cookie sheet that is greased or lined with parchment paper. Leave inch between balls to allow for spreading.

4. Bake 10-12 minutes until puffed and cracked. Cool on baking sheet 5 minutes, then transfer to wire rack to cool. Makes 16.

Calories	Fat	Protein	Carb	Chol	Sodium	Fiber
165	8g	2g	25g	0mg	124mg	2g

Egg and butter add additional 29mg cholesterol per cookie.

Celebration Cookies: Add ¼ cup coconut flakes and ¼ cup chopped nuts (pecans, walnuts, or almonds). Bake as directed.

Calories	Fat	Protein	Carb	Chol	Sodium	Fiber
215	10g	2g	34g	0mg	124mg	2g

Egg and butter add additional 29mg cholesterol per cookie.

~ Chocolate Ice Cream Sandwiches ~

These are so simple that your children or grandchildren can help make them.

Chocolate Wafers
¼ cup butter or margarine
2 Tbsp. honey
½ cup brown sugar, firmly
  packed
1 large egg or ¼ cup flax mix
  (p. 211)
1 ½ tsp. vanilla extract
1 cup brown rice flour
3 Tbsp. potato starch
2 Tbsp. tapioca flour
¼ cup cocoa (not Dutch)
½ tsp. xanthan gum
½ tsp. salt
1 ½ tsp. baking powder

Filling & Edges
1 pint ice cream of choice
1 cup chopped nuts or crushed
  gf/df chocolate chips or
  shredded coconut for
  rolling edges of cookies

1. Preheat oven to 325°. In food processor, combine butter to vanilla.

2. Add flours, cocoa, xanthan gum, salt, and baking powder and combine thoroughly. Shape batter into soft ball. Batter will be somewhat soft. Cover and refrigerate 1 hour.

3. Shape dough into 24 balls measuring 1-inch in diameter. Place balls on greased nonstick cookie sheet (or lined with parchment paper). Flatten each ball with spatula to approximately 1 ½ to 2-inch circle, depending on preferred size of cookie. The cookies will spread more when butter is used and less when oleo or canola oil spread is used.

4. Bake about 25-30 minutes or until cookies appear dry on top. Baking time depends on size of cookies, watch carefully so cookies don't burn. Makes about 2 dozen.

5. To make sandwich cookies, place 2 Tbsp. slightly softened ice cream between two cookies. Roll edges in chopped nuts, chopped chocolate chips, or coconut. Freeze until ready to eat. Serves 12.

Excluding edges

Calories	Fat	Protein	Carb	Chol	Sodium	Fiber
200	7g	3g	32g	38mg	186mg	1g

Egg and butter add additional 28mg of cholesterol per serving.

~ Colorado Chocolate Chip Cookies ~

These cookies are decadently wonderful!

½ cup butter or margarine
½ cup brown sugar
1 tsp. vanilla extract
1 large egg or ¼ cup flax mix
   (p. 211)
¼ cup buttermilk or ½ tsp. cider
   vinegar plus enough non-dairy
   milk to make ¼ cup
1 cup brown rice flour

½ cup potato starch
¼ cup tapioca flour
½ tsp. baking soda
½ tsp. salt
½ cup shredded coconut
½ cup chopped nuts
½ cup dried tart cherries or
   cranberries
1 ½ cups gf/df chocolate chips

1. Preheat oven to 350°. In large mixing bowl, use electric mixer to beat butter, sugar, and vanilla together until smooth. Beat in egg, then buttermilk. In separate bowl, combine flours, soda, and salt. Beat into egg mixture on low speed until incorporated.

2. Stir in coconut, nuts, cranberries, and chocolate chips. Drop by tablespoons (or use small spring-action ice cream scoop for evenly sized cookies) onto nonstick cookie sheet that is greased or lined with parchment paper.

3. Bake 7-10 minutes or until cookies are lightly puffed and slightly browned. Cool on rack. Store in airtight container. Serves 12.

Calories	Fat	Protein	Carb	Chol	Sodium	Fiber
350	19g	4g	46g	0mg	173mg	3g

Butter and egg add additional 38mg of cholesterol per serving.

~ "Oatmeal" Cookies ~

Ok, so these aren't REALLY oatmeal cookies, but they taste just as good. You'll find the rolled rice flakes in natural food stores. Be sure to use potato flour— not potato starch or potato starch flour.

1 cup brown rice flour
¼ cup potato flour
2 Tbsp. tapioca flour
½ cup brown sugar
½ tsp. salt
½ tsp. xanthan gum
½ tsp. baking soda
½ tsp. baking powder
1 tsp. ground cinnamon

1 large egg or ¼ cup flax mix
  (p. 211)
¼ cup butter or margarine
½ cup applesauce
2 Tbsp. molasses
1 tsp. vanilla extract
¾ cup gf/df chocolate chips or raisins
½ cup rolled rice flakes*

*Available at health food stores or www.vitamincottage.com

1. Preheat oven to 325°. Grease nonstick cookie sheet line with parchment paper.

2. Combine dry ingredients (brown rice flour through cinnamon).

3. In food processor, combine egg (or flax mix), butter, applesauce, molasses, and vanilla extract until well blended.

4. Add dry ingredients and rolled rice flakes. Pulse until thorough-ly mixed. Gently stir in chocolate chips (or raisins). Dough will be somewhat stiff.

5. Drop by tablespoons (or use spring-action ice cream scoop for evenly shaped cookies) onto prepared cookie sheet. Flatten each cookie to ½-inch thickness with wet spatula.

6. Bake 20-25 minutes or until edges begin to brown. For flavor twist, add ⅓ cup nut butter of your choice such as almond, cashew, or soy. Makes 12 cookies.

Calories	Fat	Protein	Carb	Chol	Sodium	Fiber
200	8g	2g	34g	0mg	192mg	2g

Egg and butter add additional 29g cholesterol per cookie.

~ Rocky Road Brownies ~

Absolutely and completely decadent— chocoholics will love this one. If you can think of anything else to throw in this recipe, do so. It's meant to be truly decadent. If nuts are not appropriate for your diet, omit them or substitute something else.

½ cup brown rice flour
½ cup potato starch
¼ cup tapioca flour
½ cup cocoa (not Dutch)
½ tsp. baking powder
½ tsp. salt
¼ tsp. xanthan gum
¼ cup butter or margarine or canola oil
½ cup granulated sugar

½ cup brown sugar
1 large egg*
2 tsp. vanilla extract
¼ cup warm (110°) water or coffee
½ cup gf/df chocolate chips or chocolate squares, chopped
½ cup chopped pecans
½ cup miniature Kraft Jet Puff® marshmallows
½ cup dried tart cherries or cranberries

1. Preheat oven to 350°. Grease 8-inch square nonstick pan. Stir together flours, cocoa, baking powder, salt, and xanthan gum (and Egg Replacer, if using––see below). Set aside.

2. In large mixing bowl, beat butter and sugars with electric mixer on medium speed until well combined. Beat in egg and vanilla.

3. With mixer on low speed, add dry ingredients. Mix until just blended; a few lumps may remain. Gently stir in chocolate chips, nuts, marshmallows, and cherries or cranberries.

4. Spread batter in prepared pan and bake 35 minutes or until toothpick inserted in center comes out clean. Cool brownies before cutting. Serves 12.

*Rocky Road Brownies without Eggs: Omit egg and add 2 tsp. Ener-G® Egg Replacer with dry ingredients. Increase water or coffee to ½ cup.

Calories	Fat	Protein	Carb	Chol	Sodium	Fiber
260	10g	3g	46g	0mg	130mg	3g

Egg and butter add additional 28mg cholesterol per serving.

~ Basic Cut-Out Cookies ~

There are many uses for these versatile cookies.

¼ cup butter or margarine
2 Tbsp. honey
½ cup sugar
1 Tbsp. vanilla extract
2 tsp. grated lemon peel
¾ cup brown rice flour
½ cup white rice flour
3 Tbsp. potato starch

2 Tbsp. tapioca flour
½ tsp. xanthan gum
½ tsp. salt
1 tsp. baking powder
½ tsp. baking soda
2 Tbsp. water (if needed)
Additional rice flour for rolling

1. In food processor, combine butter (room temp, not melted), honey, sugar vanilla, and lemon peel and process 1 minute. Add flours, xanthan gum, salt, baking powder, and baking soda, blending all ingredients until dough forms large clumps. Scrape down sides of bowl with spatula. Blend until dough forms ball again. Add water if necessary— 1 Tbsp. at a time. Refrigerate 1 hour.

2. Preheat oven to 325°. Using half of dough, roll to ¼-inch thickness between sheets of waxed paper or plastic wrap sprinkled with rice flour. Keep remaining dough chilled until ready to use. Cut into desired shapes (about 2 inches in diameter) and transfer to baking sheet that is greased or lined with parchment paper.

3. Bake 10-12 minutes, or until cookies are lightly browned. Remove from cookie sheet and cool on wire rack. Makes 16.

Calories	Fat	Protein	Carb	Chol	Sodium	Fiber
88	3g	.5g	15g	0mg	71mg	.5g

Butter adds additional 8 mg cholesterol per cookie.

Tips for Successful "Cut-Out" Cookies

1. To avoid sticking, use non-stick baking liners or parchment paper.
2. Insulated baking sheets assure even baking and won't buckle.
3. Metal cookie cutters work better than plastic cookie cutters.
4. If chilled dough is too stiff, leave dough at room temperature 15-20 minutes. Knead with hands to make dough more pliable. If dough is too soft after rolling, chill or freeze until firm— then cut into desired shapes. Do not roll dough thinner than ¼-inch.
5. For trouble with transferring cookies to baking sheet, try rolling dough onto parchment paper, cut desired shapes, remove scraps of dough (leave cut-out cookies on paper). Transfer paper (cookies and all) to baking sheet.

~ Chocolate Cappuccino Ice Cream ~

The coffee flavor will be more pronounced if you use espresso, rather than regular coffee.

½ cup hot brewed espresso or
  very strong brewed coffee
½ cup brown sugar
2 packages (12 oz) soft silken tofu
1 tsp. vanilla extract

¼ tsp. xanthan gum
2 Tbsp. cocoa (not Dutch)
1 tsp. espresso powder
½ tsp. ground cinnamon
⅛ tsp. salt

1. Dissolve sugar in hot espresso or coffee. Add to food processor, along with remaining ingredients. Purée until very smooth.

2. Cover and chill until mixture reaches 40°. Freeze in ice cream maker according to manufacturer's directions. Makes about 3 cups. Serves 6 (½ cup each).

Calories	Fat	Protein	Carb	Chol	Sodium	Fiber
130	3g	5g	22g	0mg	63mg	1g

~ Chocolate Sorbet ~

Use the very best cocoa you can find for this decadent, yet fat-free dessert.

1 ½ cups cocoa (not Dutch)
1 tsp. xanthan gum
2 cups brown sugar
½ tsp. salt
4 cups water

1 cup brewed espresso or coffee
  (or water)
2 tsp. vanilla extract
1 tsp. rum extract or
  1 Tbsp. gf rum (optional)

1. Stir together cocoa, xanthan gum, sugar, and salt in medium, heavy saucepan. Add water and brewed coffee and whisk to blend. Bring mixture to boil, then reduce heat and simmer 20 minutes to slightly reduce. Stir occasionally. Add vanilla (and rum or rum extract, if using.) Refrigerate mixture to 40°.

2. Pour into freezer container of hand-turn or electric freezer. Freeze according to manufacturer's directions. Makes 1 quart. Serves 8.

Calories	Fat	Protein	Carb	Chol	Sodium	Fiber
332	3g	4g	84g	0mg	238mg	8g

~ Lemon Sorbet ~

For a really special touch, use lemons as the serving dish for this delightful sorbet. Remove the peel from the top ⅓ of the lemons only. Then, slice off the top ⅓ of the lemons and juice them, saving the bottom. Using a spoon, scrape out the remaining pulp from each of the lemons. Slice off the bottom slightly so the shell sits firmly on plate. Refrigerate the empty lemon shells until ready to use. When the sorbet is ready to serve, fill each lemon shell with sorbet and garnish with fresh mint. Serve immediately.

4 large lemons	2 ¼ cups cold water
2 Tbsp. grated lemon peel	1 cup sugar
1 packet (2 ¼ tsp.) unflavored	¾ cup fresh lemon juice
gelatin powder	Fresh mint for garnish

1. With potato peeler, remove enough peel from lemons to equal 2 Tbsp. when grated. Finely mince peel by using either coffee grinder or sharp knife and cutting board. Set peel aside.

2. Squeeze lemons, extracting enough juice to equal ¾ cup. Set aside.

3. In heavy, medium-sized saucepan whisk gelatin into ¼ cup of water. Let stand 5 minutes to dissolve. Add remaining water and sugar. Cook over medium heat until sugar and gelatin completely dissolve. Remove from heat; stir in lemon juice and lemon peel. Cool to 40°.

4. Pour mixture into ice cream freezer and follow manufacturer's directions. Remove sorbet by using melon baller or spring-action ice cream scoop. Serve immediately--in dessert goblets or in lemon shells (see above). Garnish with fresh mint. Makes 1 quart. Serves 4.

Calories	Fat	Protein	Carb	Chol	Sodium	Fiber
105	0g	1g	27g	0mg	4mg	0g

~ Peach Ice Cream ~

1 box (12 oz) soft silken tofu
½ cup milk (cow, rice, soy)
½ cup sugar
1 Tbsp. butter or margarine
¼ tsp. xanthan gum

¼ cup lemon juice
2 cups sliced fresh peaches
1 tsp. vanilla extract
1 tsp. almond extract
¼ tsp. salt

1. Place all ingredients in food processor and blend until very, very smooth. Chill mixture until it reaches 40°.

2. Freeze in ice cream maker, according to manufacturer's directions. When ready to serve, use spring-action ice cream scoop or melon baller to remove balls of ice cream. Serve immediately with your favorite sauce. Makes 1 quart. Serves 8 (½ cup each).

Calories	Fat	Protein	Carb	Chol	Sodium	Fiber
110	3g	3g	20g	4mg	47mg	1g

~ Strawberry Sherbet ~

1 box (12 oz) soft silken tofu
2 cups sliced fresh strawberries
1 cup milk (cow, rice, soy)
¼ cup lemon juice
½ tsp. xanthan gum

⅔ cup sugar
1 Tbsp. butter or margarine
1 tsp. vanilla extract
⅛ tsp. salt

1. Combine all ingredients in food processor. Process until very smooth (or if you like little chunks of fruit, stop before mixture is entirely smooth.)

2. Chill mixture to 40°. Place in electric ice cream maker and freeze according to manufacturer's directions. Serve with toppings of your choice. Makes 1 quart. Serves 8 (½ cup each).

Calories	Fat	Protein	Carb	Chol	Sodium	Fiber
125	3g	3g	23g	4mg	55mg	1g

Raspberry Sherbet: Use 2 cups fresh raspberries in place of 2 cups strawberries.

~ Vanilla Frozen Yogurt without Eggs ~

If you choose to use goat milk, make sure it's appropriate for your diet.

2 cups vanilla-flavored yogurt
(cow or soy)
2 tsp. unflavored gelatin powder

1 ¾ cups milk (cow, rice, soy)
½ cup honey
3 tsp. vanilla extract

1. Place all ingredients in food processor and blend until very smooth. Chill to 40°. Freeze in ice cream maker, according to manufacturer's directions.

2. Makes 1 quart. Serves 8 (½ cup each).

Calories	Fat	Protein	Carb	Chol	Sodium	Fiber
140	1g	6g	29g	4mg	70mg	0g

~ Vanilla Ice Cream with Eggs ~

This delicious frozen treat omits dairy, however, it is the egg yolks that give it a creamy texture. So, it will be perfect for those <u>without</u> egg sensitivities.

1 tsp. unflavored gelatin powder
4 cups milk (cow, rice, soy), divided
½ cup honey

4 large egg yolks, beaten
very smooth
3 tsp. vanilla extract

1. Combine gelatin with 3 Tbsp. milk and stir until dissolved. Add gelatin mixture, honey, and remaining milk to small saucepan. Cook over low heat until mixture almost boils. Remove from heat.

2. Whisk ½ cup of hot mixture into eggs. Add eggs to mixture in saucepan. Return saucepan to low-medium heat and cook, stirring, for another two minutes. Do not boil; mixture may curdle. Remove from heat. Stir in vanilla. Chill to 40°. Freeze in ice cream maker, according to manufacturer's directions. Makes 1 quart. Serves 8 (½ cup servings).

Calories	Fat	Protein	Carb	Chol	Sodium	Fiber
140	3g	6g	24g	109mg	68mg	0g

~ Notes ~

~ SALADS ~

Salads are a marvelous way to add color, texture, and variety to our meals--not to mention that they are a source of important nutrients. And, they can transform an ordinary meal into a real showstopper.

For example, a colorful, crunchy, flavorful salad adds "pizzazz" to any meal and shows your guests that this is a special occasion— and they're special, too!

Salads	**Salad Dressings**
Cabbage Coleslaw 174	*Basic Vinaigrette 164*
Caesar Salad Without Eggs 166	*Cilantro Citrus Dressing 164*
Couscous Salad 175	*Tomato-Basil Vinaigrette 165*
Fruit Salad with Balsamic Vinegar 167	*Vinegar-Free Herb Dressing 165*
Grapefruit & Avocado Salad 167	
Herbed Rice Salad 177	
Jicama & Mandarin Orange Salad 168	
Jicama, Orange, & Avocado Salad 168	
Lettuce Salad with Pears & Feta Cheese 169	
Potato Salad 169	
Spinach Salad with Strawberries 170	
Fruit-Sweetened Gelatin Salad 171	
Waldorf Salad 170	

For additional salads dishes, see *Wheat-Free Recipes & Menus: Delicious Dining without Wheat & Gluten,* 2002

~ Basic Vinaigrette ~

¼ cup chicken stock
2 Tbsp. apple cider vinegar or
  fresh lemon juice
2 tsp. Dijonnaise mustard

1 Tbsp. extra virgin olive oil
1 garlic clove, minced
¼ tsp. salt
⅛ tsp. black pepper

In small bowl, whisk together ingredients until thoroughly mixed. Or, blend in blender or small food processor. Makes about ½ cup. Serves 4 (2 Tbsp. each.)

Calories	Fat	Protein	Carb	Chol	Sodium	Fiber
37	4g	.1g	1g	0mg	400mg	1g

~ Cilantro Citrus Dressing ~

3 Tbsp. fresh orange juice
1 Tbsp. fresh lemon juice
1 Tbsp. fresh lime juice
½ cup cilantro leaves, packed
¼ tsp. cumin powder

¼ tsp. dried thyme leaves
⅛ tsp. cayenne pepper
⅛ tsp. salt
⅛ tsp. white pepper
¼ cup olive oil or canola oil

Place all ingredients in blender. Process until mixture is very smooth. With motor running, add oil in thin, steady stream. Refrigerate, covered. Bring to room temperature to serve. Makes ½ cup. Serves 4 (2 Tbsp. each.)

Calories	Fat	Protein	Carb	Chol	Sodium	Fiber
130	14g	0g	2g	0mg	76mg	0g

~ Tomato-Basil Vinaigrette ~

2 large tomatoes (seeded, chopped)
2 Tbsp. lemon or lime juice
  or 2 Tbsp. red wine vinegar
2 Tbsp. fresh basil, packed or
  1 Tbsp. dried basil leaves
½ tsp. dried oregano leaves

2 Tbsp. extra virgin olive oil
½ tsp. garlic powder
  or 1 garlic clove, minced
½ tsp. sugar
¼ tsp. salt
¼ tsp. black pepper

Combine all ingredients in blender and purée until thoroughly mixed. Refrigerate, covered, up to 2 days. Makes about ½ cup. Serves 4 (2 Tbsp. each.)

Calories	Fat	Protein	Carb	Chol	Sodium	Fiber
83	7g	1g	6g	0mg	152mg	1g

~ Vinegar-Free Herb Dressing ~

My favorite herbs are thyme, basil, marjoram, and savory— but use the ones you like.

½ cup lemon juice
2 small garlic cloves
¼ cup extra virgin olive oil
2 tsp. honey
½ cup chopped green onions
  or chives

½ tsp. salt
¼ cup chopped fresh herbs or
  3 tsp. dried herbs of choice
⅛ tsp. xanthan gum (optional)
⅛ tsp. black pepper

Combine all ingredients in blender and purée until mixture is completely smooth. Makes about ¾ cup. Serves 6 (about 2 Tbsp. each.) Best served immediately.

Calories	Fat	Protein	Carb	Chol	Sodium	Fiber
100	9g	0g	5g	0mg	195mg	1g

~ Caesar Salad without Eggs ~

Use only half of the garlic-oil mixture to toss with the croutons, adding the remainder to the salad dressing itself.

2 garlic cloves
¼ cup extra-virgin olive oil
½ tsp. salt
1 cup gf croutons
1 Tbsp. lemon juice
1 tsp. apple cider vinegar
1 tsp. dry mustard*
*Grind mustard seeds with small coffee grinder

1 tsp. Worcestershire sauce
   (Lea & Perrins)
1 tsp. anchovy paste (Reese)
   (optional)
⅓ cup grated Parmesan cheese
   (cow, rice, soy)
1 head Romaine lettuce,
   washed and torn

1. Use garlic press to mince garlic before mashing with salt and olive oil. Brown croutons 10 minutes in 350° oven. Toss them with half of garlic-oil mixture and return to oven for another 3-5 minutes, or until golden. Remove from oven. Set aside until cool.

2. In large salad bowl, whisk together remaining garlic-oil mixture, lemon juice, vinegar, mustard, Worcestershire sauce, and anchovy paste (if using). Add Romaine lettuce and toss thoroughly. Sprinkle with Parmesan cheese and croutons, toss again, and serve immediately. Serves 4.

Calories	Fat	Protein	Carb	Chol	Sodium	Fiber
230	18g	7g	10g	11mg	999mg	2g

~ Fruit Salad with Balsamic Dressing ~

Dressing
1 Tbsp. balsamic vinegar
2 Tbsp. canola oil
¼ cup orange juice
1 tsp. grated lemon peel
⅛ tsp black pepper

Fruit
1 pink or red grapefruit
1 orange
1 red pear, cored and halved
½ cup red or green seedless grapes
4 large lettuce leaves

Dressing
In screwtop jar, combine ingredients. Shake vigorously to blend.

Fruit
1. With sharp knife, cut peel and white membrane from grapefruit and orange. Section grapefruit and slice orange crosswise into 8 slices. Cut pear in ¼-inch thick slices lengthwise. Dip slices in reserved juices from grapefruit and orange.

2. Cover large platter or 4 individual serving plates with lettuce leaves. Decoratively arrange fruit over lettuce. Drizzle with dressing. Serves 4.

Calories	Fat	Protein	Carb	Chol	Sodium	Fiber
140	7g	1g	20g	0mg	4mg	3g

~ Grapefruit & Avocado Salad ~

Dressing
¼ cup each olive oil and water
3 Tbsp. red wine vinegar
2 tsp. honey
½ tsp. dried tarragon leaves
1 tsp. Dijonnaise mustard
1 garlic clove, minced
¼ tsp. each salt &white pepper

Fruit
1 head red leaf lettuce
1 avocado, peeled and sliced
1 red grapefruit (peeled, sectioned)
½ cup toasted almonds

In screwtop jar, combine dressing ingredients by shaking vigorously to emulsify. In large salad bowl, toss lettuce with dressing. Add avocado, grapefruit, and toasted almonds. Toss gently. Drizzle with dressing. Serve chilled. Serves 4.

Calories	Fat	Protein	Carb	Chol	Sodium	Fiber
345	30g	5g	18g	0mg	322mg	7g

~ Jicama & Mandarin Orange Salad ~

1 medium jicama
  (peeled, shredded)
1 cup cilantro (coarsely chopped)
2 Tbsp. lime juice

2 Tbsp. red wine vinegar or
  rice vinegar
1 can (11 oz) mandarin oranges,
  drained

Combine jicama, cilantro, lime juice, and vinegar in medium bowl and mix well. Gently stir in oranges. Serve slightly chilled. Makes 3 cups. Serves 4.

Calories	Fat	Protein	Carb	Chol	Sodium	Fiber
150	.5g	3g	36g	0mg	19ng	17g

~ Jicama, Orange, & Avocado Salad ~

2 Tbsp. olive oil
2 Tbsp. lime or lemon juice
2 Tbsp. orange juice
1 tsp. sugar
1 tsp. red wine vinegar
1/4 tsp. chili powder
1/8 tsp. salt

1/8 tsp. cayenne pepper
1 head red leaf lettuce (torn in pieces)
2 medium oranges (peeled, sectioned)
2 chopped green onions
1 cup jicama, peeled and cubed
1 large avocado, peeled and slice

1. In screwtop jar, combine olive oil, lime juice, orange juice, sugar, vinegar, chili powder, salt, and cayenne pepper. Shake vigorously to blend. Set dressing aside.

2. Wash and dry lettuce. Place in large serving bowl. Add oranges, green onions and jicama. Toss with dressing. Add avocado and toss gently. Serve chilled. Makes about 4 cups. Serves 4.

Calories	Fat	Protein	Carb	Chol	Sodium	Fiber
200	15g	3g	19g	0mg	85mg	7g

~ Potato Salad ~

If eggs are not appropriate for your diet, omit them and use another potato instead.

3 cups cooked potatoes (peeled, diced)
4 hard-boiled eggs(peeled, chopped)
½ cup finely chopped celery
¼ cup finely chopped green onion
2 Tbsp. sweet pickle relish
   or 2 tsp. dried dill weed
½ cup Mayonnaise (p. 217)

1 Tbsp. cider vinegar
1 tsp. sugar
½ tsp. celery salt
½ tsp. celery seed
¼ tsp. white pepper
½ tsp. dry mustard*
Paprika for garnish
Grind mustard seed with small coffee grinder

Combine chopped potatoes, eggs, celery, onion, and relish (or dill) in large bowl. In small bowl, combine remaining ingredients (except paprika) until smooth. Pour over potato mixture and toss until thoroughly coated. Turn into serving bowl and garnish with paprika. Chill until serving time. Makes about 5 cups. Serves 6.

Calories	Fat	Protein	Carb	Chol	Sodium	Fiber
165	7g	6g	19g	146mg	280mg	2g

~ Lettuce Salad with Pears & Feta Cheese ~

3 cups red leaf lettuce, torn
2 Tbsp. balsamic vinegar
2 tsp. Dijonnaise mustard or
   1 tsp. dry mustard*
2 tsp. vegetable or walnut oil
2 tsp. water

1 garlic clove, minced
½ tsp. dried thyme leaves
1 red pear, thinly sliced
3 Tbsp. feta cheese, crumbled
½ cup toasted pecans
grind mustard seed with small coffee grinder

1. Place washed, dried, and torn lettuce into large bowl. Set aside.

2. In screwtop jar, combine vinegar, mustard, oil, water, garlic, and thyme. Shake vigorously to blend. Toss with greens. Arrange on salad plates. Place red pear slices decoratively in pin-wheel design on each salad. Top with crumbled feta cheese and toasted pecans. Serves 4.

Calories	Fat	Protein	Carb	Chol	Sodium	Fiber
178	14g	3g	12g	6mg	147mg	3g

~ Spinach Salad with Strawberries ~

Next time try mixing in a few green or red grapes for added interest.

3 Tbsp. orange juice
1 Tbsp. lemon juice
1 Tbsp. honey
2 Tbsp. dried basil leaves or
  ½ cup chopped fresh basil
¼ tsp. dried thyme leaves
¼ tsp. xanthan gum
⅛ tsp. cayenne pepper

⅛ tsp. salt
⅛ tsp. white pepper
¼ cup olive oil or cooking oil
10 oz. (1 pkg) baby spinach leaves,
  (rinsed, dried)
1 pint hulled strawberries, halved
1 cup toasted pecan halves
¼ cup feta cheese, crumbled

1. In small jar, whisk together orange juice, lemon juice, honey, basil, thyme, xanthan gum, cayenne pepper, salt, pepper, and oil until smooth.

2. Place cleaned spinach leaves in large bowl. Add strawberries and pecans. Add enough dressing to coat leaves and toss gently. Just before serving, sprinkle crumbled feta cheese on top. Serves 10.

Calories	Fat	Protein	Carb	Chol	Sodium	Fiber
160	15g	2g	7g	3mg	71mg	2g

~ Waldorf Salad ~

2 red delicious apples, chopped
2 stalks celery, chopped
½ cup toasted pecan halves
½ cup golden raisins

1 tsp. lemon juice
2 Tbsp. Mayonnaise (p. 217)
⅛ tsp. salt
½ tsp. sugar

Combine apples, celery, pecans, and raisins in small bowl. In another bowl, stir together lemon juice, mayonnaise, salt, and sugar. Pour mayonnaise mixture over apple mixture and toss thoroughly. Serve immediately. Serves 4.

Calories	Fat	Protein	Carb	Chol	Sodium	Fiber
225	12g	2g	32g	2mg	130mg	4g

~ Fruit-Sweetened Gelatin Salad ~

Gelatin salads (or Jello as we usually say) are almost a staple in American culture. Yet, the sugar and artificial color can be a problem for some of us. You can make this gelatin as sweet as you like, either by adding a sweetener that you tolerate— or intensifying the juice.

Juices that work especially well include pure white grape or pure apple juice, because they produce a lovely translucent look that allows fruits and vegetables to show through nicely. However, orange juice or tomato juice also work. Use whatever fruits or vegetables you prefer (but don't use fresh pineapple or it won't gel properly). Vary the colors of the fruit to achieve a pretty effect. For a festive touch, replace ¼ cup of the cold fruit juice with your favorite champagne or white wine.

You can halve this recipe so it fits nicely into a 6-cup Bundt pan to serve 8.

¼ cup unflavored gelatin powder
2 cups fruit juice, cold
6 cups fruit juice, hot
½ cup fresh blueberries

1 cup mandarin oranges
½ cup fresh raspberries
½ cup chopped celery

1. Dissolve gelatin powder in 2 cups cold fruit juice in large bowl. Add hot fruit juice, stirring thoroughly until dissolved. For sweeter salad, simmer juice until it is reduced by ⅓. Remember you'll still need 6 cups of hot juice, so if you're reducing the juice you must start with 8 cups.

2. Chill gelatin in refrigerator until it just begins to set (it will begin to resist when you try to stir it). Stir in fruit or vegetables until thoroughly distributed. Pour mixture into 10-cup pan that has been sprayed with cooking spray. Chill all day or overnight.

3. To unmold, place pan in room-temperature water 2 to 3 minutes. Remove from water, dry bottom of pan, and invert onto serving plate. If it won't release, try pressing a hot, wet towel on the pan for a few minutes. Serves 16.

Calories	Fat	Protein	Carb	Chol	Sodium	Fiber
70	0g	2g	15g	0mg	12mg	1g

~ Notes ~

~ SIDE DISHES ~

S ide dishes are often taken for granted, but they can also be the touch that transforms an ordinary meal into a spectacular event. Think of them as playing "supporting roles" alongside the main dish. They complement the main dish yet stand on their own in terms of color, texture, and eye appeal.

I've tried to make each side dish in this chapter worthy of an "Oscar" nomination for supporting role. Instead of ordinary baked potatoes try baking them into crispy rounds (Potatoes Anna) or combine them other vegetables and grill or roast them over hot coals on the grill (Roasted or Grilled Vegetables). Two different taste and texture sensations from a simple vegetable!

For additional side dishes, see *Wheat-Free Recipes & Menus: Delicious Dining without Wheat & Gluten*, 2002

~ Brown Rice Pilaf ~

1 cup brown rice
1 Tbsp. canola oil, divided
½ cup chopped onion
¼ cup chopped celery
¼ cup chopped carrots
1 medium garlic clove, minced
¼ cup currants or raisins

½ tsp. dried sage leaves
½ tsp. dried thyme leaves
¼ tsp. black pepper
2 ½ cups low-sodium gf chicken broth
1 bay leaf

1. Place first two ingredients and half of the oil in heavy saucepan. Sauté over medium heat, stirring frequently, until lightly browned— about 5 minutes. Remove rice from pan. Place remaining oil in saucepan and sauté onions, celery, and carrots over medium heat until tender--about 5-8 minutes.

2. Add remaining ingredients and bring to boil. Cover, reduce heat, and simmer mixture for 50 minutes or until liquid is absorbed. Discard bay leaf before serving. Serves 4 (½ cup servings).

Calories	Fat	Protein	Carb	Chol	Sodium	Fiber
240	6g	6g	41g	2mg	80mg	3g

~ Cabbage Coleslaw ~

1 small cabbage, shredded
1 medium carrot, coarsely grated
2 celery stalks (¼-inch diagonals)
1 bunch green onions (¼-inch diagonals)
2 Tbsp. apple cider vinegar
3 Tbsp. fresh lemon juice

1 tsp. honey
½ Tbsp. Dijonnaise mustard
⅓ cup cooking oil
½ tsp. celery seed
½ tsp. salt
¼ tsp. ground white pepper
¼ tsp. paprika

In large bowl, toss together cabbage, carrots, celery, and onions. In blender or food processor, blend remaining ingredients— except paprika. Toss vegetables with dressing. Garnish with paprika. Serve chilled. Serves 4.

Calories	Fat	Protein	Carb	Chol	Sodium	Fiber
250	19g	4g	20g	0mg	410mg	8g

~ Couscous ~

Use ½ tsp. salt if you're using commercial, store-bought broth because it's saltier.

1 cup long-grain basmati rice or
  long-grain white rice

2 cups vegetable or gf chicken
  broth
½ to 1 tsp. salt (or to taste)

1. Place half of rice in blender or food processor. Pulse machine until rice kernels are broken into smaller pieces— similar to size of couscous. Continue with remaining rice.

2. Spread rice in thin layer on baking sheet and toast in 350° oven until lightly browned, about 25-30 minutes, stirring occasionally for even browning.

3. Place rice and remaining ingredients in medium, heavy sauce-pan, bring to boil and reduce heat. Simmer, covered, until mixture has absorbed water--about 30 minutes. Fluff with fork and serve at once. Serves 4.

Calories	Fat	Protein	Carb	Chol	Sodium	Fiber
188	1g	5g	41g	0mg	639mg	1g

~ Couscous Salad ~

A great salad for picnics since it can be made ahead of time and tastes great whether it's cold or at room temperature.

2 cups cooked Couscous (see above)
½ cup diced celery
1 Tbsp. grated lemon or lime peel
1 Tbsp. chopped fresh mint
1 Tbsp. chopped fresh cilantro or
  parsley, packed

¼ cup olive oil
¼ cup lemon juice
½ tsp. onion powder
½ tsp. salt
¼ tsp. black pepper
Paprika for garnish

Combine couscous, celery, lemon peel, mint, and cilantro in medium bowl. To make salad dressing, whisk together olive oil, lemon juice, onion powder, salt, and black pepper. Mix with rice. Serve chilled. Garnish with paprika before serving. Serves 4 (½cup each).

Calories	Fat	Protein	Carb	Chol	Sodium	Fiber
322	15g	6g	42g	2mg	999mg	2g

~ Corn Bread & Sausage Stuffing ~

You'll need two batches if you use corn bread recipe on p. 67 (omit chiles/cilantro).

12-14 cups torn gf corn bread
½ lb. gluten-free sausage
3 stalks celery, finely chopped
1 medium onion, finely chopped
3 tsp. ground sage

1 tsp. celery seed
1 tsp. dried oregano
½ tsp. salt
½ tsp. white pepper
2 cups gf chicken broth

1. In heavy skillet over medium heat, brown sausage, onion and celery. Drain well. Crumble corn bread and combine with remaining ingredients, stirring well. Turn into greased 13 x 9-inch dish. Bake 30-40 minutes at 350° until browned— or loosely stuff turkey with corn bread mixture and bake remainder in 11 x 7-inch greased casserole. Makes about 8-10 cups. Serves 16 (½ cup each).

Calories	Fat	Protein	Carb	Chol	Sodium	Fiber
225	7g	7g	34g	11mg	680mg	2g

~ Bread Stuffing ~

This is the traditional stuffing for turkey, chicken, or pork chops.
Vary the spices to suit your taste.

2 loaves gf bread
1 large finely chopped onion
4 stalks finely chopped celery
1 tsp. cooking oil
4 tsp. dried sage
2 tsp. poultry seasoning

2 tsp. celery salt
2 tsp. celery seed
1 tsp. dried parsley
½ tsp. white pepper
4 cups gf chicken broth

1. Tear bread into small pieces. Sauté onion and celery in oil until tender. Combine all remaining ingredients with bread; toss lightly until moist.

2. Loosely stuff turkey with bread mixture— or bake in greased casserole dish at 350° for 30-40 minutes or until nicely browned. Makes about 10-12 cups. Serves 20 (½ cup each).

Calories	Fat	Protein	Carb	Chol	Sodium	Fiber
175	1g	6g	34g	0mg	246mg	1g

~ Herbed Rice Salad ~

Perfect for an informal picnic— or elegant enough for a wedding reception.

1 ½ cups white long grain rice
3 cups water
1 tsp. salt
2 Tbsp. lemon juice
2 Tbsp. rice vinegar
2 tsp. Dijonnaise mustard
2 Tbsp. olive oil
2 Tbsp. minced fresh dill

½ cup chopped fresh parsley
½ cup chopped green onions
½ cup fresh or frozen green peas
2 Tbsp. diced red bell pepper
1 tsp. salt
¼ tsp. black pepper
Paprika, cilantro, and red bell
   pepper strips for garnish

1. In medium pan, combine rice, water, and salt. Cover, bring to boil, reduce heat, and simmer until rice is done–about 18 minutes. Remove from heat, let stand 5 minutes, fluff with fork.

2. Chill cooked rice. Meanwhile, combine lemon juice, vinegar, mustard, olive oil, and dill weed for dressing. Set aside.

3. When rice is cool, toss thoroughly with dressing in large bowl. Stir in parsley, onions, peas, and red bell pepper. Season with 1 tsp. salt and ¼ tsp. pepper. Garnish. Serves 6.

Calories	Fat	Protein	Carb	Chol	Sodium	Fiber
228	5g	4g	41g	0mg	630mg	2g

~ Pineapple Fruit Boats ~

Use this colorful dish as a centerpiece on the table.

1 whole fresh pineapple
3 kiwi fruit (peeled, quartered)

1 pint fresh hulled strawberries
Fresh mint leaves for garnish

1. Slice pineapple in half lengthwise, leaving leafy crown attached to each half. Use grapefruit knife to slice around perimeter of each half to separate fruit from the skin. The skin forms two boats.

2. Remove core; slice pineapple into bite-size pieces. Combine with other fruit. Place mixture in two boats. Refrigerate. Garnish. Serves 6.

Calories	Fat	Protein	Carb	Chol	Sodium	Fiber
75	1g	1g	19g	0mg	3mg	3g

~ Rice Pilaf with Dill ~

For a really special presentation, grease small custard cups, timbale forms, or a single large Bundt pan. Gently press hot rice mixture into mold(s). Invert to serve.

1 Tbsp. olive oil
3 green onions, finely chopped
2 tsp. dried dill weed
1 tsp. grated lemon peel
1 cup long-grain white rice

2 cups vegetable broth
½ tsp. salt
⅛ tsp. ground nutmeg
1 Tbsp. lemon juice
Dill weed for garnish

1. In large saucepan, combine oil, onions, dill, lemon peel, and rice. Cook, stirring constantly, 1 minute to slightly cook vegetables and brown rice. Add broth, salt, and nutmeg. Bring to boil, reduce heat to low. Cover and simmer until rice is absorbed— about 15-20 minutes.
2. Add lemon juice. Garnish with dill. Serves 4 (½ cup servings).

Calories	Fat	Protein	Carb	Chol	Sodium	Fiber
220	5g	5g	39g	2mg	346mg	1g

~ Tomatillo Rice ~

Tomatillos belong to the nightshade family and are related to tomatoes, peppers, potatoes, and so on. Wear rubber gloves when chopping the jalapeño.

3 large tomatillos (husked, washed)
1 plum tomato (seeded, chopped)
2 Tbsp. chopped fresh cilantro
1 chopped jalapeño (optional)
¼ tsp. salt

1 large garlic clove
½ cup long grain white rice
1 ¼ cups low-sodium gf
   chicken broth
Additional cilantro for garnish

Chop tomatillos coarsely. Combine with remaining ingredients in medium, heavy pan. Bring to boil, reduce heat, and simmer until liquid is absorbed––about 20 minutes. Cover; let stand 5 minutes. Garnish with cilantro. Serves 4 (⅓ cup each).

Calories	Fat	Protein	Carb	Chol	Sodium	Fiber
110	1g	3g	22g	1mg	180mg	1g

~ Dilled Baby Carrots ~

My guests always enjoy these carrots, but inevitably ask me about the recipe. They are usually surprised to learn how easy it is to make this delicious vegetable.

1 lb. baby carrots (washed, trimmed) | 2 Tbsp. maple syrup
½ tsp. salt | 2 tsp. dill weed

Combine baby carrots and salt with enough water to cover in a medium saucepan. Bring to boil and simmer, covered, for 6-8 minutes. Drain thoroughly. Toss carrots with maple syrup and dill weed. Serve immediately. Serves 4.

Calories	Fat	Protein	Carb	Chol	Sodium	Fiber
70	1g	1g	16g	0mg	330mg	2g

~ Green Onion Pancakes ~

Serve these tasty pancakes in place of potatoes or rice. Roll into cylinders and garnish with paprika and chives. Or, top with your favorite creamed sauce for a special brunch.

⅔ cup milk (cow, rice, soy)
¼ cup brown rice flour
¼ cup potato starch
1 Tbsp. tapioca flour
2 Tbsp. chopped toasted
   nuts or sesame seeds
1 ¼ tsp. baking powder

¾ tsp. baking soda
1 tsp. olive oil
¼ tsp. onion salt
¼ tsp. ground white pepper
¼ cup finely chopped green onions
Additional oil for frying
Paprika and chopped chives (garnish)

1. In medium mixing bowl, whisk together all ingredients. Lightly coat small non-stick skillet with cooking oil and warm over medium heat. Add 2 Tbsp. batter to skillet. Cook until edges are golden— about 1 minute. Flip carefully. Cook another 30 seconds or until browned.

2. Transfer to plate and keep warm. Repeat with remaining batter. Serve as a side dish with fish or chicken. Serves 4 (2 pancakes each).

Calories	Fat	Protein	Carb	Chol	Sodium	Fiber
170	7g	8g	19g	138mg	178mg	2g

~ Pineapple Coconut Rice ~

1 Tbsp. olive oil
1 small onion, finely chopped
1 tsp. dried thyme leaves
½ tsp. dried savory leaves
½ tsp. salt
¼ tsp. ground white pepper

¾ cup long grain white rice
1 can (8 oz) crushed pineapple
2 Tbsp. coconut flakes
½ cup chopped chives or cilantro
⅓ cup minced red bell pepper
Paprika for garnish

1. In large saucepan over medium heat, sauté onions, thyme, savory, salt, pepper, and rice in oil until onion is translucent and rice is browned, stirring constantly— about 2 minutes.

2. Drain pineapple thoroughly, reserving juice. To reserved juice, add enough water to equal 1 ½ cups. Add juice to rice, along with pineapple and coconut. Cover, reduce heat; simmer 20 minutes or until liquid is absorbed. Stir in chives and red bell pepper. Garnish with paprika at serving time. Serve warm or chilled. Serves 4.

Calories	Fat	Protein	Carb	Chol	Sodium	Fiber
200	5g	3g	37g	0mg	295mg	2g

~ Polenta ~

1 small onion, grated
1 Tbsp. olive oil
½ tsp. dried oregano leaves
¼ black pepper
¾ tsp. salt
1 cup milk (cow, rice, soy)

¾ cup low-sodium gf chicken
 broth
½ cup yellow cornmeal
2 Tbsp. grated Parmesan
 cheese (cow, rice, soy, optional)
1 Tbsp. cooking oil

1. In large saucepan over high heat, combine onion to milk. Bring to boil. Reduce to low; gradually add cornmeal. Cook 3-5 minutes, stirring constantly until thick. Remove from heat. Add cheese.

2. Pour into greased 11 x 7-inch dish. Refrigerate, covered, until firm. Cut into wedges or squares. Heat oil in large, heavy skillet and fry over medium-heat until very crisp on both sides. Serve immediately. Serves 4.

Calories	Fat	Protein	Carb	Chol	Sodium	Fiber
165	9g	6g	18g	4mg	548mg	2g

~ Roasted Asparagus ~

Roasted asparagus has a fuller flavor and more interesting texture than simply steaming or boiling it. Use the bigger asparagus spears for this dish.

1 ½ lb. fresh large asparagus spears	¼ tsp. salt
2 Tbsp. olive oil	¼ tsp. black pepper

1. Preheat oven to 450°. Rinse spears, then snap off ends (stalks will break naturally at point where they start to get tough). Peel asparagus stalks with potato peeler to remove stringy skin, if desired.

2. Place asparagus in single layer on baking sheet. Drizzle with oil and shake to coat thoroughly. Season with salt and pepper. Roast until tender and lightly browned, about 10-15 minutes. Serve immediately. Serves 4.

Calories	Fat	Protein	Carb	Chol	Sodium	Fiber
75	7g	2g	3g	0mg	150mg	1g

~ Roasted Fennel ~

An unusual vegetable that adds lots of interest to a winter meal.

2 fennel bulbs	½ tsp. salt
¼ cup olive oil	¼ tsp. black pepper
2 Tbsp. lemon juice	

1. Preheat oven to 400°. Wash fennel. Trim tops and outer leaves. Reserve leafy fronds. Cut through fennel lengthwise into ¼ inch slices. Toss with 3 Tbsp. olive oil to thoroughly coat all pieces.

2. Place on nonstick baking sheet and roast 15-20 minutes. Turn pieces and roast another 15-20 minutes, or until caramelized. Drizzle with lemon juice and remaining olive oil. Add salt and pepper and chopped, reserved fronds and serve immediately. Serves 4.

Calories	Fat	Protein	Carb	Chol	Sodium	Fiber
155	14g	2g	9g	0mg	348mg	4g

~ Roasted (Grilled) Vegetables ~

The flavor of vegetables cooked on a grill is much fuller than if they're just steamed. In this recipe, the marinade introduces even more flavor. See next page for tips on roasting vegetables.

2 Tbsp. olive oil
⅓ cup balsamic vinegar
½ tsp. dried oregano leaves
1 large garlic clove, minced
½ tsp. ground coriander
¼ tsp. ground cumin
¼ tsp. salt
¼ tsp. pepper
2 tsp. molasses

1 large yellow onion, quartered
4 large carrots, halved lengthwise
1 large red pepper, quartered
1 large yellow pepper, quartered
4 small red new potatoes, halved
2 medium zucchini, halved
1 large onion, halved
2 small yellow squash, halved

1. Combine first 9 ingredients (olive oil through molasses) in large bowl. Add vegetables in marinate 30-45 minutes. Stir occasionally.

2. Drain vegetables, reserving marinade, and arrange in grill basket liberally coated with cooking spray. (Withhold more delicate vegetables such as red and yellow bell pepper until final 10 minutes so they don't overcook.)

3. Cook on grill over medium-hot coals with lid down about 15-20 minutes or until done, turning every 5 minutes. The type and thickness of vegetables determines cooking time. Add remaining vegetables during last 10 minutes. Meanwhile, warm marinade over low-medium heat. Remove vegetables from grill basket and toss with marinade. Serve warm. Makes about 6 cups. Serves 6 (1 cup each).

4. As an alternative to grilling, roast vegetables (uncovered) in 400° oven, turning occasionally, until desired degree of doneness.

Calories	Fat	Protein	Carb	Chol	Sodium	Fiber
135	5g	2g	23g	0mg	122mg	4g

~ Tips on Roasting & Grilling Vegetables ~

Since so many of the recipes in this chapter involve roasting, it seems appropriate to discuss this important method further.

There are two ways to roast vegetables: in the oven and on the grill. While the oven method is fairly easy, grills are more involved.

Roasting on the Grill
Roasting on the grill brings out flavor and introduces color and a pleasingly crisp exterior on vegetables. Here are some tips:

1. Wash and trim vegetables, then pat dry with paper towel so that heat grills vegetables instead of steaming them.

2. Experts advise against marinades or basting sauces to avoid flare-ups. Coat vegetables in olive oil; then sprinkle with dry spices before grilling. Add salt and pepper before or after cooking.

3. Halve vegetables such as onions and bell peppers. Leave mushrooms and carrots whole. Slicing potatoes in half lengthwise gives broad, flat surface for more complete cooking. Cut vegetables in similar-size pieces for uniform cooking.

4. Close lid for hard, dense vegetables. Leave it open for softer, tender ones. Or, use closed lid for first half of cooking period, then leave lid open for remainder. Experiment to see what works.

5. Turn vegetables when one side shows grill marks. Avoid overcooking vegetables which blackens and toughens them. Vegetables with higher sugar content, such as sweet potatoes, cook faster as do those with high water content such as zucchini or tomatoes. Add such vegetables to the grill toward the end.

Roasting in the Oven
Save your old, darkened, battered cake pans for this task. Toss vegetables in marinade or salad dressing. Roast at high temperatures until done, such as between 400° and 425°.

~ Sautéed Brussels Sprouts ~

Enjoy a change of pace with this tasty version of brussels sprouts. Sauté at the last minute so you can serve them fresh from the hot skillet.

1 lb. brussels sprouts
1 Tbsp. olive oil
½ tsp. salt

¼ tsp. black pepper
¼ tsp. ground nutmeg or mace
2 limes, juiced

1. Cut off ends and trim brussels sprouts. Cut each in half, lengthwise, then lay each half flat on cutting board and cut in narrow strips.

2. In small skillet, sauté brussels sprouts in olive oil over low-medium heat for 3-5 minutes. Add salt, pepper, ground nutmeg (or mace), and lime juice to skillet and toss thoroughly. Serve immediately. Serves 4.

Calories	Fat	Protein	Carb	Chol	Sodium	Fiber
85	4g	4g	12g	0mg	316mg	4g

~ Colcannon ~

This is a traditional dish in Ireland. Regular cabbage can be used in place of savory.

2 lb. potatoes, peeled
1 head savoy cabbage
(remove outer leaves)
¼ cup butter or cooking oil
1 small onion

2 Tbsp. chopped fresh
parsley
½ tsp. salt
¼ tsp. black pepper

1. Cut potatoes into equal-size chunks. Place in medium-size saucepan. Cover with cold water and bring to boil. Cook 20-25 minutes or until fork tender. Drain thoroughly, then mash.

2. Meanwhile, bring another pan of water to boil and cook cabbage 15 minutes or until just tender. Drain thoroughly.

3. Melt butter in large, heavy skillet. Add onion and cook until soft, about 3-5 minutes. Add mashed potato and cabbage and fry 5 minutes over medium heat, stirring occasionally, until brown around edges. Stir in parsley, salt, and pepper. Serve hot. Serves 4.

Calories	Fat	Protein	Carb	Chol	Sodium	Fiber
350	14g	6g	54g	0mg	310mg	5g

~ Duchess Potatoes ~

These potatoes are especially pretty when placed around the perimeter on a platter of roast beef or chicken. If you don't have the pastry tips, don't despair. Just use a heavy-duty plastic freezer bag with the corner cut off.

1 ½ lb. russet potatoes
3 cups low sodium gf chicken
   broth
¼ cup butter or margarine

¼ tsp. ground nutmeg
Salt & white pepper to taste
½ cup hot (115°) milk
   (cow, rice, soy)

1. Wash, peel and slice potatoes into chunks. Place potatoes and chicken broth in large saucepan, bring to boil, then cover and simmer until potatoes are done— about 20-30 minutes. Remove pan from heat and turn off heat. Drain potatoes thoroughly. Return potatoes to hot pan and place on burner 5-10 seconds to thoroughly dry.

2. Put potatoes through potato ricer (or mash thoroughly by hand with potato masher). Add nutmeg, salt, and pepper to taste. Stir in enough of the ½ cup hot milk to reach consistency of mashed potatoes. Use more milk, if necessary.

3. Preheat oven to 350°. Place potatoes in pastry bag fitted with large decorative tip (or use heavy duty, plastic freezer bag). Coat baking sheet with oleo or cooking spray and pipe 4 large rosettes (or 8 smaller ones) onto sheet.

4. Bake rosettes in the middle of oven 10-15 minutes or until lightly browned. (If you've previously prepared rosettes and chilled them, bake until they're heated through, about 15-20 minutes.) Then place under the broiler to finish browning. Serve immediately. Serves 4.

Calories	Fat	Protein	Carb	Chol	Sodium	Fiber
295	13g	7g	40g	35mg	106mg	3g

~ Garlic Mashed Potatoes ~

Garlic mashed potatoes are a trendy dish in many restaurants. However, they're nothing more than down-home mashed potatoes with roasted garlic. Easy, yet delicious. You may double this recipe to serve 8.

2 large whole garlic cloves
1 tsp. olive oil
2 lb. white potatoes, peeled
¼ tsp. salt

Low sodium gf chicken broth to
   cover potatoes
¼ tsp. white pepper
3 cups water
1 cup hot (115°) milk (cow, rice, soy)

1. Preheat oven to 350°. Place garlic cloves on small piece of aluminum foil, drizzle with 1 tsp. olive oil (or spray with cooking spray), and sprinkle with salt and pepper. Close foil loosely and bake in small baking pan or cooking sheet until garlic is done, about 30 minutes. Remove garlic from oven and loosen foil to allow garlic to cool.

2. Meanwhile, cut potatoes into large chunks. Place them in large pot with enough chicken broth to cover. Bring to boil, reduce heat, and gently boil until potatoes are done— about 20–30 minutes.

3. Drain cooked potatoes and return them to cooking pot. Shake gently over low heat few times to remove all moisture. Press through potato ricer (or blend with hand masher.) Squeeze roasted garlic into potatoes and blend thoroughly. Add hot milk to potatoes, ¼ cup at a time, until desired consistency is reached. Serve immediately. Drizzle with extra butter or oleo. Serves 4.

Garlic Mashed Potatoes with Spinach: Add 1 cup blanched spinach.

Horseradish Mashed Potatoes: Add 1 Tbsp. grated fresh horseradish or add to taste.

Calories	Fat	Protein	Carb	Chol	Sodium	Fiber
245	2g	7g	53g	1mg	192mg	3.5g

~ New Potatoes & Peas in Lemon-Dill Sauce ~

This innovative way to serve potatoes and peas together will delight everyone.

16 small new red potatoes, unpeeled
1 tsp. salt
3 Tbsp. fresh lemon juice
1 small garlic clove, minced
2 Tbsp. extra virgin olive oil
½ tsp. honey

3 Tbsp. chopped onion
½ tsp. salt
2 Tbsp. dill weed
¼ tsp. xanthan gum
⅛ tsp. black pepper
1 cup cooked green peas

1. Scrub potatoes well. In large saucepan, place potatoes and salt in water to cover. Cook, covered, until tender. Quarter potatoes while hot.

2. Meanwhile purée remaining ingredients (except peas) in blender until very smooth. Toss potatoes and peas with lemon-dill sauce. Serve hot. Serves 4.

Calories	Fat	Protein	Carb	Chol	Sodium	Fiber
240	7g	5g	42g	0mg	874mg	5g

~ Roasted Potatoes ~

The first four ingredients combine to make a tasty gremolata.

3 Tbsp. minced fresh parsley
1 Tbsp. grated lemon peel
2 tsp. minced garlic
1 tsp. extra-virgin olive oil
1 ½ lb. small red potatoes,
2 Tbsp. extra-virgin olive oil

½ tsp. salt
¼ tsp. black pepper
1 tsp. chopped fresh rosemary
1 tsp. chopped fresh thyme
¼ cup chopped flat-leaf parsley
¼ cup chopped fresh basil

1. Combine first four ingredients for gremolata. Set aside. Preheat oven to 400°. In large shallow pan, toss potatoes with remaining ingredients.

2. Bake 30 minutes, shaking pan occasionally. Then reduce temperature to 350°; bake another 15-20 minutes or until fork-tender. Combine ⅔ of parsley-lemon mixture and toss with potatoes. Sprinkle vegetables with remaining ⅓ parsley mixture. Serves 4.

Calories	Fat	Protein	Carb	Chol	Sodium	Fiber
225	8g	4g	36g	0mg	300mg	3g

~ Potatoes Anna ~

Try this easy dish for a special occasion. Your guests will appreciate the added touch, but you'll know how very easy it is. Be sure to use a deep enough cast-iron skillet or the excess juices will run over into your oven. For added flavor, sprinkle 1 tsp. crushed rosemary leaves between the potato layers.

¼ cup butter or margarine
2 lb. red potatoes
½ tsp. salt or to taste

½ tsp. black pepper or to taste
Chopped parsley or rosemary

1. Heat oven to 450°. Peel and slice potatoes in ⅜-inch slices. Heat 9 or 10-inch cast-iron skillet over medium-high heat and add 1 Tbsp. of the butter. Quickly arrange layer of sliced potatoes in overlapping, concentric circles. Drizzle with more butter and sprinkle with salt and pepper (and rosemary, if using).

2. Continue making layers of concentric circles drizzled with butter and salt and pepper. Top with aluminum foil and press down with heavy object to compress slices. Remove foil and bake in oven 30 minutes. Remove from oven; press again with foil and heavy object. Remove foil and return to oven to bake another 30-40 minutes or until potatoes are golden brown and tender when pierced with fork.

3. Remove skillet from oven and invert onto plate (be careful— it's hot). If potatoes won't come out, slide metal spatula under potatoes to loosen them. Serve immediately. Garnish with sprinkle of parsley or crushed rosemary leaves. Serves 4.

Calories	Fat	Protein	Carb	Chol	Sodium	Fiber
315	12g	5g	49g	0mg	300mg	4g

Butter adds additional 31mg cholesterol per serving.

~ APPETIZERS, SNACKS, & BEVERAGES ~

Appetizers are designed to take the edge off your hunger . . . or to whet your appetite for the main course. At other times, appetizers can be a meal in themselves. Sort of like understudies in a play— ready at any moment to take center stage, if necessary.

Finger foods, dips, crackers, beverages––you'll find a wide range of tasty tidbits to delight your family and guests at any special occasion.

~ Appetizer Meatballs ~

I like to use this recipe when I want something hot on the buffet table, yet can be prepared ahead of time. A heated chafing dish works just great, but I've also served the meatballs in a crock pot.

Meatballs
1 lb. lean ground beef
½ cup crushed gf corn flakes
  or gf cracker crumbs
2 Tbsp. ketchup
1 tsp. dried thyme leaves
1 tsp. salt
¼ tsp. black pepper
¼ tsp. chili powder
¼ cup finely chopped onion

Sauce
2 Tbsp. sweet pickle relish
8 oz. tomato sauce
2 Tbsp. finely chopped onion
2 Tbsp. brown sugar
1 Tbsp. cider vinegar
¼ cup ketchup
1 Tbsp. Worcestershire sauce
  (Lea & Perrins)
½ tsp. salt
¼ tsp. black pepper
¼ tsp. ground allspice
¼ cup water

Meatballs
1. Preheat oven to 400°. Grease baking sheet or line with parch-ment paper.

2. In large bowl, thoroughly combine beef, crumbs, ketchup, thyme, salt, pepper, chili powder, and onion. Shape into 36 small meatballs (about 1 Tbsp. each). Place on prepared baking sheet and bake until nicely browned, about 15-20 minutes.

Sauce
1. Meanwhile, in medium saucepan combine pickle relish, tomato sauce, onion, sugar, vinegar, ketchup, Worcestershire sauce, salt, pepper, allspice, and water. Bring to boil and simmer 15 minutes. Add meatballs and simmer another 15 minutes. Spear meatballs with toothpicks. Serves 12 (3 meatballs each). Double recipe for larger groups.

Calories	Fat	Protein	Carb	Chol	Sodium	Fiber
100	4g	8g	9g	14mg	470mg	1g

~ Buffalo Wings ~

You can eat these tasty wings plain or dip in your favorite dipping sauce. Have plenty of napkins handy. These wings are a little bit messy— but definitely worth it!

4 lb. chicken wings
   or drummettes
1 Tbsp. olive oil
1 Tbsp. paprika
1 tsp. black pepper
1 tsp. ground white pepper
1 tsp. garlic powder

1 tsp. onion powder
1 tsp. sugar
2 tsp. celery salt
1 tsp. dried oregano leaves
1 tsp. dried thyme leaves
½ tsp. cayenne pepper
1 tsp. dry mustard*
*Grind mustards with small coffee grinder

1. Pat chicken dry with paper towel. If not using drummettes, cut off wings at first joint and reserve discarded pieces for another use (such as chicken stock).

2. In large bowl or plastic freezer bag, toss wings with olive oil. Combine remaining ingredients. Then toss wings with spice mixture until thoroughly coated.

3. Refrigerate at least two hours or overnight. Arrange wings on shallow baking pan or cookie sheet. Preheat oven to 450°. Bake wings 12-15 minutes on middle rack of oven. Turn wings and continue baking another 12-15 minutes or until crispy. As an alternative, you may grill wings on barbecue grill until done. Serve with dipping sauce of your choice. Serves 16 as appetizers (¼ lb. each).

Calories	Fat	Protein	Carb	Chol	Sodium	Fiber
300	20g	26g	1g	79mg	77mg	.5g

~ Falafel ~

If you're using rice crackers instead of bread crumbs, add a tablespoon of olive oil to make sure the mixture sticks together.

Falafel Patties
1 can (19 oz) canned chickpeas
   (rinsed, drained)
½ cup chopped onions
⅓ cup gf bread crumbs
2 Tbsp. chopped parsley or cilantro
1 tsp. ground cumin
½ tsp. ground coriander
¼ tsp. baking soda
⅛ tsp. cayenne pepper
2 garlic cloves, minced
¼ tsp. salt
¼ tsp. black pepper
1 Tbsp. olive oil for frying

Dressing
1 cup yogurt (cow, soy) or
   soft silken tofu
¼ cup tahini paste
2 Tbsp. lemon juice
1 small garlic clove, minced
¼ tsp. salt
⅛ tsp. black pepper
1 small cucumber
   (peeled, diced)

1. Combine chickpeas, onion, bread crumbs, parsley, cumin, coriander, baking soda, cayenne pepper, garlic, salt, and pepper in food processor. Purée until well blended. Divide into 12 portions and shape into patty, flattening slightly.

2. In large skillet in 1 Tbsp. olive oil, brown falafel patties on both sides (about 2-3 minutes per side).

3. For dressing, combine yogurt, tahini, lemon juice, garlic, salt, and pepper and purée until smooth. Stir in diced cucumbers. Serve with falafel in bread, buns, or with crackers or vegetables. Serves 12 (1 patty each).

Calories	Fat	Protein	Carb	Chol	Sodium	Fiber
110	4g	5g	14g	1mg	282mg	3g

~ Miniature Focaccia Sandwiches ~

Focaccia is so simple to make. And, it makes extremely flavorful sandwiches. Try these at your next party or reserve them for a truly special occasion such as a wedding or shower. Arrange them decoratively on a large platter, garnished with sprigs of fresh parsley or your favorite herbs.

Bread
¾ cup warm milk (110°)
1 tsp. sugar
2 large eggs*
2 Tbsp. olive oil
½ tsp. cider vinegar
1 ½ tsp. active dry yeast
1 cup brown rice flour
½ cup tapioca flour

1 ½ tsp. xanthan gum
1 tsp. unflavored gelatin powder
1 tsp. dried rosemary leaves
½ tsp. onion powder
¾ tsp. salt
Topping
1 ¼ tsp. Italian herb seasoning
¼ tsp. salt
1 Tbsp. olive oil

Bread
1. Combine warm milk, sugar, eggs, olive oil, and vinegar in mixer bowl. Beat with electric mixer until very smooth— about 1 minute. Add yeast, flours, xanthan gum, gelatin powder, rosemary, onion powder, and salt. Beat dough 2 minutes. Dough will be soft and sticky— like thick cake batter.

2. Transfer dough to greased 11 x 7-inch nonstick pan. Cover with aluminum foil and let rise in warm place 30 minutes or until desired height.

Topping
Preheat oven to 400°. Sprinkle Focaccia with Italian seasoning, salt, and olive oil (or to taste). Bake 15 minutes or until top is golden brown. Cool completely before slicing.

Sandwiches
To make Miniature Focaccia Sandwiches, cut Focaccia into 12 equal pieces. Using sharp, serrated knife, carefully slice each piece horizontally. Spread filling of choice (see next page) between slices. Serve immediately or cover tightly and refrigerate up to 4 hours. Serves 6.

Without fillings

Calories	Fat	Protein	Carb	Chol	Sodium	Fiber
230	9g	5g	32g	52mg	410mg	2.5g

*Egg Alternative: Omit eggs. Use ½ cup soft silken tofu.

~ Focaccia Sandwich Fillings ~

Choose from this wide variety of savory fillings for Miniature Focaccia Sandwiches.

Chicken Salad or Tuna Salad Filling

2 cups ground cooked chicken (about 2 whole chicken breasts) or 2 cups low-salt canned tuna (about 4 small cans)
½ cup *Mayonnaise* (p. 217)
1 tsp. dried thyme leaves

1 tsp. dried dill weed
1 tsp. onion powder
½ tsp. celery salt
¼ tsp. black pepper

Combine all ingredients in a bowl and mash together with fork. Chill until serving time. Serves 16 (2 Tbsp. per sandwich).

Calories	Fat	Protein	Carb	Chol	Sodium	Fiber
60	2g	3g	7g	8mg	205mg	<1g

Additional Fillings (recipes for italicized ingredients are in this book)

• Thin sliced cucumber, red onion, *Sunny Tomato-Basil Dip*, lettuce

• Paper-thin slices of prosciutto and Granny Smith apples, fresh basil leaves, mayonnaise, lettuce

• Softened goat cheese with raisins, *Orange Marmalade* or *Apricot Ketchup*, whole mint leaves, lettuce. (Goat cheese is not dairy-free.)

• Paper-thin slices of roast beef and red onion, gf horseradish sauce, butter or margarine, lettuce

• Thinly sliced plum tomatoes, red onion, guacamole dip, lettuce

• Thinly sliced smoked turkey, red onion, Dijonnaise mustard, lettuce

• Paper-thin slices of smoked ham, *Tuscan Bean Spread*, lettuce

• Crumbled crisp bacon, finely chopped *Oven-Dried Tomatoes*, *Tuscan Bean Spread*, lettuce

~ Grilled Shrimp with Wraps ~

1 cup olive oil
¼ cup rice vinegar
½ cup lemon juice
2 Tbsp. dried basil leaves
20 jumbo shrimp (shelled, deveined)

20 whole large basil leaves
20 Oven-Dried Tomatoes (p. 214)
20 fresh cilantro sprigs
20 prosciutto strips
(2-inches wide)

1. Mix together oil, vinegar, lemon juice, and dried basil. Set aside.

2. Wrap each shrimp, first with basil leaf, then sun-dried tomato, then a sprig of cilantro, then strip of prosciutto. Use toothpicks to fasten prosciutto in place. Pour marinade over shrimp in large, shallow container. Refrigerate, covered, for 4 hours.

3. Remove shrimp from marinade (reserving marinade). Place shrimp in fish basket or lay carefully on grate. Grill shrimp, basting often with reserved marinade, about 5 minutes each side— or to desired doneness. Serve immediately. Serves 10 (2 each).

Calories	Fat	Protein	Carb	Chol	Sodium	Fiber
251	25g	5g	3g	37mg	207mg	1g

~ Grilled Quesadillas ~

2 corn tortillas
2 tsp. olive oil
¼ cup shredded cheese
(cow, rice, soy)

3 tomatillos (grilled, smashed flat*)
¼ cup finely chopped green onion
¼ cup chopped fresh cilantro

Brush one side of tortilla with oil. Place oil-side down on cutting board. Top tortilla with half of cheese— then smashed tomatillos, onion, and cilantro. Top with remaining half of cheese and remaining tortilla, coated with olive oil on top side. Carefully slide quesadilla onto grill, 4-5 inches from heat. Grill until browned on underside, about 5 minutes. Turn and grill other side. Remove, cut into wedges with kitchen shears. Serves 4 (¼ each).

Calories	Fat	Protein	Carb	Chol	Sodium	Fiber
160	10g	5g	14g	13mg	84mg	1.5g

*Grill tomatillos, 5 inches from heat until soft. Remove from heat and smash.

~ Oven-Baked Crab Cakes ~

Crab cakes are featured here as an appetizer; make them larger for a main course.

1 lb. shelled crabmeat,
  (picked over)
1 celery stalk, finely chopped
1 Tbsp. dried minced onion or
  2 Tbsp. grated fresh onion
2 tsp. Seafood Seasoning (p. 221)
1 Tbsp. chopped fresh parsley

1 Tbsp. Worcestershire sauce
  (Lea & Perrins)
1 tsp. Italian herb seasoning
½ cup mayonnaise
1 Tbsp. baking powder
1 cup gf bread crumbs
Cocktail Sauce (see below)

1. Preheat oven to 400°. Combine all ingredients in food processor. Process until ingredients are thoroughly mixed. Shape mixture into 16 small crab cakes. Arrange on cookie sheet coated with cooking spray or parchment paper.

2. Bake on lower rack in oven about 10 minutes per side, or until both sides are gently browned. Serves 8 (2 crab cakes each).

Calories	Fat	Protein	Carb	Chol	Sodium	Fiber
265	4g	30g	26g	115mg	999mg	1g

~ Shrimp with Cocktail Sauce ~

This simple sauce is moderately spicy; add more horseradish to jazz it up.

2 lb. large cooked shrimp
1 tsp. horseradish sauce
  or grated fresh horseradish

1 tsp. lemon juice
2 Tbsp. Dijonnaise mustard
3 Tbsp. ketchup

Peel and devein shrimp. Chill until ready to use. Thoroughly combine all remaining ingredients in small bowl or blender. Serve with shrimp. Serves 8 (about ¼ lb. each).

Calories	Fat	Protein	Carb	Chol	Sodium	Fiber
130	2g	24g	3g	170mg	330mg	0g

~ Avocado Bean Salsa ~

Serve this great dip to complement a Southwestern meal.

1 firm ripe avocado, diced
1 plum tomato (seeded, diced)
1 small red onion, minced
2 Tbsp. lime juice
¼ cup chopped fresh cilantro,
  packed

½ small jalapeño, finely chopped
1 Tbsp. olive oil
1 small garlic clove, minced
¼ tsp. black pepper
1 can (16 oz) white beans, drained

Combine all ingredients in small bowl and toss thoroughly. Serve with tortilla chips, crackers, or fresh vegetables. Or, serve on lettuce leaf as side salad to a Southwestern inspired meal. If cooking your own beans, you may want to add salt to taste. Serves 4.

Calories	Fat	Protein	Carb	Chol	Sodium	Fiber
210	12g	9g	24g	0mg	25mg	8g

~ Dried Apple Rings ~

Dried apples are great in a "survival" kit. But if you who don't want the sulfites found in the commercial variety, here's an easy version you can make yourself— and they're completely natural. You can also omit the sweetener, if you wish.

4 large Granny Smith apples,
  cored and sliced in ⅛-inch slices
4 cups water

¼ cup sugar
¼ tsp. ground cinnamon
Juice of 1 lemon

1. Preheat oven to 200°. In large saucepan, bring water, cinnamon and lemon juice to boil. Stir until sweetener is dissolved.

2. Reduce heat to low, add apple slices, and simmer until just tender, about 2-5 minutes. Transfer to baking sheet lined with parchment paper. Bake apples 1 hour. Reduce heat to 150° and bake until apples are dry. Watch carefully because apples will dry quickly toward end of baking. Serves 4.

Calories	Fat	Protein	Carb	Chol	Sodium	Fiber
160	0g	0g	44g	0mg	2mg	3g

~ Chutney Appetizer Spread ~

The sweet, yet spicy flavor of chutney melds wonderfully with creamy, mellow cream cheese (or tofu.) This duo seems unlikely, yet produces a wonderful taste sensation. And, if you have the chutney on hand you can whip this dish up in seconds. If you're not using cream cheese, add a teaspoon of gf butter-flavored extract to lend a "dairy" taste.

8 oz. cream cheese
  or soft silken tofu
¼ cup chopped fresh cilantro,
  packed
2 Tbsp. grated fresh onion

¼ tsp. salt
¼ tsp. white pepper
⅔ cup Mango Chutney (p. 22)
  or your favorite gf chutney
¼ tsp. crushed red pepper

In food processor, blend together cream cheese, cilantro, onion, salt, and pepper. Stir in chutney and red pepper flakes. Makes slightly less than 2 cups. Serves 6 (about ⅓ cup each).

Calories	Fat	Protein	Carb	Chol	Sodium	Fiber
76	15g	3g	11g	0mg	415mg	.5g

Cream cheese adds additional 90 calories and 42mg cholesterol per serving.

~ Tuscan Bean Spread ~

For a dramatic, colorful presentation, serve in a hollowed out red cabbage half that nestles in a bed of greens.

1 can (16 oz) garbanzo beans
1 garlic cloves, minced
3 Tbsp. olive oil
¼ cup lemon juice
1 tsp. salt
1 tsp. ground cumin

1 tsp. dried dill weed or 1 Tbsp.
  fresh chopped dill weed
2 Tbsp. fresh cilantro
½ tsp. black pepper
¼ tsp. crushed red pepper

Place beans (undrained) and remaining ingredients in food processor and purée until smooth. Scrape down sides of bowl often. If mixture is too thick, add water, 1 Tbsp. at a time. Makes 1 ½ cups. Serves 6 (¼ cup each).

Calories	Fat	Protein	Carb	Chol	Sodium	Fiber
135	8g	3g	13g	0mg	547mg	4g

~ Hot Seafood Dip ~

If you don't use cream cheese, yet want to replicate the dairy taste, try adding a teaspoon of gf butter flavored extract. Whether you use 1 or 2 tsp. of the seafood seasoning is up to you. You might use 1 tsp. at first and add more, later.

1 cup cooked crab meat
8 oz. cream cheese (cow, soy)
  or soft silken tofu
2 Tbsp. Dijonnaise mustard
1 Tbsp. lemon juice
1 tsp. horseradish sauce or
  ½ tsp. fresh grated horseradish

2 Tbsp. finely chopped onion
1-2 tsp. Seafood Seasoning
  (recipe on p. 221)
1 stalk finely chopped celery
2 Tbsp. fresh chopped
  parsley for garnish
1 tsp. paprika for garnish

1. Prepare seafood by discarding any cartilage or bones. If seafood has been previously frozen or contains a lot of water, drain in sieve by pushing meat firmly with paper towel. Chop finely. Set aside.

2. Combine cream cheese, mustard, milk, lemon juice, horseradish sauce, and onion in food processor. Purée until very smooth. Stir in celery and prepared seafood.

3. Spoon mixture into oven-proof bowl and heat to serving temperature, either by baking in 350° oven 15-20 minutes or in microwave oven at low-medium setting until mixture reaches desired temperature.

4. Garnish with chopped parsley and dash of paprika. Serve hot with crackers or crisp bread. Makes about 2 cups. Serves 8 (not quite ¼ cup each).

Calories	Fat	Protein	Carb	Chol	Sodium	Fiber
125	11g	6g	2g	46mg	342mg	.5g

~ Mexican Tomato Salsa Dip ~

I've been making this salsa for at least 20 years. Although I usually serve it with corn chips or vegetables, I've also thickened it slightly with cornstarch or arrowroot and used it as a sauce for Southwestern main dishes. If you prefer a less spicy version, reduce the chiles to 2 Tbsp.

4 medium tomatoes or 10 plum
   tomatoes
½ cup chopped onion
½ cup chopped celery
¼ cup green pepper
2 Tbsp. olive oil
1 can (4 oz) green chiles or ¼ cup
   finely chopped fresh chiles

2 Tbsp. red wine vinegar
1 Tbsp. mustard seeds
1 tsp. crushed coriander seed
   or ½ tsp. dried coriander
1 tsp. salt
¼ tsp. black pepper
¼ tsp. sugar

1. Combine all ingredients in food processor or blender and whirl until mixture reaches desired texture.

2. For a chunky texture, reserve half of the onion, celery, and green pepper until the other ingredients are blended. Add reserved onion, celery, and green pepper and whirl or pulse just a few times to incorporate them into salsa. Refrigerate in glass container for up to one week. Makes 2 pints. Serves 16 (¼ cup each).

Calories	Fat	Protein	Carb	Chol	Sodium	Fiber
60	4g	1g	6g	0mg	310mg	1g

~ Sunny Tomato-Basil Dip ~

You can use sun-dried tomatoes packed in oil (be sure to drain them well). However, they may contain unacceptable ingredients. In that event, use the sun-dried tomatoes that are dry. Reconstitute by simmering in ⅓ cup hot water. Let stand 15 minutes. Drain thoroughly before using. Or make your own using the recipe on p. 214. If using tofu but you really like the taste of cream cheese, add a teaspoon of butter-flavored extract to help replicate that "dairy" taste.

8 oz. cream cheese
  or soft silken tofu
½ cup sun-dried tomatoes
⅓ cup chopped fresh basil or
  2 Tbsp. dried basil leaves
1 tsp. grated lemon peel

1 small garlic clove, minced
2 Tbsp. Parmesan cheese
  (cow, rice, soy)
¼ tsp. onion salt

Combine all ingredients in food processor and purée until smooth. Transfer to serving bowl and chill at least 2 hours. Return to room temperature before serving. Serve with crackers, French bread, or fresh vegetables. Makes 1 cup. Serves 4 (¼ cup each).

Calories	Fat	Protein	Carb	Chol	Sodium	Fiber
65	3g	7g	6g	2mg	316mg	1g

Cream cheese adds 100 calories, 12g fat, and 41mg cholesterol per serving.

~ Savory Crackers ~

These crackers are very easy to make and also travel well. Try adding your favorite dried herbs for variety.

¼ cup brown rice flour
¼ cup potato starch
¼ cup sweet rice flour
½ tsp. xanthan gum
¼ tsp. baking soda
½ tsp. salt
2 Tbsp. Parmesan cheese
(cow, rice, soy)

1 tsp. onion powder or 1
  Tbsp. grated fresh onion
2 Tbsp. butter or canola oil
1 Tbsp. honey
3 Tbsp. toasted sesame seeds
2 Tbsp. milk
1 tsp. cider vinegar

1. Preheat oven to 350°. Grease baking sheet.

2. In food processor, combine flours, xanthan gum, baking soda, salt, Parmesan cheese, and onion powder. Add butter, honey, sesame seeds, milk, and vinegar. Mix until dough forms soft ball.

3. Shape dough into 20 balls, each 1-inch in diameter, and place on baking sheet at least 2 inches apart. Using bottom of drinking glass or rolling pin, flatten balls to approximately ⅛ -inch thick. Use your fingers to smooth edges of circle.

4. If you prefer not to hand-shape the crackers, roll dough to ⅛-inch thickness on cookie sheet. Then, using cookie cutter or biscuit cutter, cut cookies to desired shapes. Peel off unused dough and hand shape these scraps into crackers.

5. Bake 12-15 minutes, or until crackers look firm and slightly toasted. Turn each cracker and bake another 5-7 minutes or until golden brown. (Sprinkle with additional sesame seeds and salt, if desired). Makes about 20 crackers. Serves 10 (2 crackers each).

Calories	Fat	Protein	Carb	Chol	Sodium	Fiber
95	5g	2g	11g	1mg	175mg	1g

~ Rosemary-Thyme Pecans ~

If you love rosemary, you'll be absolutely intoxicated by the aroma of these delicacies toasting in the oven. Serve them warm. If you prefer less salt, just reduce it to your liking. And, you may substitute walnuts or cashews for the pecans.

2 cups pecan halves
2 Tbsp. olive oil
2 tsp. dried rosemary leaves

½ tsp. dried thyme leaves
¼ tsp. salt
⅛ tsp. cayenne pepper

1. Preheat oven to 300°. Sort nuts to remove any hulls or debris. Pulverize rosemary leaves with mortar and pestle or use coffee grinder to crush leaves to coarse powder. In large bowl, toss nuts and rosemary with remaining ingredients until nuts are thoroughly coated.

2. Spread nuts in single layer on large baking sheet or pan. Bake 10-15 minutes or until lightly toasted. Serve warm. Makes 2 cups. Serves 16 (⅛ cup or about 6 whole pecans).

Calories	Fat	Protein	Carb	Chol	Sodium	Fiber
65	7g	1g	1g	0mg	33mg	1g

~ Spicy "Nuts" ~

These spicy "nuts" are excellent for traveling

1 can (16 oz) garbanzo beans (drained)
2 tsp. olive oil
1 tsp. chili powder
¼ tsp. ground cumin

½ tsp. garlic powder or
  1 garlic clove, minced
½ tsp. salt

1. Preheat oven to 325°. Rinse and drain beans thoroughly.

2. In large bowl, toss olive oil with remaining ingredients. Add beans and toss until thoroughly coated. Bake on large baking sheet or pan approximately 1 hour, shaking pan occasionally to promote even browning. Store in airtight container. Serves 4 (¼ cup each).

Calories	Fat	Protein	Carb	Chol	Sodium	Fiber
125	5g	5g	18g	0mg	538mg	6g

~ Cranberry Grapefruit Punch ~

If you have cranberry juice cocktail on hand, it is most likely already sweetened— probably with sugar. If that works for your diet, fine. You can omit the white grape juice, which provides sweetness, and substitute carbonated mineral water, instead. If not, look for unsweetened cranberry juice. It will be very, very tart and will need the sweetness provided by the white grape juice.

2 cups cranberry juice (unsweetened)
3 cups grapefruit juice (unsweetened)

2 cups pure white grape juice, (reconstituted)
Lime wedges for garnish

Mix ingredients together and serve over ice, garnished with fresh lime wedges. You may halve or double this recipe, depending on the number of guests. Serves 12 (½ cup each).

Calories	Fat	Protein	Carb	Chol	Sodium	Fiber
50	0g	1g	12g	0mg	2mg	0g

~ Frozen Coffee Slush ~

This comes pretty close to the frozen drinks you buy at popular coffee houses. If you can't use sweetened condensed milk, then use ⅔ cup non-dairy milk, plus ¼ cup sweetener of choice, plus 1 Tbsp. cooking oil.

¼ cup brewed espresso or 3
   Tbsp. instant coffee powder
   dissolved in ¼ cup hot water
1 cup ice cubes

2 Tbsp. gf chocolate syrup
   or Chocolate Syrup (p. 136)
1 cup fat-free sweetened
   condensed milk (see above)

Place all ingredients in blender and blend until very smooth. Serve immediately. Serves 4 (½ cup each).

Calories	Fat	Protein	Carb	Chol	Sodium	Fiber
330	4g	9g	65g	0mg	108mg	0g

Sweetened condensed milk adds additional 15mg cholesterol per serving.

~ Fruit Punch ~

Non-alcoholic and light, this is the perfect drink for a luncheon, shower, or wedding. If you prefer, you may add your favorite alcohol such as gf rum or vodka. For a pretty ice ring in the punch bowl, combine pineapple and orange juice in a small Bundt pan and add pineapple rings, mandarin oranges, and sprigs of mint. Freeze overnight.

2 cups Simple Syrup for Beverages
  (p. 207)
¾ cup fresh lemon juice
1 qt. pineapple juice

2 cups orange juice
Fresh mint leaves for garnish
Strips of fresh lemon peels
  for garnish

Combine ingredients in large pitcher or punch bowl, stir, and chill. Serve chilled with ice. Serves 10 (about ¾ cup each).

Calories	Fat	Protein	Carb	Chol	Sodium	Fiber
270	0g	1g	71g	0mg	81mg	0g

~ Fruity Mint Punch ~

Jazz up ordinary tea (such as orange pekoe and pekoe) with fruit and spices and you have a drink appropriate for the finest occasion. Vary the fruit juice as you wish— perhaps pineapple or orange juice. Best of all, it's alcohol-free— but you could always add a dash of your favorite gluten-free spirits!

4 cups hot brewed lemon herb tea
6 cups apple or white grape juice
¼ cup sugar

1 bunch fresh mint sprigs (bunch
  measures 1-inch in diameter)
Fresh mint leaves for garnish

1. In pitcher, combine hot brewed tea, fruit juice, sugar, and mint leaves (that have been tied together with kitchen string or dental floss). Cover and chill until ready to serve.

2. Serve over ice, garnished with fresh mint leaves. Serves 10 (1 cup each).

Calories	Fat	Protein	Carb	Chol	Sodium	Fiber
100	0g	0g	26g	0mg	4mg	0g

~ Iced Coffee ~

Refreshing and distinctively different. If you can't use dairy topping, try one of the many Whipped Toppings in the Dessert chapter. You may add sweetener to taste. If your ice cubes dilute the coffee taste, use ice cubes made of brewed coffee.

6 cups water
⅓ cup ground coffee
½ tsp. ground cardamom

½ tsp. ground cinnamon or
   a 2-inch cinnamon stick
¼ tsp. ground nutmeg

Place coffee, cardamon, and cinnamon in brew basket of coffee maker. Add water and brew coffee according to manufacturer's directions. Chill brewed coffee at least 1 hour. Divide among 4 ice-filled glasses. Garnish with dash of ground nutmeg. Serves 6 (1 cup each).

Calories	Fat	Protein	Carb	Chol	Sodium	Fiber
6	<1g	<1g	1g	0mg	5mg	0g

~ Lemon Mint Punch with Raspberries ~

Pretty as a picture, this lightly-sweetened lemon punch is accented with fresh raspberries. You may increase the size of this recipe for larger groups. Add a dash of your favorite of liquor (gin or vodka), if you wish.

2 cups lemon juice
1 ½ cups Simple Syrup
   for Beverages (p. 207)
¼ cup fresh mint leaves,
   packed

2 cups seltzer water or club soda
½ cup fresh raspberries
Lemon slices, fresh mint for garnish

Combine lemon juice, syrup, and mint in pitcher and stir until completely smooth. Add seltzer water and ice cubes. Place a few raspberries in each glass of punch (or float several in a large punch bowl.). Garnish each glass with lemon slices or fresh mint leaves. Serves 6 (about 1 cup each).

Calories	Fat	Protein	Carb	Chol	Sodium	Fiber
200	0g	0g	71g	0mg	115mg	1g

~ Minty Ginger Iced Tea ~

Even plain old black tea (known as Orange Pekoe & Pekoe) takes on new life in this refreshing drink. For an alcoholic version, try adding your favorite gf gin, vodka, or rum.

6 cups boiling water
3 Tbsp. loose tea of choice
½ cup honey

1 bunch fresh mint leaves
  (about ½ cup)
1 piece fresh ginger (½-inch thick)

Bring water to boil. Remove from heat. Add tea, honey, mint, and fresh ginger. Steep for 3-5 minutes, or to taste. Strain. Serve over ice. You may halve or double this recipe, as you wish. Serves 6 (1 cup each).

Calories	Fat	Protein	Carb	Chol	Sodium	Fiber
88	0g	0g	24g	0mg	8mg	0g

~ Simple Syrup for Beverages ~

This syrup is used in several beverages and punches but you'll see several different variations of this syrup, depending on which cookbook you consult. This version is decidedly less sweet than others. If you prefer sweeter syrup, simply increase the sweetener accordingly.

2 ¼ cups sugar

5 cups water

Combine ingredients in small saucepan. Bring to boil. Reduce to medium heat and cook for 5-8 minutes. Remove from heat and cool thoroughly before using. Refrigerate, covered, for up to 1 month. Serves 14 (½ cup each).

Calories	Fat	Protein	Carb	Chol	Sodium	Fiber
170	0g	0g	47g	0mg	5mg	0g

~ Notes ~

~ INGREDIENTS & CONDIMENTS ~

E ver notice how some of the minor actors in a play or movie are critical to its success? So it is with condiments and other ingredients that play "bit parts". Their role is small, but their impact is mighty.

The recipes in this chapter play "bit parts" in a meal. They are designed to help you with other recipes in this book. For example, condiments play a very important role in several recipes but many commercially prepared condiments have forbidden components.

~ Applesauce ~

I prefer using Granny Smith apples because of their tart flavor, but you can use any apples you happen to have on hand. Applesauce can be used to sweeten hot cereal, as a binder in baking, or as a spread on toast or rolls.

1 lb. apples (3 medium)	⅛ tsp. ground cinnamon
1 cup apple juice or cider	⅛ tsp. ground allspice
2 Tbsp. lemon juice	⅛ tsp. salt
2 Tbsp. orange juice	1 strip orange peel (3 inches long)
2 Tbsp. brown sugar	1 strip lemon peel (3 inches long)
½ tsp. vanilla extract	

1. Core, peel, and chop apples. Place all ingredients in medium sized, heavy saucepan and bring to boil. Reduce heat, cover, and simmer 15-20 minutes or until apples are done. Remove cover and mash apples with potato masher.

2. Continue simmering until applesauce reaches desired consistency. Cool. Refrigerate, tightly covered, for up to 1 week. Makes about 2 cups. Serves 8 (½ cup each).

Calories	Fat	Protein	Carb	Chol	Sodium	Fiber
44	0g	0g	11g	0mg	42mg	2g

~ Vegetable Spice Rub ~

Sprinkle this boldly flavored mix on your favorite vegetables before you roast them. Or, sprinkle after steaming them.

1 Tbsp. paprika	1 tsp. cayenne pepper
2 tsp. salt	1 tsp. onion powder
2 tsp. garlic powder	1 tsp. dried oregano leaves
1 tsp. black pepper	1 tsp. dried thyme leaves
1 tsp. white pepper	

Combine all ingredients and store, tightly covered, in cool, dark place. Sprinkle on vegetables. Serves 4 (1 Tbsp. each).

~ Baking Powder with Corn ~

If you can't eat corn, try the grain-free version below.

¼ cup cream of tartar　　　**2 Tbsp. baking soda**
3 Tbsp. cornstarch

Mix together in glass jar and store in cool, dark place up to 1 month.
Use in same proportions as baking powder. Makes about ½ cup.

~ Baking Powder without Corn ~

When the recipe calls for 1 tsp. baking powder, you may use 1 ½ tsp. of this corn-free version.
Make this frequently rather than doubling it— it loses potency over time.

3 Tbsp. baking soda　　　**⅓ cup arrowroot**
⅓ cup cream of tartar

Mix together in glass jar and store in cool, dark place up to1 month.
Makes about ¾ cup.

~ Flax (Flaxseed) Mix ~

This egg substitute works best in recipes with a darker color where you are replacing 1 egg
rather than two. It works best as a binder and moisturizer, but it is not a leavening agent—
as are eggs. Therefore, baked goods will be heavier and denser.

3 tsp. flaxseeds or flaxseed meal　　　**1 cup boiling water**

Grind seeds into fine powder with coffee grinder or use flaxseed meal.
Whisk into boiling water, remove from heat, and let stand for 5 minutes.
Use as substitute for eggs— ¼ cup flax mix equals 1 large egg.

Calories	Fat	Protein	Carb	Chol	Sodium	Fiber
12	1g	<1g	0g	0mg	3mg	1g

~ Beef Stock ~

This version produces a deeper, more fully flavored beef stock because the beef and vegetables are roasted. If you don't have time to roast the ingredients— or prefer a milder stock— simply simmer the ingredients together for a couple of hours. I prefer to use an ovenproof Dutch oven that goes from oven to stove top, thus eliminating an extra pan. For chicken or vegetable stock, see next page.

1 lb. beef stew meat (1-inch cubes)
1 large onion, peeled and quartered
1 large carrot, sliced lengthwise
1 large celery ribs, halved
2 large garlic cloves, peeled
4 qt. cold water
1 bunch parsley

1 tsp. dried thyme leaves
¼ tsp. dill seeds
1 tsp. salt
6 whole black peppercorns
1 large bay leaf
1 large tomato, halved

1. Place beef, onions, and carrot in large baking pan and roast 20-30 minutes in 400° oven until nicely browned. Transfer vegetables to large stockpot and add remaining ingredients. Pour off any extra fat from roasting pan and add just enough water to cover bottom of pan. Deglaze pan over medium-high heat, scraping up browned bits. Add this mixture to stockpot.

2. Bring mixture in stockpot slowly to simmer, cover, and continue to simmer for 3 hours. (Avoid bringing to boil rapidly since this produces foam that you'll have to skim off.)

3. Strain stock through sieve. Chill stock and remove fat that rises to top. If you're not using all the stock immediately, freeze for up to 3 months. Makes about 4 quarts. Serves 16 (1 cup each).

Calories	Fat	Protein	Carb	Chol	Sodium	Fiber
8	1g	0g	2g	0mg	156mg	1g

~ Chicken Stock ~

Save the bones from Sunday's roast chicken and use them to flavor this stock. If you refrigerate the stock, the fat can easily be skimmed off the following day and frozen in containers. For beef stock, see the previous page. For vegetable stock, see below.

3 qt. water
2 lb. chicken pieces or bones
1 Tbsp. salt
1 small onion, halved
4 ribs celery, leaves left on
4 large peeled carrots
2 small parsnips (optional)

6 dill seeds
6 whole black peppercorns
1 large tomato, halved
1 bunch fresh herbs (thyme, savory, marjoram, etc.) or 2 tsp. dried herbs of choice

Combine all ingredients in large stockpot. Bring to simmer slowly, cover tightly, and let cook 2-3 hours. Let stock cool in refrigerator. Skim off fat. Strain stock through fine mesh sieve and discard solids. Freeze in tightly covered containers. Makes 3 quarts. Serves 12 (1 cup each).

Calories	Fat	Protein	Carb	Chol	Sodium	Fiber
40	<1g	1g	9g	0mg	670mg	2g

~ Vegetable Stock ~

Keep jars of this flavorful stock in your freezer and you'll always be prepared.

3 qt. water
1 Tbsp. salt
1 small onion, halved
4 ribs celery, leaves left on
4 large carrots, peeled
2 small parsnips (optional)

6 dill seeds
6 whole black peppercorns
1 large tomato, halved
1 bunch fresh herbs (thyme, marjoram, savory, etc.) or 2 tsp. dried herbs of choice

Combine all ingredients in large stockpot. Bring to simmer slowly, cover tightly, and let cook 2-3 hours. Let stock cool in refrigerator. Strain stock through fine mesh sieve and discard solids. Freeze in tightly covered containers until ready to use. Makes 3 quarts. Serves 12 (1 cup each).

Calories	Fat	Protein	Carb	Chol	Sodium	Fiber
40	0g	0g	9g	0mg	670mg	2g

~ Oven-Dried Cherries ~

If you love dried cherries but don't want to use the commercial variety, then dry your own. It is really quite simple. You can use either fresh or canned tart cherries.

2 cans (16 oz each) red tart cherries,   **1 Tbsp. honey**
   drained or 4 cups fresh tart cherries   **Parchment paper**

1. Heat oven to 250° Line large baking sheet with parchment paper.

2. Check each cherry for stones. Toss cherries with honey and arrange on prepared baking sheets.

3. Bake 1 hour or until cherries appear wrinkled but still moist. As cherries bake, remove those that dry faster. If cherries are still not dry after 1 hour, turn oven off— but leave cherries in oven another 30 minutes or until desired degree of dryness. Serves 8 (about ½ cup each).

Calories	Fat	Protein	Carb	Chol	Sodium	Fiber
257	1g	3g	89g	1mg	1mg	5g

~ Oven-Dried Tomatoes ~

Plum tomatoes dry thoroughly and evenly and have a wonderful flavor. Use these flavorful little morsels in tossed salads or salad dressings--or any dish you choose.

12 plum or cherry tomatoes   **½ tsp. dried basil**
1 Tbsp. olive oil   **¼ tsp. salt— or to taste**

1. Wash and pat tomatoes dry with paper towel. Remove stems and slice in half, lengthwise (from stem to bottom of tomato). Remove seeds and pulp with melon baler.

2. Toss with olive oil. Place on baking sheet lined with parchment paper. Sprinkle with basil and salt.

3. Bake at 200° 2 to 4 hours or to desired degree of dryness. Store in refrigerator. Makes 24 dried tomatoes. Serves 4 (6 tomato halves each).

Calories	Fat	Protein	Carb	Chol	Sodium	Fiber
68	4g	2g	9g	0mg	160mg	2g

~ Nut Milk ~

The nice thing about making your own nut milk is that you can vary the ingredients to achieve the desired result. For example, for a sweeter version simply increase the sweetener. Likewise, for a less sweet version to be used for savory dishes, omit the sweetener altogether. Vary the density of the milk by increasing the nuts and/or decreasing the amount of water.

½ cup raw cashews or almonds   1 tsp. honey
2 cups water   ½ tsp. vanilla extract
                                                     (optional)

Combine ingredients in blender and blend until completely smooth, about 10 minutes. Strain through cheesecloth to remove any remaining nuts. Refrigerate, covered, for up to 1 week. Use in dishes as you would use any non-dairy milk substitute. Makes about 2 cups. Serves 4 (½ cup each).

Calories	Fat	Protein	Carb	Chol	Sodium	Fiber
105	8g	3g	7g	0mg	6mg	1g

~ Rice Milk ~

The advantage to making your own rice milk is that you can vary the density of the milk by increasing the rice and/or decreasing the amount of water. The cashews add flavor and body, but they can be omitted. I prefer using basmati rice, but you can use plain white or brown rice, also.

⅔ cup hot cooked rice   1 tsp. vanilla extract
3 cups warm water   1 Tbsp. honey— or to taste
⅓ cup raw cashews (optional)   ⅛ tsp. xanthan gum

Blend all ingredients in blender until very, very smooth. Strain through cheesecloth to remove any remaining rice particles. Refrigerate, covered, for up to 1 week. Makes about 3 cups. Serves 12 (¼ cup each).

Calories	Fat	Protein	Carb	Chol	Sodium	Fiber
23	0g	0g	5g	0mg	3mg	0g

~ Tomato Sauce ~

If you can't eat commercial canned tomato sauce (it often contains several other ingredients), make your own with this easy recipe.

2 Tbsp. chopped onion
1 small garlic clove, minced
1 can (14.5 oz) whole peeled tomatoes
  or 4 large peeled fresh tomatoes

¼ tsp. salt
½ tsp. sugar
⅛ tsp. black pepper

Purée all ingredients in blender until very smooth. Place in small saucepan and cook over low-medium heat 20-25 minutes or until desired consistency. Makes 1 cup, which is equivalent to 1 can (8 oz.) of commercial canned tomato sauce. Serves 4 (¼ cup each).

Calories	Fat	Protein	Carb	Chol	Sodium	Fiber
40	.5g	2g	8g	0mg	158mg	1g

~ Apricot Ketchup ~

Experts on food trends say that exotic-flavored ketchup will be very popular.

1 can (16 oz) apricots in fruit juice,
  undrained
½ cup finely chopped onion
½ cup white wine vinegar
1 small garlic clove, minced
½ tsp. ground cinnamon

½ tsp. salt
¼ tsp. ground cloves
¼ tsp. ground allspice
⅛ tsp. cayenne pepper
⅛ tsp. ground nutmeg
⅛ tsp. ground white pepper

1. Drain apricots, reserving juice in small saucepan.

2. Cook juice over low-medium heat, stirring occasionally, 7-10 minutes— or until reduced to ½ cup.

3. Add apricots and remaining ingredients. Mash apricots slightly. Bring to boil, reduce heat; simmer 40-50 minutes— or until thickened. Cool.

4. In food processor, purée apricot mixture until very smooth. Refrigerate in glass container, covered, 1 day before serving. Keeps in refrigerator 1 week. Makes 1 cup. Serves 8 (2 Tbsp. each).

Calories	Fat	Protein	Carb	Chol	Sodium	Fiber
32	0g	1g	8g	0mg	148mg	1g

216

~ Mayonnaise ~

After you make this easy mayonnaise recipe once, you may alter the ingredients to achieve your preferred taste. Here, it's really more like a tangy salad dressing. For a less-tangy version reduce the vinegar or increase the sugar for a sweeter spread. Use this mayonnaise the same way you would use commercial mayonnaise. Remember, it's free of gluten, dairy, and egg.

¼ cup canola or safflower oil
¼ cup water
2 Tbsp. lemon juice
2 Tbsp. cider vinegar
2 tsp. sweet rice flour
1 tsp. arrowroot
½ tsp. xanthan gum

½ tsp. sugar
¼ tsp. dry mustard*
¼ tsp. salt
⅛ tsp. white pepper
⅛ tsp. cayenne pepper
Grind mustard seeds in small coffee grinder

Combine all ingredients in blender and blend until mixture thickens. Flour. Makes about 1 cup. Store in refrigerator up to 1 week. Serves 8 (2 Tbsp. each).

Calories	Fat	Protein	Carb	Chol	Sodium	Fiber
65	7g	0g	2g	0mg	72mg	0g

~ Mustard ~

3 Tbsp. tapioca flour
⅔ cup water, divided
¼ cup dry mustard*
⅓ cup cider vinegar
2 Tbsp. honey

½ tsp. salt
2 Tbsp. fresh grated horseradish
¼ tsp. ground turmeric
⅛ tsp. paprika
*Grind mustard seeds with small coffee grinder

1. Mix tapioca flour in ¼ cup of the water until paste forms. Set aside. In small saucepan over low-medium heat, mix together dry mustard, vinegar, honey, salt, and remainder of water. Gradually whisk in tapioca flour paste until well blended. Bring to boil, stirring constantly, until mixture thickens.

2. Remove from heat and stir in horseradish, turmeric, and paprika. Refrigerate in airtight container up to1 week. Makes 1 cup. Serves 8 (2 Tbsp. each).

Calories	Fat	Protein	Carb	Chol	Sodium	Fiber
30	0g	0g	8g	0mg	145mg	0g

~ Tomato Ketchup ~

Adjust the spices to suit your family's tastes. You may halve the recipe, if you wish.

1 can (35 oz) canned tomatoes
2 garlic cloves, minced
2 Tbsp. grated fresh ginger
¼ cup cider vinegar
½ tsp. ground cinnamon
¼ cup brown sugar

1 tsp. ground cumin
¼ tsp. cayenne pepper
⅛ tsp. ground allspice
⅛ tsp. ground cloves
½ tsp. salt
¼ tsp. black pepper

1. Place all ingredients in medium, heavy saucepan and bring to boil. Reduce to low and simmer, uncovered, 1 hour or until liquid evaporates. Stir occasionally to avoid scorching. Cool 15 minutes.

2. Transfer mixture to food processor and purée until very smooth. Refrigerate, covered, 2 weeks. Makes 4 cups. Serves 32 (2 Tbsp. each).

Calories	Fat	Protein	Carb	Chol	Sodium	Fiber
11	0g	0g	3g	0mg	39mg	.5g

~ Asian Seasoning ~

Combine with oil and rub on seafood or other meat. One of the easiest ways to crush the toasted sesame seeds is to use a small coffee grinder used only for grinding spices.

2 Tbsp. toasted sesame seeds,
   crushed
1 tsp. ground coriander
1 tsp. ground allspice
1 tsp. onion powder
½ tsp. ground cumin

½ tsp. dried thyme leaves
¼ tsp. ground cinnamon
¼ tsp. ground nutmeg
¼ tsp. cayenne pepper
¼ tsp. salt

Combine ingredients in tightly closed glass container. Store in cool, dark place up to 3 months. Best if used quickly. Makes ¼ cup. Serves 12 (1 tsp. each).

~ Curry Powder ~

Fenugreek and whole curry leaves are unusual and sometimes hard to find— you can omit them, if necessary, with some loss of flavor.

2 tsp. whole coriander seeds
1 tsp. whole cumin seeds
1 tsp. whole fenugreek seeds
½ tsp. whole mustard seeds
4 whole red chiles (or 1 tsp.
   crushed red peppers— not
   cayenne pepper)

1 tsp. whole black peppercorns
10 dried curry leaves (optional)
1 tsp. ground turmeric
½ tsp. ground ginger

1. In small frying pan, toast coriander, cumin, fenugreek, and mustard seeds over medium heat 2-3 minutes until spices become fragrant. Watch carefully; shake pan frequently to prevent burning.

2. Put toasted spices in spice grinder (or small coffee grinder reserved just for spices) and add chiles, peppercorns, curry leaves, turmeric, and ginger. Grind until spices are smooth. Store in airtight glass container in cool, dark place up to 3 months. Makes 3 Tbsp. Serves 8 (1 tsp. each).

~ Fines Herbes ~

Keep this flavorful seasoning on hand to sprinkle on meat, vegetable, or salads.

1 tsp. dried chervil
1 tsp. chives, freeze-dried
1 tsp. dried parsley

¼ tsp. dried tarragon
¼ tsp. salt

Combine all ingredients in airtight, glass container. Store in cool, dark place up to 3 months. Makes 1 ½ Tbsp.

~ Herbes de Provence ~

This is excellent on roasted chicken, steamed vegetables, or in salad dressings.

1 tsp. dried basil leaves
½ tsp. fennel seed, crushed
1 tsp. dried marjoram leaves
1 tsp. dried rosemary, crushed

½ tsp. dried sage leaves
½ tsp. dried thyme leaves
½ tsp. dried lavender (optional)

Combine all ingredients in glass, airtight container. Store in cool, dark place up to 3 months. Makes about 2 Tbsp.

~ Italian Bread Crumbs ~

Italian bread crumbs are so easy to make and add so much flavor to our dining. If you prefer them dry, toast them in a slow oven to desired degree of dryness.

4 cups gf bread torn in small pieces
1 tsp. onion powder

4 tsp. Italian herb seasoning

Place bread in food processor and pulse on/off until crumbs reach desired consistency. Toss with remaining ingredients. Store tightly covered, in refrigerator, up to 2 weeks. Makes 2 cups. Serves 16 (½ cup each).

Calories	Fat	Protein	Carb	Chol	Sodium	Fiber
63	1g	2g	12g	1mg	114mg	1g

~ Italian Herb Seasoning ~

The advantage of making your own spice mixes is that you know they're safe. If any of these spices disagree with you or your family, omit them— or substitute a similar one.

1 Tbsp. dried basil leaves
1 Tbsp. rosemary, crushed
2 tsp. dried majoram leaves
2 tsp. dried thyme leaves
2 tsp. dried oregano leaves

1 tsp. dried sage leaves
1 tsp. onion powder
¼ tsp. black pepper
¼ tsp. cayenne pepper
⅛ tsp. ground nutmeg

Combine all ingredients and store, covered, in dark, dry place. Use within 3 months. Makes 5 Tbsp.

~ Seafood Seasoning ~

Use this seasoning on your favorite seafood by rubbing it on all sides of the fish and then refrigerate for at least 1 hour. Cook as directed.

1 Tbsp. dried thyme leaves
1 Tbsp. dried sage leaves
1 Tbsp. dried marjoram leaves
1 Tbsp. dried savory leaves
2 tsp. freeze-dried chives
1 small bay leaf, crushed
1 tsp. paprika
1 tsp. celery salt

½ tsp. mustard powder*
½ tsp. onion powder
¼ tsp. ground ginger
¼ tsp. ground nutmeg
¼ tsp. ground cardamom
¼ tsp. cayenne pepper
⅛ tsp. ground cloves
Grind mustard seeds with small coffee grinder

Combine all ingredients in glass jar with tightly sealed lid. Store in dark, cool place up to 3 months. Makes about 6 Tbsp.

~ Notes ~

~ APPENDICES ~

Baking with Alternative Sweeteners

Recipes may need some experimenting to achieve desired results.

Liquid Sweeteners

SWEETENER	AMOUNT TO USE	WHEN TO USE
Agave Nectar Honey-like liquid from cactus plant.	1 c. for 1 c. sugar. Reduce liquid ¼ c. per 1 c. agave nectar.	All baked item. Puddings, drinks.
Brown Rice Syrup Made from brown rice. Lundberg is gf. Half as sweet as sugar. Refrigerate.	1 ⅓ c. for 1 c. sugar. Reduce liquid ¼ c. per c. rice syrup. Add ¼ tsp. baking soda per c. of syrup.	Cookies, pies, puddings. Use with other sweeteners in cakes. Crisps baked goods.
Honey From bees. Color, taste depend on flower. 20- 60% sweeter than sugar.	⅔ - ¾ c. for 1 c. sugar. Reduce liquid ¼ c. per c. honey. Add ¼ tsp. baking soda per c. honey. Lower oven 25°.	All baked goods. Don't give honey to children under age 2 because of possible botulism.
Maple Syrup (pure) Maple tree sap. Grade B best in baking. Dark brown.	⅔ - ¾ c for 1 c. white sugar. Reduce liquid by 3 Tbsp. per c. syrup. Add ⅛ tsp. baking soda per c. syrup.	All baked goods, especially cakes. Use organic to avoid formaldehyde and other additives. Refrigerate.
Frozen Fruit Juice Concentrate (apple, white grape, orange, pineapple) Look for *pure* concentrate.	2/3 c. for 1 c. white sugar. Add ¼ tsp. baking soda per recipe. Reduce liquid ⅛ c. per c. concentrate.	Cakes, cookies, bars. For sweeter flavor, simmer juice on low heat until reduced by ⅓. Cool.
Fruit Purée Use baby food fruits or purée fruits in blender.	Prune, apple, apricot, banana, pear. Best as substitute for ½ (not all) sugar or fat.	Baked goods, e.g., prunes in "dark" colored foods, pears in light foods, etc.
Molasses Concentrated sugar cane juice. Strong flavor.	Use ½ c. molasses for 1 c. sugar. Reduce liquid by ¼ c. per c. molasses.	All baked goods; best with spiced cakes, muffins, cookies.

Note: Ask your health professional if these alternative sweeteners are safe for your diet.

Baking with Alternative Sweeteners

Granular Sweeteners

SWEETENER	AMOUNT TO USE	WHEN TO USE
Date Sugar Ground, dehydrated dates. Coarse, sweet brown granules.	⅔ as much as sugar. Best used in combination with other sweeteners. Keep dry, cool. Sift.	Dissolve in hot liquid before using. Burns if baked long time. Use on fruit desserts.
Dried Cane Juice (Sucanat®) Sugar cane. Coarse, amber grains. Molasses taste.	Same amount as sugar. Add ¼ tsp. baking soda per c. dried cane juice. Sift before using. Keep dry, cool.	Cookies, cakes, pies, puddings; not white cakes. Dissolve in hot liquid ingredient for less graininess.
Maple Sugar From maple syrup boiled down to light brown granules.	1 c. maple sugar for 1 c. sugar. Add ⅛ tsp. baking soda for each c. maple sugar.	Dissolve in hot liquid from recipe before using in batters, if possible.
Stevia (white powder) Sweet-leafed herb from Paraguay.	Pinch. 30 to 40 times sweeter than sugar. Slight licorice after-taste.	Recipes need total revision for best results. Best in low-sugar recipes.

FOS (Fructooligosaccharides). White, low-calorie powder— about half as sweet as sugar. Derived from fruit carbohydrates. Best used in combination with caloric sweeteners in baking, but can be used alone to sweeten cereals, beverages, sauces. May cause gas.

Note: Ask your health professional if these alternative sweeteners are safe for your diet.

Baking with Alternative Sweeteners

The following sweeteners are believed to be more highly refined than those on the previous pages. Here are some guidelines to assure successful results.

More Highly Refined Sweeteners

SWEETENER	AMOUNT TO USE	WHEN TO USE
Brown Sugar White sugar with added molasses. May use light or dark version.	1 c. brown sugar in place of 1 c. white sugar.	Lends heartier flavor and darker color in baked goods.
Corn Syrup Produced enzymes on cornstarch. Used in many commercial products.	1 c. corn syrup in place of 1 c. white sugar. Reduce liquid by ¼ to ⅓ c. per c. syrup.	Any baked item that can use honey.
Fructose Granular version usually refined from corn syrup or from fruit sources. Bit sweeter than white sugar. Liquid version also derived from corn.	1 c. fructose in place of 1 c. white sugar. 1 c. liquid fructose in place of 1 c. white sugar. Reduce liquid ¼ - ⅓ c. per c. liquid fructose.	Cakes, cookies, bars, breads, muffins, or any baked item where honey is also appropriate. Use liquid fructose in same way as corn syrup.
Turbinado Raw sugar with impurities removed.	1 c. turbinado in place of 1 c. white sugar.	Any recipe, but works better in darker colored baked goods.

Note: Ask your health professional if these alternative sweeteners are safe for your diet.

Baking with Dairy Substitutes

Milk is one of the easiest ingredients to make substitutions for in baking, although some milk substitutes lend a subtle flavor to baked goods and may affect the degree of browning while baking. In addition, read labels to avoid problem ingredients such as casein or barley malt. Choose low-sugar versions when making savory dishes.

In place of 1 cup of cow's milk, use:

SUBSTITUTE	AMOUNT TO USE	WHEN TO USE
Rice Milk (rice beverage) Choose fortified, gf brands.	1 c. Mild flavor, white color. Looks like skim milk from cows.	Any recipe, but slightly sweet-tasting. Reduce by 2 Tbsp. per c. if used as buttermilk substitute.
Soy Milk (soy beverage) Choose fortified, gf brands.	1 c. Slight soy flavor, light tan in color. Buy in liquid or powder form (to mix with water.) Powdered version makes lighter color milk.	Best in recipes with stronger flavors to mask soy and in baked goods with darker colors since soy milk darkens with heat.
Nut Milk (usually almond) Not for nut allerg-ies or intolerances.	1 c. Mild, slightly nutty flavor. Light brown color.	Best in dessert recipes. Tastes slightly "off" in savory dishes.
Goat Milk Available in pow-der and liquid form (and low-fat liquid) by Meyenberg. Not for milk allergies or lactose-intolerant.	1 c. Most closely resembles cow's milk in color (pure white.)	Any recipe. Works especi-ally well in ice cream, pud-dings and other milk-based dishes. Aseptic and powder-ed varieties have stronger flavor.
Oat Milk	Not recommended for those with gluten-intolerance.	
Coconut Milk	Very high in fat. Not tested with baked goods in this book. However, many people use coconut milk successfully.	

NOTE: Ask your health professional if these alternatives are safe for your diet.

Baking with Dairy Substitutes

In place of 1 cup evaporated skim milk, use:

SUBSTITUTE	AMOUNT TO USE	WHEN TO USE
Ener-G® Nut-Quik or SoyQuik or other non-dairy milk powder.	1 c. Mix at double strength by using twice as much powder.	Recipes using evaporated skim milk. Flavors are stronger. Calories, nutrients double.

In place of 1 cup buttermilk, use:

SUBSTITUTE	AMOUNT TO USE	WHEN TO USE
Use 1-2 Tbsp. fresh lemon juice or cider vinegar and enough rice, soy, or nut milk to equal 1 c.	1 c. Some non-dairy milks produce thinner buttermilk. If so, use 2 Tbsp. less non-dairy buttermilk per c. specified in recipe.	Any recipe calling for buttermilk

If recipe calls for Dry Milk Powder: Use same amount of non-dairy milk powder by Solait, Better Than Milk, or DariFree. Some brands are available in both soy and rice form. Read labels to avoid problem ingredients such as casein. Or, omit dry milk powder and add same amount of sweet rice flour or almond flour (finely ground blanched almonds). Baked goods won't brown as much without dry milk powder. In yeast breads, rising and browning are diminished without milk.

Density of Milk: Reduce liquid by 1 Tbsp. per cup if using skim milk instead of whole milk, or very thin rice milk instead of thicker version. Liquid milk varies by brand. Ratio of powder to water will affect density of milks made from non-dairy powders. Also, increase thickener by 25% when rice milk is used in recipe that is thickened such as pudding Note that plain milk may contain one set of ingredients but flavored versions may contain different ingredients.

Lactose-Reduced Milk: Lactose-reduced milk may be used in these recipes. Be certain to read labels to avoid other offending ingredients. Also, some recipes may not produce the same results as those with "regular" cow's milk or non-dairy milks.

Note: Ask your health professional if these alternatives are safe for your diet.

Baking with Dairy Substitutes

In place of 1 cup yogurt, use:

SUBSTITUTE	AMOUNT TO USE	WHEN TO USE
Goat Yogurt Not for milk allergies or lactose intolerant persons.	1 c.	Any recipe calling for yogurt. However, tapioca in some goat yogurt may make baked item "doughy".
Soy Yogurt	1 c.	Doesn't bake well, but use in dips, ice cream, and other non-baked items. Won't drain.
Non-Dairy Milk Liquid	⅔ c.	Any recipe calling for yogurt. Best to add liquid in ⅓ c. increments to avoid adding too much.

The suggestions offered in this section on dairy substitutes are primarily for baking. However, the same amount of milk beverage substitute such as rice, soy, or nut milk can be used in non-baked items—like milkshakes, puddings, ice cream, or smoothies.

Cheese: Although there are several "non-dairy" cheeses such as Parmesan cheese made from rice, soy, or nuts, it is difficult to find one that doesn't have additional problem ingredients. For example, they may contain milk proteins called calcum caseinate, sodium caseinate, or casein. Others include oats (which is off-limits for celiacs).

Sour Cream and Cream Cheese: Soyco makes rice-based version, but check label for problem ingredients—the milk protein, casein, is present in both items. Soymage makes casein-free sour cream alternative.

Keep in touch with your natural food store. New, non-dairy cheeses are being developed.

Note: Ask your health professional if these alternatives are safe for your diet.

Baking with Egg Substitutes

Eggs are one of the hardest ingredients to exclude because they play such critical roles in baking. They are binding agents (hold ingredients together), moisturizers (add moisture), or leavening agents (make things rise). Generally speaking, egg-free baked goods rise less and have a denser texture. Here are some general guidelines when excluding eggs.

Eggs as Binders:
If recipe has only one egg but contains fair amount of baking powder or baking soda, then the egg is the binder.

In place of 1 large egg as a binder, use:

SUBSTITUTE	AMOUNT TO USE	WHEN TO USE
Tofu (soft silken) by Mori-Nu®	¼ c. for each egg. Blend with recipe liquid until very smooth.	Cakes, cookies, breads. Baked goods won't brown as deeply. Makes very moist, heavy baked goods.
Puréed fruits /vegetables Baby food without fillers (apples, pears)	3 Tbsp. to replace each egg. Increase liquid in recipe by 1 Tbsp.	Baked goods where purée flavor complements or doesn't detract from dish's flavor.
Unflavored Gelatin Powder Knox or Grayslake brand	Mix 1 envelope gelatin in 1 c. boiling water. Use 3 Tbsp. for each egg. Refrigerate.	Baked goods such as cookies, cakes, breads. Microwave to liquefy.
Arrowroot, Soy, Lecithin (liquid or granular lecithin)	Mix ¼ c. warm water, 2 Tbsp. arrowroot, 1 Tbsp. soy flour, and ¼ tsp. lecithin.	Stronger flavored dishes since soy flour and lecithin may affect overall taste of dish.
Flaxseed (brown or golden seeds or ground flaxmeal). Refrigerate all flax products.	¼ c. flax mix. Soak 1 tsp. ground flaxseed in ¼ c. boiling water 5 min. Bake slightly longer; 25° lower. Reduce oil 1 to 2 Tbsp.	Cool before using Best in dark color dishes. Mild flavor. Baked goods heavier, denser. Best in cookies, bars. Slight laxative.

Note: Ask your health professional if these alternatives are safe for your diet.

Baking with Egg Substitutes

Liquid Egg Substitutes: You may use liquid egg substitutes in place of fresh eggs, but they still contain eggs. The yolks have been removed to reduce fat and cholesterol. *People with egg allergies must not eat these products because they still contain eggs. Also, some egg substitutes contain other problem ingredients— which may or may not be wheat-based.* Read the label.

Eggs as Leavening Agents:
If there are no other ingredients to make baked item rise, then the egg is the leavening agent.

In place of 1 egg as leavener, use:

SUBSTITUTE	AMOUNT TO USE	WHEN TO USE
Ener-G ® Egg Replacer	Ener-G® suggests 1 ½ tsp. powder mixed in 2 Tbsp. water. 2-3 times as much powder gives better results.	All baked goods. Flavorless; won't affect taste of recipe. For added lightness, whip in food processor or blender for 30 seconds.
Buttermilk-Soda	Replace recipe liquid with same amount of buttermilk or thinned yogurt. Replace baking powder with ¼ as much baking soda.	All baked goods; works best in dishes that don't require lot of "rising", such as cookies, bars and flatbreads.

Other Hints when Omitting Eggs (if eggs are leavening)
1. Add air to lighten recipe by creaming fat and sweetener together with electric mixer. Then add dry ingredients.

2. Whip liquid ingredients in food processor or blender for 30 seconds.

3. Add extra ½ tsp. baking powder per egg, not to exceed 1 tsp. baking powder per cup of flour. Too much baking powder produces bitterness.

4. Recipes with acidic liquids such as buttermilk, molasses, lemon juice, or vinegar tend to rise better than those with non-acidic liquids such as water or milk.

Note: Ask your health professional if these alternatives are safe for your diet.

Baking with Egg Substitutes

Eggs as Moisture:
The egg's purpose is to add moisture if there are leavening agents in the recipe, but not much water or other liquid in the recipe.

Generally speaking, baked goods without eggs are somewhat heavier and more dense. Slightly increase the leavening agent in egg-free recipes to compensate for the egg's natural leavening effect. In addition, using liquid sweeteners such as honey or molasses for part of the sugar in a recipe helps compensate for the loss of the "binding" effect of eggs.

In place of 1 egg as a moisturizer, use:

SUBSTITUTE	AMOUNT TO USE	WHEN TO USE
Fruit juice, milk, or water	2 Tbsp. Increase leavening by 25-50%. May need to bake items slightly longer.	Baked goods such as cakes, cookies, bars
Puréed fruit: Bananas, applesauce, apricots, pears, prunes. (The natural pectin in fruits, especially prunes, traps air which helps "lighten" baked goods.)	Use ¼ c. Increase leavening agent by 25-50%. May need to bake items slightly longer.	Baked goods where the fruit's flavor complements the overall dish such as applesauce in spice cakes, bananas in banana bread, apricots and pears in mild-flavored items, and prunes in dark, heavily-flavored items such as chocolate or spice cakes.

Note: Ask your health professional if these alternatives are safe for your diet.

Baking with Wheat-Free Flours

This table presents a summary of the baking characteristics, color, flavor, and storage recommendations for gluten-free flours and grains.

FLOUR	CHARACTERISTICS
Arrowroot	
Baking	Good in baking; adds no flavor of its own and lightens baked goods. Produces golden brown crust in breading. Twice the thickening power of wheat flour.
Color/Flavor	Snow white in color. Looks like cornstarch. Flavorless.
Comments	Silky, fine powder from West Indies root. Replaces cornstarch or tapioca flour in baking.
Storage	Air-tight containers in cool, dry, dark place.
Bean	
Baking	Two kinds (1) pure garbanzo or chickpea flour, and (2) blend of garbanzo(chickpea) and broad (fava) beans Provide beneficial protein for baking. May replace rice flour.
Color/Flavor	Light tan or yellowish. Slight "beany" flavor with pure chickpeas or garbanzo beans—less with garbanzo/fava bean combination. Latter lends slightly sweeter taste in baking.
Comments	Adds beneficial protein to "starchy" gluten-free flour blends.
Storage	Air-tight containers in cool, dry, dark place.
Cornmeal	
Baking	Excellent in corn bread, muffins, and waffles—especially when blended with other flours.
Color/Flavor	White or yellow. Tastes like corn.
Comments	Coarser than corn flour. Often used in Mexican dishes. Used in Polenta.
Storage	Air-tight container in cool, dry, dark place.

Note: Ask your health professional if these alternatives are safe for your diet.

Baking with Wheat-Free Flours

FLOUR	CHARACTERISTICS
Cornstarch	
Baking	Lightens baked goods, but use only in combination with other flours—not alone. Thickens sauces and gravies.
Color/Flavor	Snow white. Flavorless, but more noticeable than arrowroot.
Comments	Highly refined; contributes little nutritional value.
Storage	Air-tight container in cool, dry, dark place.
Potato Starch	
Baking	Excellent baking properties, especially when combined with eggs. Lumps easily, so stir before measuring.
Color/Flavor	Very white. Bland flavor.
Comments	Very fine, powdery texture. Made from starch in potatoes. Not potato flour, which is made from dried, whole potatoes.
Storage	Air-tight container in cool, dry, dark place.
Rice–White	
Baking	Dry, gritty; better when combined with other flours. Should be about ⅔ of total flour. Coarser grinds need more liquid.
Color/Flavor	White. Bland, pleasant-tasting flavor.
Comments	Milled from broken hulls of rice kernel. Bran layers milled away; mostly starch. Among least "allergenic" of flours.
Storage	Air-tight container in cool, dry, dark place.
Rice–Brown	
Baking	Dry, gritty— but excellent in baked goods.
Color/Flavor	Off-white. Mild flavor. Baked goods slightly ivory-colored.
Comments	More nutrients than white rice; still contains bran. Refrigerate to avoid rancidity.

Note: Ask your health professional if these alternatives are safe for your diet.

Baking with Wheat-Free Flours

FLOUR	CHARACTERISTICS
Sorghum	Also called milo.
Baking	Somewhat dry--increase liquid and oil by 5-15%. Works very well in egg-free recipes.
Color/Flavor	Light tan. Mild flavor, somewhat closer to wheat.
Comments	Introduces variety and more protein into gluten-free diet.
Storage	Air-tight container in cool, dry, dark place.
Soy	
Baking	Excellent. Works well in baked goods with nuts, fruits, or chocolate. Adds moisture to baked goods.
Color/Flavor	Yellow. Bland, somewhat nutty or beany flavor. Can be camouflaged by mixing with spices, fruit, nuts, or chocolate.
Comments	Makes crispy breading. Higher in protein, fat than other flours. Short shelf life; buy small amounts to avoid spoilage.
Storage	Air-tight container. Refrigerate.
Sweet Rice	
Baking	Not the same as white rice flour. Use in small amounts in blends. Helps bind baked goods because of its sticky nature.
Color/Flavor	White, bland in flavor. Easily confused with white rice flour.
Comments	Sometimes called sticky glutinous rice but contains no wheat gluten. Good thickener; sauce won't separate when chilled.
Storage	Air-tight container in cool, dark, dry place.
Tapioca	
Baking	Excellent in baked products as 25-50% of total flour. Lightens baked goods; adds "chewiness" to breads. Browns crust.
Color/Flavor	Snow-white, velvety powder. "Anonymous" flavor.
Comments	From cassava plant. Use like arrowroot.
Storage	Air-tight container in cool, dark, dry place.

Note: Ask your health professional if these alternatives are safe for your diet.

Substitutes for Wheat as Thickener

In place of 1 tablespoon of wheat flour, use the following:

INGREDIENT	TRAITS	SUGGESTED USES
Agar (Kanten) 1 ½ tsp.	Use package directions. Colorless/flavorless. Sets at room temp. Gels acidic liquids. Thin sauces need less.	Puddings, pie fillings, gelatin desserts, ice cream, glazes, cheese. Holds moisture and improves texture in pastry products.
Arrowroot 1 ½ tsp.	Mix in cold water first. Thickens at lower temps. Don't boil. Add during last 5 min. of cooking. Serve immediately. Clear, shiny. Semi-soft when cool.	Any food requiring clear, shiny sauce, but good for egg or starch dishes where high heat is undesirable. Gives appearance of oil even if none used.
Bean Flour 3 tsp.	Produces yellowish, rich-looking sauce.	Soups, stews, gravies but lends "bean" flavor.
Cornstarch 1 ½ tsp.	Mix in cold water first. Stir just until boiling. Makes clear, shiny sauce. Firms when cool.	Puddings, pie fillings, fruit sauces, soups. Gives appearance of oil if none used.
Gelatin Powder 1 ½ tsp.	Dissolve in cold water, then heat until liquid is clear before using.	Jello puddings, aspics, cheesecakes. Won't gel acids like fresh pineapple.
Guar Gum 1 ½ tsp.	Mix with liquid first.	Large amounts are laxative.
Kudzu (kuzu) Powder ¾ tsp.	Dissolve in cold water first. Odorless, tasteless. Makes smooth, transparent, soft sauces.	Puddings, pie fillings, and other dishes that must have "gelatin-like" consistency
Sweet Rice Flour 1 Tbsp.	Excellent thickener. Called "glutinous" rice.	Sauces such as vegetable sauces. (Has no gluten)
Rice Flour (brown or white) 1 Tbsp.	Mix with cold liquid first. Somewhat grainy.	Soups, stews, or gravies or hearty, robust sauces

Note: Ask your health professional if these alternatives are safe for your diet.

Substitutes for Wheat as Thickener

In place of 1 tablespoon of wheat flour:

INGREDIENT	TRAITS	SUGGESTED USES
Tapioca Flour 1 ½ Tbsp.	Mix with cold water first. Add during last 5 min. of cooking. Produces transparent, shiny sauce. Thick, soft gel when cool.	Soups, stews, gravies, potato dishes
Quick-Cooking Tapioca – 2 tsp.	Mix with fruit, let stand 15 min. before baking.	Fruit pies, cobblers, and tapioca pudding
Xanthan Gum 1 tsp.	Mix with dry ingredients first; add to recipe.	Puddings, salad dressings, and gravies

Wheat Flour Equivalents

Use this table to convert your own recipes to gluten-free—or to modify recipes in this book. Each flour has unique characteristics that affect the texture, taste, and appearance of baked goods.

In place of 1 cup of wheat flour, use:

FLOUR	AMOUNT
Corn	1 cup
Cornmeal	¾ cup
Cornstarch	¾ cup
Garbanzo (chickpea)	¾ cup
Garbanzo/fava (broad) bean	⅞ cup (use 1:1 ratio if <1 cup flour)
Nuts (ground fine)	½ cup
Potato starch or potato starch flour	¾ cup
Rice (brown or white)	⅞ cup
Sorghum (milo)	⅞ cup
Soy	½ cup + ½ cup potato starch flour
Sweet rice	⅞ cup
Tapioca or tapioca starch	1 cup

Flours from reputable sources usually measure consistently time after time, although differences in flour milling processes may affect consistency and texture. As you become more experienced with these flours, you can judge if the dough is too dry, too moist, or just right.

NOTE: Ask your health professional if these alternatives are safe for your diet.

Hidden Sources of Wheat & Gluten

Wheat flour is present in many products, but it isn't always listed as such. Avoid products containing ingredients such as all-purpose flour, unbleached flour, bread flour, cake flour, whole-wheat flour, semolina, or durum — these are alternate terms for wheat flour. And, yes—white bread contains wheat. Check whether your food is prepared in the same receptacle or manufacturing line as gluten-containing foods or somehow contaminated with gluten—even though not listed as an ingredient. This list may change over time, so continue to read labels.

• **Beverages:** See www.celiac.com for an updated list of gluten-free beverages.

• **Breads:** Unless label says "gluten-free", avoid biscuits, breads, crackers, croutons, crumbs, doughnuts, tortillas, or wafers. Avoid breads made of oats, spelt, kamut, barley and rye because they contain gluten.

• **Candy:** Wheat may be an ingredient (for example, licorice contains wheat flour) or used in shaping or handling of candy.

• **Caramel Color:** Manufactured by only two companies in the U.S. and generally believed to be gluten-free, whether in liquid or powdered form.

• **Caramel Flavoring:** Made by several different companies, processes may vary. Therefore, it <u>may</u> contain malt syrup or wheat starch.

• **Cereal:** Avoid those made from wheat, rye, oats, barley, spelt, and kamut or if they contain malt flavoring or malt syrup. Cereals from amaranth, sorghum, buckwheat, and Montina are gluten-free.

• **Coffee:** Some flavored and instant coffee beverages aren't gluten-free.

• **Condiments and Baking Ingredients:** Check labels, especially on baking powder, mayonnaise, salad dressings, and most soy sauces. Look for gluten-free versions (e.g., wheat-free tamari soy sauce)

• **Dairy Products:** Some flavored yogurts contain modified food starch (which could be wheat). Look for those with pectin (this is fruit). Malted milk, processed cheese spreads, and chocolate milk may contain wheat. Low-fat sour cream may contain wheat.

Hidden Sources of Wheat & Gluten

• **Desserts and Other Sweets:** Avoid commercial pudding mixes, cake decorations, and marzipan because wheat flour is a thickener or binder.

• **Distilled Vinegar:** Basic vinegar (except malt) is gluten-free because gluten peptides cannot survive the distillation process.

• **Hydrolyzed Plant Protein (HPP):** Can be made from wheat starch.

• **Hydrolyzed Vegetable Protein (HVP):** Label must list source.

• **Flavorings and Extracts:** Vanilla is safe for same reason as vinegar.

• **Meat, Fish, and Eggs:** Avoid any meat that's breaded or where fillers might be used such as sausage, luncheon meats, or hot-dogs. Avoid self-basting turkeys. Buy low-salt tuna in spring water rather than oil. Egg-substitutes are not pure eggs but often contain many other additional ingredients—possibly wheat flour.

• **Modified Food Starch:** In U.S.-made foods, this is corn but could be other grains if made outside U.S. Label should list source.

• **Pastas**: Oriental rice noodles, bean threads, and commercial pasta made from rice, corn, tapioca, or potato are safe. Read labels since some pasta contains wheat along with gluten-free flours.

• **Soups and Chowders:** Many canned soups, soup mixes, and bouillon cubes/granules contain hydrolyzed vegetable protein (HVP) which may contain wheat.

• **Texturized Vegetable Protein (TVP):** Can contain wheat.

• **Vegetables:** Avoid vegetables that are breaded, creamed, or scalloped because this usually involves wheat flour or bread crumbs made from wheat flour. When you see "vegetable starch" or "vegetable protein" on a label, this could mean protein from corn, peanuts, rice, soy—or wheat.

An excellent resource to help you know which commercial products are gluten-free is the Celiac Sprue Association's Cooperative Gluten-Free Commercial Products Listing or the guide from Tri-County Celiac Support Group. See Associations & Resources in the Appendix.

Hidden Sources of Dairy Products

Milk and milk products are hidden in many foods. Your food choices should be guided by whether you are lactose-intolerant or allergic to milk proteins. Many words indicate milk— casein is a milk protein; whey, another protein, is the liquid derived from drained yogurt. Other terms to avoid are: acidolphilus, caseinate, calcium caseinate, hydrolyzed milk protein or vegetable protein, lactalbumin, lactate, lactoglobulin, lactose, and potassium caseinate. Below is a partial list of hidden dairy sources.

Baked Goods/Cooking Ingredients
Bread
Biscuits
Cakes
Caramel Coloring or Flavoring
Chocolate
Cookies
Doughnuts
Hot Cakes
Malted Milk
Mixes for Cakes, Cookies, Doughnuts,
       Muffins, Pancakes, etc.
Ovaltine (and other cocoa drinks)
Pie Crust (made with milk products)
Soda Crackers
Zwieback

Casseroles/Side Dishes
Creamed Vegetables
Hash
Mashed Potatoes
Scalloped Dishes
Dishes in Au Gratin Style
Fritters
Rarebits

Dairy
Buttermilk
Cheese
Condensed Milk
Cream
Cream Cheese
Evaporated Milk
Ice Cream
Ghee (clarified butter)
Milk (all forms)
Non-Dairy Creamer
Skim Milk Powder
Sour Cream
Yogurt
Whey

Desserts
Bavarian Cream
Candies
Custard
Ice Cream, Sherbet
Sorbet (some versions)
Spumoni
Pudding

Egg Dishes
Omelets
Scrambled Eggs
Soufflés

Meats/Fish
Canned Tuna
Deli Turkey
Hamburgers
Meats Fried in Butter
Sausages

Sauces/Salad Dressings
Butter Sauces
Cream Sauces
Gravies
Hard Sauces
Mayonnaise (some brands)
Salad Dressings (some)

Soups
Bisques
Chowders

Pharmaceuticals

Hidden Sources of Eggs

Many commercially prepared foods— or ingredients used to prepare your own dishes— contain eggs. Here is a partial list of those items. Be sure to read labels and remember that the ingredient list may not specifically mention the word eggs, but instead use words such as albumin, livetin, ovaglubin egg albumin, ovamucin, ovumucoid, ovovitellin, lysozyme, or egg whites, egg yolks, egg solids, or egg powder.

Baked Goods/Cooking Ingredients
Baking Powder
Batters for Deep-Frying
Breads
Breaded Foods
Cakes
Cake Flour
Cinnamon Rolls
Cookies
Donuts
French Toast
Fritters
Frostings
Icings
Malted Cocoa Drinks
Marshmallows
Muffins
Pancake Flour
Pancakes
Pancake Mixes
Pretzels
Waffles
Waffle Mixes

Condiments/Sauces
Hollandaise Sauce
Salad Dressings (especially boiled ones)
Sauces (may be thickened with eggs)
Tartar Sauce

Desserts
Bavarian Cream
Ice Cream
Ices
Macaroons
Meringues
Pies (Cream pie filling and
    some pie crusts)
Puddings
Sherbets
Soufflés

Meats/Meat-Related Dishes
Bouillon
Hamburger Mix
Meat Loaf
Meat Balls
Meat Jellies
Meat Molds
Pate (also called Fois Gras)
Patties
Sausages
Soups (e.g., consommés)
Spaghetti & Meatballs

Beverages
Eggnog
Malted Cocoa Drinks (e.g. Ovaltine)
Wines (may be "cleared" with egg
    whites)

Other
Pasta (and dishes containing pasta)
Tartar Sauce

Hidden Sources of Corn

Corn appears in many unsuspecting places as an emulsifier, sweetener, or main ingredient.

Baked Goods/Cooking Ingredients
Baking Mixes for Biscuits, Doughnuts,
    Pancakes and Pies
Baking Powder
Batters and Deep-Frying Mixtures
Bleached Wheat Flour
Breads and Pastries
Cakes
Cookies
Cereals
Corn Syrup
Cream Pies
Glucose Products
Graham Crackers
Oleo
Powdered Sugar
Tortillas
Vanilla
Vinegar (distilled)
Xanthan gum

Beverages
Ales, Beer
Bourbon, Whisky
Carbonated Beverages
Instant Coffee
Milk (in paper cartons)
Fruit Juices
Grape Juice (look for pure grape juice)
Soy Milk
Tea (instant)
Wines (some contain corn)

Non-Food Items
Adhesives and Glue
Bath Powder
Envelopes, Stamps
Plastic Food Wrappers
Talcum Powder
Toothpaste

Condiments/Sauces/Snacks
Catsup
Cheese
Commercial Syrups (e.g., Karo)
Fritos, Tortilla Chips
Peanut Butter
Popcorn
Salad Dressings (e.g., French)
Soups (cream-style)

Desserts
Candy
Frosting
Gelatins or Jello
Ice Cream, Sherbet
Jams, Jellies
Puddings or Custards
Sauces for Cakes or Sundaes

Meats/Side Dishes
Bacon
Bologna
Canned Peas
Chili
Chop Suey
Gravies, sauces for meats
Grits
Hams
Sandwich Spread
Sausage
Vegetables (in cream sauces)

Pharmaceuticals/Drugs/Additives
Aspirin, Cough Syrup, and other tablets
Dextrin, Dextrose
Mannitol
MSG (Monosodium Glutamate)
Nutra-Sweet, Splenda
Sorbitol
Vitamin C Preparations

Hidden Sources of Soy

Soy appears in many commercially prepared foods as well as many ingredients.

Baked Goods/Cooking Ingredients
Breads
Cakes
Cereals
Cooking Spray
Crackers
Lecithin (derived from soy)
Oils
Oleo or Margarine
Pastries
Rolls
Shortening

Beverages
Coffee Substitutes
Lemonade Mix
Soy Milk

Condiments/Sauces/Snacks/Soups
Butter Substitutes
Cheese
Soy Sauce (and other Oriental sauces)
Worcestershire Sauce
Salad Dressings
Soup

Desserts
Caramel
Candies
Candy Bars
Custards
Ice Cream
Nut Candies

Meats/Meat-Related Dishes
Luncheon Meats
Sausage (certain kinds)

Miscellaneous
Baby Foods
Bean Sprouts
Pasta from Soy Flour
Tempura
Tofu

Associations & Resources

The following is a partial list of resources for people on gluten-free diets. Ask your physician about local support groups for people with food allergies, celiac disease, diabetes, or other conditions where certain ingredients must be omitted from one's diet. This partial list is offered as a resource and is not intended as an endorsement of any kind.

Allergy/Asthma Network, MOA Inc. 3554 Chain Ridge Road, Suite 200 Fairfax, VA 22030-2709 (800) 878-4403 (help line) (703) 385-4403	Amer. Acad. Allergy, Asth/Immun.. 611 E. Wells Street Milwaukee, WI 53202 (800) 822-2762 (help line) (414) 272-6071
American Diabetes Association 1660 Duke Street Alexandria, VA 22314 800.DIABETES or 800.232.3472 www.diabetes.org	American Dietetic Association 120 S. Riverside Plaza, Suite 2000 Chicago, Ill., 60606 312.899.0040 or 800.366.1655 www.eatright.org
Asthma/Allergy Foundation of America 1125 15th Street, N.W., Suite 502 Washington, D.C. 20005 800.7ASTHMA; 202.466.7643 fax aafasupgr@aol.com or www.aafa.org	Celiac Disease Foundation 13251 Ventura Blvd., Suite 1 Studio City, CA 91604-1838 818.990.2354; 818.990.2379 fax www.celiac.org/cdf
Celiac Sprue Association/USA PO Box 31700 Omaha, NE 68131-0700 402.558.0600; 402.558.1347 fax www.csaceliacs.org	Food Allergy & Anaphylaxis Network (FAAN) 10400 Eaton Place, Ste.107 Fairfax, VA 22030 800.929.4040 or 703.691.3179 www.foodallergy.org
Gluten-Free Living (newsletter) PO Box 105 Hastings-on-Hudson, NY 10706 914.969.2018;914.969.2018 fax	Gluten Intolerance Group of NA - (GIG) 15110 10th Ave. SW Suite A Seattle, WA 98166-1820 206.246.6652; 206.246.6531 fax www.gluten.net
Living Without (magazine): A lifestyle guide for people with food/chemical sensitivities PO Box 2126 Northbrook, IL 60065 847.480.8810; 847.480.8819 fax www.livingwithout.com	National Jewish Center/Medical Research 1400 Jackson Street Denver, CO 80206 (800) 222-5864 (LungLine) (303) 388-4461 www.njc.org

Mail Order Sources
For Gluten-Free Ingredients & Products

If you don't have a natural food or specialty food store nearby, the following are mail-order companies. This list is offered as a convenience and is not intended as an endorsement of any particular company. Nor is it intended to be a complete list of mail-order sources. The names, addresses, phone (or fax) numbers, and e-mail addresses of these companies may have changed as well as the product lines they carry.

Authentic Foods 1850 W. 169th Street, Suite B Gardena, CA 90247 800.806.4737; 310.366.6938 fax www.authenticfoods.com flours, ingredients, mixes	Bob's Red Mill Natural Foods 5209 S.E. International Way Milwaukie, OR 97222 800.553.2258; 503.653.1339 fax www.Bobsredmill.com flours, grains, mixes
Cybros, Inc. 417 Barney Street Waukesha, WI 53186 800.876.2253 bakery items	Dowd & Rogers 1641 49th St. Sacramento, CA 95819 916.451.6480; 916.736.2349 fax www.dowdandrogers.com chestnut flour mixes
Dietary Specialties 1248 Sussex Tnpke, Unit C-2 Randolph, NJ 07869 888.640.2800 www.dietspec.com foods, ingredients	Ener-G Foods, Inc. P.O. Box 84487 Seattle, WA 98124-5787 800.331.5222; 206.764.3398 fax www.ener-g.com flours, ingredients, mixes
Enjoy Life Foods 1601 Natchez Avenue Chicago, IL 60707-4023 888.50.ENJOY; 773.889.5090 fax www.enjoylifefoods.com cookies, bars, bagels	Gluten-Free Exchange www.gfexchange.com T-shirts, stickers, magnets

Mail Order Sources
For Wheat-Free/Gluten-Free Ingredients & Products

Gluten Solutions, Inc. 737 Manhattan Beach Blvd, #B Manhattan Beach, CA 90266 888.845-8836; 810.454.8277 fax www.glutensolutions.com mixes, ingredients, books, food	Gluten Free Market Rt. 83 and Lake Cook Rd Buffalo Grove, IL 60089 847.419.9610; 847.419.9615 fax www.glutenfreemarket.com foods, ingredients, books
Gluten-Free Pantry PO Box 881 Glastonbury, CT 06033 203.633.3826; 860.633.6853 fax www.glutenfree.com mixes, ingredients, appliances	Gluten Free Mall www.glutenfreemall.com many vendors offering flours, ingredients, mixes, food, bakery items, books, etc. (also see www.celiac.com)
Gluten-Free Trading Co., LLC 604A W. Lincoln Avenue Milwaukee, WI 53215 888.993.9933; 414.385.9915 fax www.gluten-free.net flours, ingredients, mixes	Glutino.com (DEROMA) 1118 Berlier, Laval, Quebec Canada H7L-3R9 800.363.DIET; 450.629.4781 fax www.glutino.com mixes, ingredients, baked items
Goodday Health 514A North Western Ave. Lake Forest, IL 60045 877.395.2527; 847.615.1209 fax gooddayglutenfree@msn.com gluten-free items, all major vendors	Jo's Spices (Healthy Exchanges) PO Box 124, 110 Industrial St. DeWitt, IA 52742 319.659.8234; 319.659.2126 fax www.healthyexchanges.com spice blends
King Arthur Flour PO Box 876 Norwich, VT 05055-0876 800.827.6836; 800.343.3002 fax www.bakerscatalogue.com flours, xanthan gum, mixes	Miss Roben's PO Box 1434 Frederick, MD 21702 800.891.0083; 301.631.5954 fax www.missroben.com baking mixes, ingredients
Montina (Amazing Grains) 405 West Main Ronan, MT 59864 877.278.6585; 406.676.0677 fax www.montina.com Indian rice grass flour and foods	Pamela's Products (cookies, mixes) 364 Littlefield Avenue South San Francisco, CA 94080 415.952.4546; 415.742.6643 fax www.pamelasproducts.com available from gluten-free vendors

Mail Order Sources
For Wheat-Free/Gluten-Free Ingredients & Products

Kinnikinnick Foods 10940-120 Street Edmonton, AB,Canada, T5H 3P7 877.503.4466 www.kinnikinnick.ca flours, foods, ingredients	Sylvan Border Farms P.O. Box 277 Willits, CA 95490-0277 800.297.5399; 707.459.1834 fax www.sylvanborderfarm.com mixes using quinoa, amaranth, etc.
Tri-County Celiac Support Group 47819 Vistas Circle Canton, MI 48788 gluten-free product list	Twin Valley Mills, LLC R.R. 1, Box 45 Ruskin, NE 68974 402.279.3965 www.twinvalleymills.com sorghum flour
Vance's Foods P.O. Box 255734 Sacramento, California 95865 800.497.4834; 800-497-4329 fax www.vancesfoods.com gluten-free milk powder and liquid	

Internet Support Lists
These Internet news groups provide discussions on important topics:

Celiac Disease, Wheat Sensitivities, and Celiacs with Diabetes
http://www.enabling.org/ia/celiac/index.html

Dairy Sensitivities: To join, in the body of an e-mail to:
listserv@MAELSTROM.stjohns.edu send the following:
SUB NO-MILK firstname lastname

Also, see www.celiac.com for a wealth of information on the gluten-free diet.

Cooking Oils

Consult with your health professional about which oil is best for you. Use this chart to help in your decision. The lower the smoking point, the more quickly the oil burns.

Oil	% Saturated	% Poly-unsaturated	% Mono-unsaturated	Smoking Point
Canola	6	32	62	400°
Safflower (refined)	10	77	13	450°
Sunflower	11	69	20	450°
Corn (unrefined)	13	62	25	320°
Olive	14	9	77	350°
Soy	15	61	24	450°

Source: *Compositions of Foods*, USDA

Raw & Cooked Food Equivalents

This handy chart shows how much raw food converts to cooked food.

Amount	Measure	Amount	Measure
Berries		Flour	
1 pt.	2 ¾ c.	1 lb.	4 c.
Butter/Margarine		Herbs	
1 stick	½ cup (8 Tbsp.)	1 Tbsp. fresh	1 tsp. dried
1 lb.	4 sticks/2 c.		
Cheese		Pasta	
8 oz. cream cheese	1 c.	8 oz elbow	4 c. cooked
8 oz. cottage cheese	1 c.	8 oz. noodles	3 ¾ c. cooked
4 oz. Parmesan	1 ¼ c.	8 oz. angelhair	5 ½ c. cooked
		8 oz. spaghetti	4 c. cooked
Chocolate		Rice	
1 square	1 oz.	1 c. white	3 c. cooked
1 square	3 Tbsp. cocoa + 1 Tbsp. oil	1 cup brown	3-4 c. cooked
		1 cup instant	1 ½ c. cooked
Cream		Sugar	
1 c. heavy cream	2 cups whipped	1 lb. granulated	2 c.
		1 lb. brown	2 ¼ c.
		1 lb. powdered	4 ½ c.
Dried Beans/Peas			
1 c.	2 ¼ c. cooked		

Appliances, Pans, & Utensils

Appliances

People often ask me what type of appliances I use when developing recipes for my cookbooks. I use Breadman, Welbilt, and Zojirushi bread machines. When mixing large recipes or heavy bread dough by hand, I use a 4.5 quart KitchenAid stand mixer with regular beaters— not dough hooks.

For cake, cookie batters, and cooking class demonstrations, I use a hand-held Hamilton Beach mixer. My KitchenAid food processor (using knife blade) is fabulous for blending batter. It is very fast and does a better job of distributing the moisture throughout the ingredients than an electric mixer. In fact, I wouldn't be without this indispensable appliance (cheaper versions are $40 at discount stores.)

My range is an electric Jenn-Air and I have two ovens: a Jenn-Air and a KitchenAid. Remember that different brands and types may produce slightly different outcomes. Follow the directions exactly the first time you make any recipe; then make changes as needed— such as longer or shorter baking times.

I love my small, handheld coffee grinder. About $10, it grinds mustards seeds into mustard powder perfectly. To clean coffee grinder, pulverize a tablespoon of white rice kernels, discard rice, and wipe clean with damp paper towel. Avoid using the same grinder for grinding coffee. I use a microplane zester to grate lemon peel.

Pans

I bake almost exclusively in gray (not black) nonstick pans because gluten-free batters tend to stick and their finish helps the browning process. Insulated baking pans tend to make baked goods somewhat soggy (except for some cookies). Be sure to use non-scratch utensils. Baking in several smaller pans in place of one large pan assures that the finished product will rise and bake thoroughly.

Pan Substitutions

When choosing pan sizes, measure across top of pan, from inside edge to inside edge. For fluted baking molds, measure from inside edge of outward curve to inside of exact opposite curve. Measure depth on inside vertical from bottom of dish or pan to top edge. To determine volume of pan or dish, fill with water. Then, pour water into measuring cup.

Pan or Dish	Equivalent in Cups
13 x 9-inch baking dish	12 - 15 cups
10 x 4-inch tube pan	12 cups
10 x 3 1/2-inch Bundt pan	12 cups
9 x 3-inch tube pan	9 cup
9 x 3-inch Bundt pan	9 cups
11 x 7-inch baking dish	8 cups
8-inch square baking dish	8 cups
9 x 5-inch loaf pan	8 cups
9-inch deep-dish pie plate	6 - 8 cups
9 x 1 1/2-inch cake pan	6 cups
7 1/2 x 3-inch Bundt pan	6 cups
9 x 1 1/2-inch cake pan	5 cups
8 x 1 1/2-inch cake pan	4 - 5 cups
8 x 4-inch loaf pan	4 cups

Here are the most common sizes for various pots and pans.

Dutch Ovens
Small = 2 qt.
Medium = 6 qt.
Large = 8 qt.

Shallow Baking Dishes
Small = 1 qt.
Medium = 2 qt.
Large = 3 qt.

Roasting Pans
Small = 13 x 9 x 2 in.
Medium = 14 x 11 x 2 in.
Large = 16 x 13 x 3 in.

Skillets
Small = 7 or 8- in. diameter
Medium = 9 or 10-in. diameter
Large = 11 or 12-in. diameter

Saucepans
Small = 1 quart
Medium = 1 ½ - 2 quarts
Large = 4 quarts

Stockpots
Small = 6-8 quarts
Medium = 12 quarts
Large = 16-20 quarts

Utensils & Other Helpers
Use serrated knives or electric knives for cutting breads or pie crust. Use waxed paper or parchment paper for baked goods that must be removed from the pan whole, rather than sliced.

~ INDEX ~

Meet Carol Fenster, Ph.D.

What began as a solution to her own wheat intolerance grew into an internationally-recognized publishing house serving people with food allergies, celiac disease, and autism.

Today, Carol has published five books and is actively involved and recognized as a leader in the area of food sensitivities:

▪ She is Associate Food Editor of the magazine, *Living Without: A Lifestyle Guide for People with Food & Chemical Sensitivities.*

▪ She appears on several episodes of "Food for Life", an allergy-free cooking show on The Health Network.

▪ She developed the new gluten-free mixes for Bob's Red Mill Natural Foods, an industry leader. She consults with other manufacturers, teaches cooking classes, and lectures at the University of Colorado @ Denver's Business School.

▪ She is an international consultant, traveling to Japan on behalf of the U.S. Grains Council to conduct seminars on the use of sorghum in gluten-free diets.

▪ Her articles appear in *Veggie Life* magazine and the *Food Allergy & Anaphylaxis Network* (FAAN) newsletter.

▪ Her books are recognized by the Gluten Intolerance Group of North America, Celiac Disease Foundation, and Celiac Sprue Association as important resources for celiacs. Many autism organizations support her work. York Nutritional Laboratories, an international allergy testing firm, recommends her books to patients.

▪ She has a home economics degree from the University of Nebraska. Her doctorate is in Organizational Sociology from the University of Denver, where she was also a faculty member. To contact her:

Savory Palate, Inc.
8174 South Holly, #404
Centennial, CO 80122-4004
(800) 741-5418
http//www.savorypalate.com   carol@savorypalate.com

~ Notes ~

~ Notes ~

~ Notes ~

Go Gluten-Free Today! Order Now!

Name_____

Address_____

City/State/Zip_____

Telephone (_____)_____ E-mail_____

Money-back guarantee!	HOW MANY	PRICE (Canada & UK add $6)	TAX (Colorado Residents only)	TOTAL
Gluten-Free 101		$19.95	$.76 per book	
Wheat-Free Recipes & Menus		$19.95	$.76 per book	
Special Diet Solutions		$15.95	$.61 per book	
Special Diet Celebrations		$18.95	$.72 per book	
Food Allergy Field Guide		$19.95	$.76 per book	
Bookmarks Baking With Wheat-Free Flours Baking With Alternative Sweeteners Baking With Dairy Substitutes Baking With Egg Substitutes	_____ _____ _____ _____	$1.00 each $1.00 each $1.00 each $1.00 each	$.04 $.04 $.04 $.04	_____
Buy 2 books–get bookmarks free!			**SUB-TOTAL**	
		Shipping & handling ($4 per book)		
		(Canada: $6); (UK: $12)		
		Total Amount Enclosed		

Please allow 2 weeks for delivery

☐ Check
(payable to
Savory Palate, Inc.)

☐ Visa, MasterCard, Discover
Account Number_____
Expiration Date_____
Customer Signature_____

SAVORY PALATE, INC.
8174 South Holly, #404, Centennial, CO 80122-4004

In Denver Metro Area	FAX (303) 741-0339	**Outside Colorado**
(303) 741-5408	info@savorypalate.com	(800) 741-5418 (orders only)

Available at health food stores, **www.savorypalate.com**, & **www.Amazon.com**

~ Notes ~